Jacob's Dream is a sequel to *The Call of the Awe, Rediscovering Christian Profundity in an Interreligious Er*a, also published by iUniverse. In the first book, Gene W. Marshall describes how Awe-happenings in our everyday lives are the key to understanding both the renewal of Christianity and the need for non-bigoted dialogue among all the religions on Earth.

Here are Reader responses to this earlier volume:

I loved reading it and finding my own journey woven through it. You are a poet!

Ted Farrar, a pastor in Montgomery, Maryland

Having been on a journey of trying to understand my Christian upbringing and its outdated language in today's world, I found this book hard to put down and a refreshing encouragement. Gene Marshall picks up where such writers as Marcus Borg, Brian Swimme, and John Shelby Spong leave off. I expect their readers will be delighted to find this book. It is a book that will stimulate the renewal of Christianity and increase the common ground for dialogue among all religions.

Richard H. Adams from Central New York

For years I have been embarrassed to affiliate in any way with the category of "Christianity." The current mainstream of fundamentalism, literalism, sentimentalism, and moralism have robbed me of some of the deepest poetry by which I understand myself. Gene Marshall's, *The Call of the Awe*, has helped me to reconnect with the center of my being . . . the same center that has inspired all of humanity's religious creations over the centuries.

Michael D. May of Bloomington, Indiana

I read it with admiration and passed it along to a colleague. The book is worthy of study and discussion in today's church.

Bishop C. Joseph Sprague, retired Bishop of the Chicago Area of The United Methodist Church.

Exactly what is needed during these tumultuous transitional times in history! Marshall's concept of Awe is what we hunger for in the deep parts of ourselves as we raise questions about and grapple with our new awareness of a world that is truly interreligious.

Marsha Buck, retired school principal and musician

Clearly, recent international events have shown that vital conversation among the adherents of the religions of the world is a compelling necessity. Unfortunately, very few persons of any religious persuasion are equipped to engage in this undertaking. Gene W. Marshall's book *The Call of the Awe* helps to fill this void. For decades I have used 'Awe' as the basic religious experience available to all. This searching and sensitive volume is a splendid tool upon which effective dialogue may be pursued.

Bishop James K. Mathews, Bishop of the United Methodist Church-retired, Ph.D. in the History of Religion, Author of a book on Gandhi, *The Matchless Weapon: Satyagraha (Truth Force)*

Gene W. Marshall starts from his journey into the Christian faith in this country. This continues in his many years of work in other cultures resulting in his experiential dialogue with Christianity and the world religions. This is not just an intellectual dialogue but also a dialogue of one's life covering the last fifty years. . . . It is a radical journey of seriously living in the 21st Century and at the same time digging deep into the Christian faith with one's total being until the profundity of that faith flows through him. . . . If you long to move beyond the old clichés and live in the world as it is, then this book is for you.

Joseph Slicker, founding member of the Order Ecumenical, The Ecumenical Institute, and the Institute of Cultural Affairs

JACOB'S DREAM

Jacob's Dream

A Christian Inquiry into Spirit Realization

Gene W. Marshall

iUniverse, Inc.
New York   Bloomington

Jacob's Dream
A Christian Inquiry into Spirit Realization

Copyright © 2008 by Gene W. Marshall

iUniverse books may be ordered through booksellers or by contacting:

iUniverse
1663 Liberty Drive
Bloomington, IN 47403
www.iuniverse.com
1-800-Authors (1-800-288-4677)

ISBN: 978-1-4401-1355-0(pbk)
ISBN: 978-1-4401-1354-3 (ebk)

Printed in the United States of America

iUniverse revision date 03/23/2009

Cover Art by Lee Sax
Cover Design by Wayne Marshall
www.marshallarts.com

To everyone who is opening

to a thoroughgoing

journey toward

Spirit maturity

Contents

Acknowledgments

My warmest appreciation goes to Marsha Buck who has enthusiastically assisted with this work for many years. She has made important writing suggestions and spent long hours editing this manuscript.

I also want to thank my fellow workers in The Symposium on Christian Resurgence who have studied early drafts of this work with me and provided invaluable feedback.

I also want to thank my companions in the Bonham Christian Resurgence Circle who have studied parts of this book with me and who share weekly with me in ongoing exploration of the journey of Spirit.

My wife Joyce has not only contributed editing and writing assistance but has also led me to and accompanied me in attending retreats and workshops that have inspired and deepened my understanding of these topics. Her contributions to this book are incalculable.

There have been scores of personal teachers and authors who have contributed wisdom and inspiration for this book. As a representative of them all I want to acknowledge A.H. Almaas, whose many remarkable books and whose trained workshop leaders have greatly enriched my own personal journey and given me fresh vision of the basic Spirit journey that characterizes our species.

Introduction

Jacob's Dream

The stories of Jacob are among the most intriguing and beloved stories of the Bible. This collection of stories took centuries to build. They are stories about humanity, that part of humanity that is being restored to authenticity, that part of humanity that is surrendering to realistically living their lives. The charm of these stories is that Jacob is a very ordinary figure who struggles with all the mundane issues of sibling rivalry, survival, marriage, work, intrigue and counter-intrigue, cheating and being cheated, enmity and reconciliation, fear and courage, and more.

The title of this book is taken from the story about Jacob as a very young man, forced to leave home and journey alone to a place where he has never been. On the way he has a dream about a staircase or ramp stretching from where he is sleeping to Eternity. Angels are coming down and going up this apparently huge ramp. In this book I will explain why today we no longer have to dream in the two-story, up-and-down imagery. We can use fresh religious metaphors that point to the same experiences.

My interpretation of this story is that Jacob was dreaming about his true being, that these angels symbolize states of Spirit that define our profound humanity – states like Trust, Love, and Freedom. This discovery of his deep being enabled Jacob to become a mature person who handled a conniving uncle, won the woman he loved, and became a Spirit leader with descendants as numerous as the grains of sand on the seashore. Each of us can experience Jacob's realization. In our essence each of us is also a mysterious ramp from here to Eternity. In our contemporary religious metaphors, Eternity can be envisioned as that boundless Mystery behind every tree, every squirrel, every event in our lives. Awe approaches us from this Eternity, and Awe moves back toward Eternity from the core of our being.

With help from his mother, Rebecca, Jacob is fleeing for his life from his father, Isaac, and his brother, Esau, whom he has profoundly angered. He is traveling alone, with only what he can carry, toward the home of his uncle, Laban. The first night out he lies down to sleep on the ground with a rock for a pillow. He dreams about a ladder or staircase (ramp may be the best translation) extending from the place where he is sleeping all the way to Eternity.

This dream has a profound effect on Jacob. Jacob sees his own true soul, and this vision gives him a new sense of who he is and his power for living. We who read this story now can see that the soul of every human being is a ramp from here to Eternity with angels moving up and down upon it. In this book I am going to say what I mean by "soul," by "Eternity," by "angels," by "angels moving down," and by "angels moving up." I am going to name some of these angels. There is a whole family of angels with the family name "Trust." Jacob consents to trust the Final Reality he meets in his dream. "Spirit Love" is another family of angels, and "Freedom" is a third. All these angels are symbols of our Awe-responses to Awesome Eternity.

In Part One of this book I introduce some of these angels, some very stern angels (states of Awe) and some that are more delightful. I describe how holes appear in who we think we are, and how we can surrender our old fixations of self and move out into wider spaces of being our true selves, our Spirit Being, our ramp from here to Eternity.

In Part Two I describe in ordinary life experiences the nine major groupings of our Awe response to Eternity. I describe three major aspects of Ultimate Trust, three major aspects of Spirit Love, and three major aspects of Complete Freedom.

In Part Three I show how these nine major aspects of Spirit living are associated with nine ways we fall away from being our True Being. These nine ways or patterns of personality have been described in great detail in a heritage of Spirit discovery called "the Enneagram," the nine-diagram. The Enneagram heritage is a powerful teaching tool, drawing on ancient Sufi wisdom as well as the work of many contemporary psychologists and religious thinkers. I have been surprised by the discovery that the nine states of profound essence indicated in the Enneagram heritage parallel the nine major aspects of Spirit response that I describe in Part Two.

In Part Four I describe how the Spirit life is a journey from our entire, almost unconscious, identification with our personality fixation to a conscious, thoroughgoing identification with our Spirit Being. This is a solitary journey that entails meeting our own personality in all its gifts and in all its horrific rigidities. And this journey is a journey home to our profound Being – a Being that we do not have to accomplish, but which is simply given to all who surrender into being who they already are.

In Part Five I describe the communal aspects of our Spirit journey, how others give us guidance, how we give guidance to others. Jacob, also called Israel, is a communal figure. He is a symbol for that part of humanity that is being restored to full realism. Jacob is a symbol for the People of God, the Body of the Resurrected Messiah, the Enlightened Ones, the Awe-filled Ones, the Commonwealth of Full Realism. The renewal of biblical heritage as well as the healing of our planet is crucially dependent upon our overcoming our individualistic overemphasis and finding again our communal quality as companions in Spirit realization.

Later in the collection of Jacob stories, Jacob wrestles with a nameless angel who gives Jacob a new name, Israel. This wrestling match takes place on the dark night before Jacob meets, after a two-decade absence, his estranged brother Esau who is coming to meet him with 400 men. This story I will tell in detail at the end of the book. But even in this brief telling, we can intuit that the Spirit journey is never over, but continues on as a life and death struggle with both stern and glorious angels.

PART ONE:

The Discovery of Soul

1.

The Ramp from Here to Eternity

Spirit realization can be described with various religious vocabularies and enabled with many religious practices. In this book I will focus on the Christian heritage, but I will do so in a manner that I hope will be useful to anyone who is seriously interested in pursuing the journey of Spirit toward ever-fuller realization.

> Christian theology begins with Jesus –
> Jesus as an ordinary human being,
> living at a space/time coordinate in history,
> part of the biological life of the planet Earth,
> inseparable from the plants, animals, fungi, and microbes,
> inseparable from the rocks, soil, air, water, and energy
> exchanges of physical reality.
>
> Jesus is a biological being capable of dying –
> a finite human person
> living in a specific finite and passing culture,
> thinking with the ideas of his time,
> dealing with the issues coming up in that time and place.

Each one of us is just like Jesus in all these respects. To the extent that we are not in touch with our bodies, we are not followers of Jesus.

To the extent that we are not in touch with our residence in time and space, we are not followers of Jesus. To the extent that we are not wholehearted participants in the realm of mass and energy, we are not followers of Jesus. To the extent that we are not a living presence of biological life with all its finite qualities of consciousness, we are not followers of Jesus.

> *Jesus was not a soul substance trapped in a physical Earth suit,*
> *nor are we.*
> *And Jesus was not a biological being with no Eternal reference,*
> *nor are we.*

In addition to being biologically human, Jesus, and each of us, is a relationship with the Eternal. Imagine Jesus as a stick figure drawn on a large piece of paper. Imagine the whole piece of paper as the Eternal. Then imagine a line drawn from the stick figure to the whole piece of paper on which the stick figure rests.

Here is Christian theology in one diagram. God Almighty is the whole paper, Jesus is the stick figure, and the line connecting them is the Holy Spirit. What does this diagram point to in our actual experience? We understand having a relationship with our pets, our spouse, or our children. We also have a relationship with the Whole of Reality. This Whole, this Mysterious Whole is a process moving towards us in every moment, challenging the depths of our being. And we are responding to this challenge, either in flight, fight, or openness. This active, often fierce process is our relationship with God, the "God" that Jesus worshiped, the "God" that the Bible insists is our appropriate worship. This God is not a being among other beings, not a supernatural thing among other supernatural things, not a thing at all – not a person, not a being, but BEING-AS-A-WHOLE.

GOD

The whole piece of paper is only a rough symbol for the Wholeness of Being. Like all symbols for the Infinite, this is an inadequate symbol. Perhaps we would have a more adequate symbol if we imagine the paper extending forever in all directions. God is not a thing located somewhere on the paper. God is not a thing or a collection of things. God is that EVERY-THING-NESS that transcends every thing and yet is present in every thing. Each and every thing is contained within this EVERY-THING-NESS. I am using the word "thing" in a very broad sense, including Jesus, including you, including me.

Each of us is a specific finite being on the paper, yet each of us is also a being that is not separate from, but is related to, the EVERY-THING-NESS in which all things cohere.

Many Christians tend to see God as a supernatural thing – a thing alongside other things – a super-being in another world of things who can interfere in this world of things and help us handle the things we want to arrange differently. This view is not the biblical view of God. When the Bible and other Christian classics seem to be talking about an otherworldly person, we need to remember that these writings are poetry. They are using mythic language. We need to remember that people who lived in pre-modern times had no difficulty using mythic language. It was their way of talking about their life experiences. They were not literalists in the sense of believing that they might be able to pull on God's beard in some future life. Literalism is a modern construction – a heresy – a departure from the origins of Christianity.

Paul Tillich, Rudolf Bultmann, Richard Niebuhr, Dietrich Bonhoeffer, and many other great theologians all reject viewing God as a thing or a person. They reject literalism in all its subtle forms. When we use personal language to talk about God, we are talking mythically about our own personal relationship with the Infinite EVERY-THING-NESS that cannot be contained within any human imagery, personal or non-personal.

God is the Wholeness that is totally beyond everything, yet manifest in everything. And this Wholeness or EVERY-THING-NESS is a real experience that you and I, like Jesus, can have. We are the sons and daughters of EVERY-THING-NESS. We are a relationship with that inescapable Wholeness. Each of us is a relationship established for us by that Wholeness, a relationship from which we cannot escape, a relationship that is our glory.

I am not saying something unscientific. Scientists who are also humanly sensitive experience Infinite Mystery behind-beyond-within-surrounding all the things they study. Many an honest scientist has said something like this, "The more we know about nature, the more we know we don't know." This awareness of Mystery is an experience of God, the God of the Bible.

Even our curiosity and openness to know more about nature and humanity is an experience of the Infinite Mystery. When we are open to know more, we are open to Mystery. Curiosity about Reality is openness to God.

Imagine lying on a cot on a clear dark night viewing the wonder of the stars. Suppose you remember your post-Einsteinian cosmology and thus know that some of the dimmest lights in the sky, viewed through a powerful telescope, are whole galaxies of billions of stars. Suppose you know that it has been empirically shown that these galaxies are traveling away from one another at vast speeds, that the cosmos is expanding through time. And if you imagine running time backwards, all these galaxies would approach a single point of white-hot potential. All this vast wonder had a beginning, an initial flaring forth – "the Big Bang" physicists have called it.

Then suppose that you call out to the night sky, "**What was before the Big Bang?**" As you listen for the answer, no sound comes back to you. All you can hear is the Infinite Silence. Paradoxically, that is the answer to your question. Before the Big Bang there was Infinite Silence. Even at the present time, all vibrations, all noises, all bangs, big or little, take place within this Infinite Silence. God is the Infinite Silence in which all sounds sound.

The Infinite Silence not only spoke forth the Big Bang of Beginning, the Infinite Silence continues to speak every day. Here is a short poem I wrote about the ever-present quality of the Infinite Silence:

The Infinite Silence Speaks
through every rustle of tree leaves,
through every singing bird,
through every sound of any kind,
and through the silent spaces between the sounds.

The Infinite Silence is Void and Darkness
but also Fullness, a dazzling backlight
that shines through
every gleaming tree, every shimmering squirrel
and surrounds every human being
with a halo.

Our everyday experience of this living relation with the Infinite Silence is an experience of that actuality that the Bible points to with the word "God."

God can also be spoken of as The Infinite Stillness in which all motions move. Meditation practices can help us get in touch with our experience of this Stillness. Perhaps it is frightening at first to enter the place of Stillness and within that Stillness watch all the activity taking place, including the activity of our own minds. Our minds are always busy. Our minds are an aspect of our biological being, which is always in motion. Our life processes, including our minds, never stop. Yet if we pay close attention to our minds, to our bodies, to all our inner being, we can also discern that all this motion is taking place within something deeper, the Infinite Stillness. We can access this Stillness as an actual experience.

Finding this Stillness in which all motions move is finding God. It is within this Still point that we find the Trust, the Love, and the Freedom from which truly creative living can emerge.

God can also be spoken of as the Infinite Void out of which all finite things come and into which all finite things return. Both birth and death are experiences of this Void. When we are born, where do we come from? We come from the Void, from the NO-THING-NESS. When we die, where do we go? We go to the Void, to the NO-THING-NESS. The Void is a real experience that travels with us all the time. Our being is always surrounded by the NO-THING-NESS from which we have come and to which we will return.

Our lives can be likened to a hallway with a door on each end. We enter at one end and exit at the other. And if we look out the windows of our hallway as we walk from the entry door to the exit door, we see that NO-THING-NESS is traveling with us along the way. Indeed, our hallway is like a plank suspended over NOTHING. Indeed, the entire cosmos is like a plank suspended over NO-THING-NESS.

And this Void, this NO-THING-NESS, is also the EVERY-THING-NESS in which all things cohere. God is both NO-THING and EVERY-THING. The NO-THING-NESS surrounds every thing, and the EVERY-THING-NESS is no singular thing. All of us have experienced or can experience this actuality. "God" is just a word. "God" is just a devotional concept indicating what we worship. But in the biblical heritage, the word "God" also points to an unavoidable actuality that confronts us in all the moments of our living. God is a devotional word for Reality, and Reality is that Infinite Mystery, that NO-THING-NESS that is also the EVERY-THING-NESS.

HOLY SPIRIT

And so who are we? We are the God experiencers. We are the Mystery experiencers. We are a line on the whole paper of Reality, a line that extends from our conscious, biological, physical space-time coordinate all the way to this Wholeness of Eternity. This line is the Holy Spirit. This line is like a highway with two lanes. On one lane the Awesome Eternal is coming at us. In the other lane our own Awe is traveling away from us toward the Eternal.

This picture is reminiscent of Jacob's dream about a "ladder" extending from the place where Jacob slept to Eternity with angels moving down and up this ladder. What is the ladder? What are these angels? What is this dream about?

In my childhood Sunday school classes, we clearly did not under-stand this ladder. We sang the song "We are climbing Jacob's ladder." This was presented to us as some sort of moral ladder that we could climb, getting better and better by our own efforts. Nothing like this is actually contained in the original story.

The word translated "ladder" could also be translated "ramp." Jacob dreamed of a ramp from here to Eternity with angels traveling down and up this ramp, this two-lane highway for states of Awe. In one lane angels are coming from Eternity to here. In the other lane angels are going from here to Eternity.

What are the angels? Angels are symbols of the Holy, of the Holy movements of God. "Holy" is also another word for Awe. Angels are Awe figures. Angels are the messengers of Awe coming from the Awesome Wholeness of Reality. And angels are also the energy of Awe moving from each of us toward the Awesome Wholeness. Awe is a two-way movement: Awe-inspiring encounter and Awe-inspired response. Awe is the quality of our relationship with God. Every aspect of this relationship is a quality of Awe. When we are captured in some state of wonder or Awe, we are experiencing the God of the Bible.

The young Jacob, all alone, the first night away from home, had a dream in which he became aware of his own Spirit Being. Jacob saw himself as a two-lane highway from Eternity to here and from here to Eternity. He saw himself as a relationship to God. In this dream he discovered his true soul. This story is about us, as well as an extensively elaborated tale of an ancient ancestor. Every moment, each of us is having an encounter with Eternity and is being a response to Eternity. We may not always be aware of this angel-populated highway; nevertheless, a host of angels is always moving towards us and another host of angels is always moving back in response. Awe is present in our deepest encounters with Reality. And Awe is our deepest action in response. This is the I-Thou relationship spoken of by Martin Buber and the entire Biblical heritage. At particular moments we, like Jacob, become aware of our deep lives. We can image that experience as a ramp from our biological particularity to the Wholeness of Eternity. This ramp is real. It is our human essence. It is you. It is I.

And the whole ramp is our true being, not just one end of it. The materialist wants us to believe that each human is just a biological being. And the spiritualist wants us to believe that our body is not real or not important, that we are just a spirit spark lost in the material world of space/time – mass/energy. Christianity is a materialistic religion in the sense that it affirms that we are both human and divine, both biological and Eternal in our essential being.

JESUS

Not just Jesus, but each of us, is both fully human and a divine ramp from here to Eternity. If we can resonate with Jacob's experience of becoming aware of this two-way ramp, we can begin to grasp the wisdom of the Christian Trinity:

1. The ramp represents the Holy Spirit.
2. The upper end of the Ramp represents God, the Infinite Papa or Infinite Mama, who accepts us into the Divine family of all beings.
3. And the Earth-based end of the Ramp represents Jesus, the ordinary human who experiences the Infinite Mystery as Papa/Mama and is filled with the Holy Spirit. Jesus is the one who is open to being this ramp – to being who he is – to being who she is. If you are open to being this ramp (your true soul, your true Spirit Being), then you can identify with Jesus in his being both human and divine. The entire community of those who identify with Jesus in this way are both human and divine.

The Christian Trinity can be summarized in just three words: the *Awesome*, the *Awe*, and the *Awed*. The Mysterious Wholeness of Reality is the *Awesome*. This ramp of ever-moving angels is our states of *Awe*. And the *Awed* human is the biological being of you and me and Jesus. This is the Christian Trinity: God, the *Awesome*; *Awe*, the Holy Spirit; and *Awed* human life, the resurrected body of the *Awed* One.

It is meaningful to ask ourselves, "Have we experienced this Trinity?" "Are we experiencing this Trinity today?" The Trinity is not a doctrine about three supernatural persons; it is an experience that we might access at any moment. It is like a great Sun that is always shining. We see it whenever we crawl out of our caves. We see it whenever we sweep the clouds of illusion out of the way.

Every good religion explores this same Trinity – this same Spirit essence of the human being, this same Awesomeness, these same states of Awe, the same Awed humanity. I give many examples of this in my book *The Call of Awe*. Every Spirit-expressive religion deals with the Awesome, the Awe, and being Awed.   In this sense every healthy religion is Trinitarian.   Christianity is simply a tradition that has made a point of naming this whole dynamic "The Trinity."

THE BOX OF PERSONALITY

But seeing the Trinity is not the end of Christian theology. **More needs to be said**. Human beings, as a rule, **do not live their Spirit being**. They retreat into the little box of the personality they have developed since infancy.

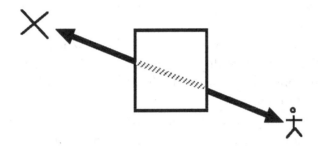

If the entire line drawn from here to Eternity represents our soul, then our whole soul cannot be contained in this box. Living within our box, we have a reduced soul, a soul or self that is conscious of itself, but not conscious of the whole of itself.   It is a soul in a box. Typically, we do not know that we are in a box. We think that the soul we experience in the box is who we are. We also think that the box contains Reality. We think that this little soul relating to this little reality is really who we are. We do not know that the little soul is just a fragment of the soul we really are. For us to become fully conscious of our full soul (of our full Spirit Being) we need to become conscious of the box in which we live.

Each of us has constructed our box, board by board, since infancy. This box is our personality. This box is our well-practiced set of habits. We often call this box our social conditioning, because most of what makes up our personality is not unique to us. We learned it from our society. Our society is also a box, a set of habits that have become customary for those of us who are members of this particular society.

A set of habits has a certain importance. We would not want to be without any habits at all. But our habits are not our true being. Our customs are not our true being. Our morals are not our true being. Our beliefs are not our true being. Our entire personality is not our true being. Our personality is a human creation: it is the particular habits we learned in the past. We put this personality together over the course of our lives. Therefore, the personality is past oriented. Though we use our personality to predict the future, the actual present and future are beyond personality.

We do not live in the past. We live in the NOW. And the real person living in the NOW has a capacity to break habits, to do something different. We built our personality pattern with our essential Freedom. Yet when we identify with the personality that we have built, it functions as a box that excludes our Freedom. When we choose to be no more than our personality, we become a set of robotic patterns that function unconsciously, automatically, and inappropriately within the actual NOW of our living.

Our personality patterns, though useful at times, do not apply in every situation of our lives. These patterns are like blocks of ice that won't move through some of the narrow places in the stream of living. The same water of soul when melted will flow through any spot in the stream. Our true being is like flowing water. But when living in our self-constructed box, we become a block of ice, rigid and unprepared for the whole challenge of living.

FREEDOM

A Spirit-realized person lives in the NOW of Freedom rather than in the habits of the past. **Freedom** is a whole family of angels that move up our Spirit ramp. Spirit Freedom means freedom from our habits, freedom from the personality that we have built. The same Freedom that built our personality has been lost when we exchange that Freedom for living in the box we have built.

Though we may call this box our "social conditioning," we need to notice that we have chosen to be socially conditioned. We have submitted to being a fit rather than a misfit in our society. Or perhaps we chose to be a misfit. Whoever we are, personality-wise, we chose it. We may not have been fully conscious of having chosen it. We may have never been fully conscious of the Freedom that we are. But we are that Freedom. We have always been that Freedom. And to the extent that we can transcend our box, we can be that Freedom in the living NOW.

But Freedom is scary to the person who identifies with being his or her personality. For it means that we do not have to be that person. If we think we are a shy person, if we have always behaved in a shy manner, seeing our Freedom means seeing that we do not have to be shy. And this is true even though shy remains our default pattern for the rest of our lives. If we have always been an angry fly-off-the-handle person, Freedom means seeing that we do not have to be compulsively angry. We can experience our anger, watch it come and go, without flying off the handle.

Whatever it is that we think we are, we don't have to be that. We are not some definite thing. We are Freedom. Beneath all our habits and customs, we are Freedom.

In the movie "The Remains of the Day," Anthony Hopkins played the role of a perfect butler. His character was stuck in this role. Even after he learned that he worked for a British conspirator with the German Nazis, even after he had to separate from the woman he loved to be this perfect butler, he chose his old familiar box. He played the perfect butler for the remains of his days.

This is a picture of a despairing person who does not even know that he is in despair. Many of us have come to the place of openly despairing over being whoever it is we think we are. If so, we may be ready to hear some good news. The perfect butler is not a complete picture of who we are. We are Freedom. We live much of our time in our box, perfect butler or whatever it is. But we need no longer despair over being trapped in our box. We can step outside our box. We are Freedom. The box will remain in our lives, but it is no longer the self we identify as who we are. We are Freedom, Freedom from the box. Freedom is one of the angels that is moving up this ramp of our soul from here to Eternity. Freedom is a state of Awe. Freedom is the Holy Spirit, the real you, the real me.

TRUST

Trust is another family of angels moving up this ramp. For me to participate in Trust means that I am open to being this ramp rather than hiding in my box. Trust means believing that the Awesome Mystery that posited me as this ramp from here to Eternity did not goof. This Mysterious Wholeness is trustworthy. The Mysterious Wholeness is my papa, my mama, my friend, my shepherd, my rock, my foundation, my beloved, my devotion, my God. Trust is a courageous commitment of my whole life to being the Spirit being that I truly am.

Many children exhibit Trust. They are open to life and to whatever they can become. Most adults have built a strong box and trust that box instead. In this primal sense, we need to become children again. We can become open again. We can Trust again.

Consider Jacob as a frightened young man leaving home for the first time, all alone, and going somewhere he had never been before. During his dream about the ramp from here to Eternity with the angels going up and down, Jacob heard words about the trustworthiness of the God who met him in this dream.

This Trust transformed Jacob the frightened boy leaving home for the first time into a spunky youth who was willing to be his ramp, his Trust, his Freedom, his power to carve out a life for himself, to marry, to become skilled at work, to grapple with his conniving uncle, to meet and reconcile with his still angry brother, to become the father of a spirit community. We are all a potential Jacob. We are all a potential Jesus. We are just hiding in our boxes.

LOVE

And when we insist on hiding in our boxes, we are also *defensive and malicious*. Some people will even kill to stay in their box. Jesus called people out of their boxes. That was why they killed him. Those who love their box do not like the implication that their box is ungodly – that their box is part of "Satan's kingdom," that living in their box is rebellion against the God of Moses and the prophets. So they killed Jesus.

Box dwellers are malicious, especially toward those who abandon their own boxes. Everyone who insists on being in their box is malicious toward even the people they think they love. ***But malicious is not who you and I really are in the essence of our being.*** **Love** or **Compassion** is another angel that moves up this ramp. Compassion is who we truly are. We do not have to work at being compassionate. We do not have to try to be loving. We just have to give up living in our box. We just have to give up self-promotion, and be who we are. "Who we are" is a compassionate being. "The real me" is Spirit Love, a love that affirms all beings.

DEAD TO SELF

As long as we think we have to make something of ourselves, that we have to improve ourselves, that we have to achieve something to be worth something, we are into self-promotion. And as long as we are into self-promotion, we are malicious. But our Holy-Spirit "Self," our Jesus "Self," is not malicious, defensive, or self-promoting. Our True Self is a realistic servant – a leader of others perhaps, but a servant leader. This Real Self is devoid of self-promotion. There is no need for it. Our True Self does not need recognition or praise. We may notice these affirmations; we may enjoy them. But our Real Self is devoid of "self" as that term is ordinarily used.

In other words, being fully our Spirit Being entails being dead to self, to ego, to personality. Here is the apostle Paul's repeated statement: "We were crucified with Christ that we might also be raised up with him to newness of life." What is killed here? It is the illusion that the personality is the real me. It is slavery to the compulsion of grinding out my current set of habits as my only possible life. Redemption means death to this compulsion – death to this illusion – death to life in this box.

Only after we have passed through such a death can we discover the resurrection. And here is the meaning of resurrection: being this Ramp from here to Eternity, being Trust, being Freedom, being Compassion. These are your higher angels. These are my higher angels. And we do not have to create them. They are already the real you, the real me. ***All*** that is required is surrender to being who we really are.

2.

Messengers from the Eternal

The ramp in Jacob's dream has angels coming down the ramp from Eternity to his specific here and now and angels moving up the ramp from his specific here and now to Eternity. I see these descending angels as the messengers of encounter with the Unfathomable Final Reality, and I see the ascending angels as communications of response to the Unfathomable Final Reality.

"Ascending" and "descending" are metaphorical images that are part of a very old metaphor that pictures Final Reality as up – up above the ordinary realities of our lives. Until fairly recently, this metaphor seemed logical and useful. In the flat-earth era, it seemed obvious that the earth (here below the sky) was full of changes. The sun, moon and planets also moved. The stars were seen as stationary, but they were potentially movable since they were seen as creatures who might fall. Final Reality, however, was changeless; it did not move at all; it was beyond the stars. Therefore, in a flat-earth era, when we wanted to symbolize the changeless, we looked up. But Final Reality does not have to be pictured as up, it can just as well be pictured as standing behind each ordinary reality and shining through it. The ramp leading up to heaven is symbolic talk about the Unfathomable; Jacob dreamed in the symbolic language of his era. Only if the reader will remember that "up" is symbolic talk, will I be able to communicate my meaning using this symbol of a ramp from here to Eternity, with angels moving up and down upon it.

One of the continuing challenges within contemporary Christian theology is recognizing that the ancient two-story metaphor of heaven and earth is a metaphor. It did not come into being as a literal belief in the existence of an empirically verifiable upper place. Heaven was not understood by Moses or Jesus or Thomas Aquinas as a literal place up above our ordinary place. Heaven was understood by them as metaphorical talk. And this did not mean false or superstitious talk. Metaphorical talk existed alongside empirical talk as a natural part of discourse.

For example, Jesus used the familiar experience of the patriarchal family of his time as a metaphor for speaking of the "Father in heaven." He was saying that Final Reality is like a father who welcomes wayward sons and daughters home. Twelve centuries later, Thomas Aquinas was still using this two-story metaphor. He was surprisingly explicit in his awareness that "heaven" is a metaphor. He spoke of an *analogy* with an earthly king and said (I am paraphrasing), "*suppose* there is an Eternal King who promulgates an Eternal Law, a law that is unknowable to the human mind." In other words, this Eternal King and his Eternal Law are sheer Mystery. This is not literalism. This is metaphorical talk about the unfathomable.

Today we are experiencing the passing of the up-there metaphor and learning to speak of the Eternal as more like a brilliant light that shines through our ordinary experiences. When our consciousness is released to see beyond the boxes of our own personality construction, we can have a full experience of Reality in which the ordinary is transparent to the shining quality of Mysterious Eternity. Using this new metaphor we no longer picture the Eternal as transcending the ordinary but as shining through it. That is, we are experiencing and speaking of Eternal Reality with what we might call the "transparency metaphor." We admit, as so many have said, that the "transcendent metaphor" is dead, that we killed it and are still killing it because it does not fit well into the rest of our post-modern cultural fabric. But this death does not mean that the transcendence metaphor was not alive in earlier centuries. Intelligent and highly conscious human beings like

Moses, like Jesus, like Augustine, like Thomas Aquinas, like Luther used the transcendence metaphor with great power. These persons and thousands of others were not stupid. They simply lived in another era. We can listen to them speak in their own language and then translate their words into our own language. Similarly, we can listen to them speak in their own metaphors and then translate those metaphors into contemporary metaphors that are compatible with the culture of our times.

When I speak of angels in this book, I am dialoguing with the metaphors of the past. The use of "angels" is an aspect of the transcendence metaphor. Angels or messengers of God come down from the Eternal into our ordinary lives. Then other angels move from our ordinary lives back up toward the Eternal. An angel is a messenger or communicator. It is an active motion moving on the "ramp" of relationship between Eternity and the space-time here and now of your or my actual life. The Bible continually uses the metaphor of an I-Thou dialogue to speak of our experience of Final Reality. The Awesome Final Reality is encountered by us as a Thou sending messenger angels (that is, states of Awe) toward us. And then the deep "I" who is Awed by this "Divine" encounter makes responses that are also states of Awe. This Awed response can be pictured as motion back toward the Awesome Final Reality.

The numerous states of Awe that human beings are capable of experiencing have been diagramed in various ways. An important mentor of mine, Joseph W. Mathews, drew four charts that he named the Land of Mystery, the River of Consciousness, the Mountain of Care, and the Sea of Tranquility. On each of these charts were sixteen separate but closely related states of Awe. In other words, he described 64 different states of Awe, 64 different angels that move on the ramp that is our true soul.

I have reordered the information contained in Mathews's charts and in other patterns of analysis into my own rational model of these transrational actualities. My model depicts various families of angels that move up and down the ramp of our soul. Here is a chart of these families of angels:

The Angels of Encounter	The Angels of Response
The Angels of The Void Ever-present Nothingness Inescapable Limitation Unrecoverable Past **The Angels of The Fullness** Connecting Wholeness Enduring Sustainment Unimaginable Possibility **The Angels of The Total Demand** Unavoidable Response Futuric Radicality Inclusive Obligation	**The Angels of Ultimate Trust** Transparent Attention Universal Forgiveness Effortless Letting Be **The Angels of Spirit Love** Autonomous Strength Enchantment with Being Out-Flowing Compassion **The Angels of Complete Freedom** Primal Merging Inherent Purity Attuned Working

Trust, Love, and Freedom are states of Being (or Awe) that are central in Christian theology. These three terms are relatively familiar to us. In Part Two I will describe these states of Awe in more detail. In this chapter I will describe the Angels of Encounter.

The angels of encounter are infinite in number. Nevertheless, they can be grouped into families. Such is the capacity of the human mind – to describe the unfathomable while remaining clear that the unfathomable is indescribable. Based on many years of reflection upon this, I have concluded that the encounter with Final Reality can be described in three inclusive ways, three families of angels: (1) the family of The Void, (2) the family of The Fullness, and (3) the family of The Total Demand. In Chapter 6 I will why this organization is meaningful. But in this chapter I will simply focus on the experiences that these descending angels point to in our everyday lives.

THE ANGELS OF THE VOID

Western literature is filled with references to the angel of death. We might wonder why death can be called an "angel." Why not a demon? Death is an angel because it brings us the truth, the truth about our finitude. When we have crawled into our personality box, into that pseudo-reality of our own creation, we have most often left our consciousness of death out of that box. Especially, we omit our present-time consciousness of our own death. In our own half-conscious and silly way, we are inclined to assume that we are the exception to the rule that all things die. Since we do not have the courage, the skills, or even a reason for being realistic on this topic, we need the angel of death to remind us that all things die, including everything in our outer and inner life that makes up what we usually call "me." The angel of death communicates to us the invincible power of Final Reality. We often picture the angel of death as a skeleton swinging a scythe, but humanity has created other pictures. In India the goddess Kali with her belt of skulls and her two edged sword is another symbol of death as well as a symbol of destruction – destruction being half of what goes on in our lives. Kali is also the slayer of falsehood. As we approach the final detachment from our box of personality habits, Kali appears as the redemptive, purifying slayer of the last remnants of falsehood in our lives. When we see our own selves in the role of slaying all falsehood in order that the sober truth may reign in our lives, then we have embraced the angel Kali and other angels of death and destruction.

The Angels of Ever-present Nothingness

The angels of death and destruction belong to a family of angels I am calling "Ever-present Nothingness." Even at the moment of birth, we can notice that we are born out of a void, out of a black hole of Nothingness. As Nikos Kazantzakis put it, "We come from a dark abyss, we end in a dark abyss, and we call the luminous interval life."[1] Birth is an entry from the abyss. Death is an entry into the abyss. And as we walk from birth to death, the infinite abyss walks with us.

We are surrounded by an ever-present Nothingness out of which we have come and into which we are returning. Each galaxy, each star, each planet, each squirrel, each human had a beginning and will have an end. The Angels of Ever-present Nothingness travel with us at all times, smiling, grinning, constantly reminding us that we were not always here and will not always be here. Carlos Castaneda suggests that death is a constant companion walking just behind our left

---

[1]   Kazantzakis, Nikos; *The Saviors of God* (Simon and Schuster, New York: 1960) page 43

shoulder. If we turn our head quickly, perhaps we can catch a glimpse of this constant companion.

The Angels of Inescapable Limitation

The angels of ever-present Nothingness have some cousins in a family of angels I will label "inescapable limitation." These angels remind us that we are never secure, no matter how much money we have, how smart we are, how much we have accomplished, how many people love us, how much effort we have expended toward being good. All our pleasant moments do not last. Everything in our life that we might be tempted to consider necessary for our happiness is vulnerable to loss. And all the things we currently retain are limited. Few of us are as beautiful as we might like to be. Few of us are as smart as we might like to be. Few of us are as successful as we might like to be. The angels of inescapable limitation communicate to us that no particular part of our life is infinite in any way whatsoever. Perhaps one of the angels in this family is named "unavoidable futility." Futility is unavoidable because we are inescapably limited by the All-powerful Actuality. This power, this holiness, this truth is communicated to us by the family of guardian angels I have named "inescapable limitation."

The Angels of Unrecoverable Past

A third subfamily of the angels of the Void can be named "the angels of unrecoverable past." We often say that what is past is past, but we do not always believe it. And even when we do believe it, we do not always accept it. Whatever we had yesterday, we no longer have today, at least not in the same way. Whoever we were yesterday, we no longer are today. Even though there are continuities, there are also big differences. Actual life in the living now is a continual departure from earlier moments of NOW that never return. The angels of unrecoverable past communicate to us over and over that this is so. Life is a flow onwards, forcing each realistic person to become detached from all things, lest he or she be ripped in two by the Power of time that relentlessly moves forward. We cannot willingly live in the here and now of our lives until we see that all the other options are subject to the invincible wrath of time. The angels of the unrecoverable past communicate to us that we need to live each moment, each day, not the day before, not the day after. This NOW is our life. The content of this NOW, pleasant and unpleasant, will soon be gone forever. It will return into the Void out of which it came.

* * * * * * * * * *

Most of the time, all these angels of the Void seem like angels of wrath to our familiar living in the supposedly safe box of our enduring personality habits. But if we are to take the Spirit journey, we need to leave this box. If we yearn for Spirit fulfillment, we must open ourselves to leaving the box of personality as our primary identification. When such openness is present, the angels of the Void are experienced as healing agents, as gifts of grace that show us the futility of clinging to the passing orders of existence.

THE ANGELS OF THE FULLNESS

The angels of the Void are not the only angels who are coming down the ramp from Eternity to here. We also encounter the angels of the Fullness. These angels communicate the EVERY-THING-NESS of the Final Awesome Actuality. They communicate to our consciousness the details of encountering Wholeness.

The Angels of Connecting Wholeness

The Unfathomable Final Reality comes toward us as the connectedness of all things, as the EVERY-THING-NESS in which all things cohere. The gravity of the sun, moon, and Earth shapes the space/time in which we live. The light of distant galaxies reaches our telescopes. In the more intimate aspects of our lives, all the people we know are residents in our own heads, haunting us, instructing us, demanding responses from us. We are connected to all things: a robbery in our neighborhood, the AIDS pandemic in Africa, the squirrels in our trees, the coyotes in our fields, the sun, the moon, the stars. We are each connected to all things. We are not separate. We are embraced by the cosmos, by the Wholeness of Reality. Even our own deep autonomy and Freedom do not separate us. That very Freedom is posited in us by the Wholeness in which we dwell and in which we exercise our autonomy and Freedom. If we use our Freedom to separate ourselves from the Whole, we create an unreality. "Connecting wholeness" is a useful name for a major subfamily of the angels of Fullness.

The Angels of Enduring Sustainment

The angels of Fullness also include a subfamily we might call "enduring sustainment." Whatever is sustaining the sun, moon, and stars is also sustaining you and me. We began our lives through no effort of our own. We have a cosmos to live in through no effort of our own. We might be able to affect the time of our death, but if we choose to live a while longer, we do so by allowing ourselves to be sustained by the Sustainer of all things. These angels communicate the welcome we have from Final Reality: the forgiving embrace, the ever-present support, the foundation and underpinning of our existence. Our very desires, longings, and drives are gifts of this Enduring Sustainment. When we insist on being a separate person isolated in our little box, we may experience the states of Enduring Sustainment as angels of wrath. But for those who are open to be their Spirit wholeness, the angels of Enduring Sustainment welcome us home to our true lives, our true nature, our actual Spirit journey. Notice the birds; they are fed. Observe the field flowers; they are clothed.

The Angels of Unimaginable Possibility

The angels of Fullness also include a subfamily of angels we might call "unimaginable possibility." When we insist on living in our box, we eventually run out of possibilities. Hopelessness ensues. Despair yells out loud or hides in our unconsciousness. The boxed person cannot see most of the actual possibilities, cannot even imagine them. Imagination is restrained by the box. The angels of unimaginable possibility bring us this truth: *there is always another way to look at the matter*. Reality and possibility are always bigger than we thought. The possibilities that actually stand before us are truly unimaginable. To access this fullness, we have to step off into the unknown, the unknown unknown of the actual future. The angels of unimaginable possibility beckon us into the fullness of our actual lives. A boxed person will tend to resist these angels. We feel secure in our box; we may not want to sacrifice security for fullness. But Final Reality loves us with unimaginable possibilities and sends angels to lead us forth onto paths which we have never trod before. Consider a professional athlete who sustains a career-ending injury. As long as being a professional athlete is the whole game, only despair is possible. Imagination must be expanded – coaching, sports casting, restaurant owning, etc. Consider a military superpower that is unable to win its wars. There are other possibilities for that nation. Seemingly unimaginable possibilities can appear, such as practicing cooperative participation and truly open negotiation.

THE ANGELS OF THE TOTAL DEMAND

The angels of the Void and the angels of the Fullness are joined by a third family of angels coming down the ramp from Eternity to here – the angels of the Total Demand.

The Angels of Unavoidable Response

The future is moving towards us as an uncompromising demand for response. The actual content of that response has options, but response is necessary. If unconscious reactions characterize our living, that is the quality of our responding. Even what we call "no response" is actually a response. Being alive means making responses. Response is required, demanded. There is no escape from making a response. The Angels of Unavoidable Response reveal to us that we don't have the option of standing on the sidelines of history. We are in history. We respond to history and have historical consequences. We can attempt to back away, but that is a response to history and it has historical consequences. We can follow the path of laziness, fear, and addictions, but that would be our response, our choice for our presence in history. We are unavoidably in this business of living as an agent of response. The Angels of Unavoidable Response reveal to us that embracing this responsibility and being this responsibility is what Spirit living looks like. Such self-aware responding is often called "intentionality." The experience of being intentional is more like a surrender than a heroic effort. The experience of being intentional is poorly described with the term "struggle." It is more like a willingness to be spontaneous and creative. If someone tells you that they are struggling to be intentional, ask them what the struggle is about. If they can be honest, they will have to admit that they are struggling to quit struggling to be unintentional. Intentionality itself requires no struggle. Intentionality is a gift of our true being. This gift must be enacted, and yet it is like a mighty river already in motion. The Total Demand of Final Reality first appears to us as a demand for total surrender to the gift of intentionality as the quality of our unavoidable responding. This set of Awe-messengers from the Eternal is moving down the ramp from Eternity to our specific temporal here and now.

The Angels of Futuric Radicality

Furthermore, we do not control the Reality to which we must respond. Our response is made within the limits and possibilities of an impending and irresistible future. Yes, we live in an enduring NOW, but this NOW is embedded in the flow of time. The specific qualities of our NOW move toward us with or without our consent. We cannot stop time. We cannot avoid new challenges. Just as the moments of the past are unrecoverable, so the moments of the future are unavoidable. This relentless future demands openness and this demand is another experience of the descending angels, the Awe-messengers from Final Reality. "Futuric radicality" is my name for this family of angels. The word "radicality" points to the fact that none of us is allowed to be fully conservative. If we opt to live realistically, we are thrust into continual change. The present state of things is always being overturned and superseded. Our familiar habits are being undermined by the challenging future that relentlessly approaches. This is Awesome. This is another powerful flock of Awe messengers.

The Angels of Inclusive Obligation

The future that is coming at us is not simply my or your individual future; it is the inclusive future that contains everybody and everything. We face together everything that humanity faces. This inclusiveness is a personal experience for each of us. For example, my life does not take place in the narrow box of my own personal issues or in the box of US domestic issues. I am part of a planetary drama that includes Muslim fundamentalists and Muslim moderates, Israeli fundamentalists and Israeli moderates, an earthquake in Pakistan, a tsunami in Asia, an AIDS pandemic in Africa, the growth of oil usage in China, the needs of women all over the world to find a greater place of dignity and participation, the needs of the poor all over the world to have even the simplest form of life, liberty, and the pursuit of happiness. I simply do respond to all these things. And because I can respond, I am **response-able**. I am responsible for my responses, and I am thereby **responsible** for everything. This is a Spirit-state, an Awe-state. I am not talking about morally beating myself over the head. I am not talking about deciding what my specific vocation needs to be. I am talking about a **quality of my Spirit being and your Spirit being.** Nikos Kazantzakis pointed to this state of Being/Awe/Spirit in this bit of poetry: "Learn to obey. Only he who obeys a rhythm superior to his own is free. Learn to command. Only he who can give commands may represent me here on earth. Love responsibility. Say: 'It is my duty, and mine alone, to save the earth. If it is not saved, then I alone am to blame.' "[2] That is an angel of Inclusive Obligation speaking.

* * * * * * * * * *

Hosts of angels move down our ramp from Eternity to here. These are the angels of encounter with Final Reality. Also, hosts of angels move up our ramp from here to Eternity. These are the angels of response to Final Reality. This ramp of moving angels represents our true soul, our Spirit Being. These angels define what I mean by the word "Spirit." Spirit is not a structure of our own making. We did not intend it. We did not choose it. We are constructed with it, and we are stuck with it. We may be trying to escape from Spirit, but since Spirit is our own true soul, it is inescapable. Our true soul is posited (created) by Final Reality. Our true soul is an expression of the creativity of that Mysterious Wholeness that is also the far end of that ramp that is our true soul. When we are living in our box, all this is unclear. We experience a restricted soul. Indeed, we have incarcerated ourselves within a prison of our own construction. In the imagination of our

---

[2] Kazantzakis, Nikos, *The Saviors of God* (Simon and Schuster: 1960) page 68

ego-limited consciousness, we see ourselves as something more modest than all this host of Awe-messengers-from-and-to-Eternity. What we call our "ego" is a stand-in, a facsimile, a replacement for the true soul. Indeed, our ego is only a creature of our own imagination; it is a working model of who we think we are. And it is far less than who we truly are. Our true soul, the self we actually are, is a ramp from here to Eternity with angels aplenty moving down and up upon this ramp.

If the ancient term "angel" is still a difficult symbol for you, perhaps the language of Awe is more to your liking. The Awesome is moving toward us from the Overall to our specific here and now. This inspires Awe in our inner core that then moves in response to the Awesome. Our true soul is the Awe of Encounter with Final Reality (the movement from The Awesome Final Reality to the center of our conscious being). And our true soul is also the Awe of Response to Final Reality (the movement of Awe initiated in our conscious center and returning through all the layers of our being toward the Awesome Final Reality). My and your true soul is a dialogue of Encounter and Response, a living, moving, flowing actuality.

If you count yourself a student of physics, perhaps you have noticed the Awesome Mysterious Reality traveling toward you (down your ramp) as you study the enigmas of space and time, mass and energy. Contemporary physics has opened insights and mysteries unthinkable a hundred years ago. If you count yourself a biologist, perhaps you have noticed the Awesome traveling toward you as you have tried to use the ideas of physics to explain the origin of life. Perhaps you have seen that the enigmatic actualities of life and consciousness are a mystery no physics can encompass. Perhaps something more pedestrian has brought you face-to-face with yourself as a ramp from here to Eternity. Jacob had a dream about this on his first night away from home, traveling alone to a place he had never been before.

3.

The Mysterious Essence of You

I was struck by these opening words in Adyashanti's book *Emptiness Dancing*[3]

> This book is for you and about you. Has no one ever addressed you as you truly are? Have *you* ever addressed you as you truly are? Or have you been fooled by the mere appearance of you, your name, gender, family affiliation, personality, past and secret hopes for a better future or maybe a better you? I assure you these trivialities do not describe or reveal you as you truly are. Not even close.
>
> Now tell the truth. Have you not suspected that there is more to you, or less, than the image that you produce in the mirror? Have you not secretly yearned in your quietest moments to peer beyond the veil of appearances, both your own and others?
>
> There is something about you more bright than the sun and more mysterious than the night sky. You have surely suspected such things in secret, but have you fallen completely into your mysterious essence?

---

[3] Adyashanti, *Emptiness Dancing* (Sounds True, Inc.: 2006) page xix

Adyashanti arrived at his mature awareness through a practice of Zen Buddhism, but he, like most prominent Spirit teachers, has widely explored the various religious traditions of our planet. Adyashanti claims to have been deeply addressed by the autobiography of Teresa of Avila. I say this about him as a reminder to all of us that the Spirit journey into our true Being is a universal journey spoken about in many religious languages. The restoration of the Christian vocabulary can be deeply enriched by our dialogue with these explorers from other traditions.

In dialogue with what I believe to be the rich core of Christian heritage, I have come to understand that "Holy Spirit" is a term that points to that "mysterious essence of you" about which Adyashanti speaks. In the following diagram, the large circle is a symbol for that mysterious essence of you. You or I, each human being, is a vastness that greatly exceeds our customary view of ourselves as well as our view of other people.

PERSONALITY

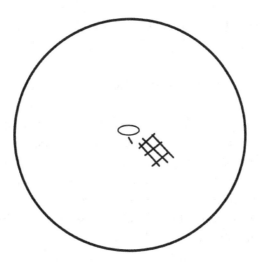

Within this vast circle of you, I have drawn a small array of intersecting lines. This represents the *structure of habits* I will call "*personality*." This structure was built line-by-line, piece-by-piece since infancy. None of us has a full knowledge of our personality. It is a very complex structure built from all the significant events, dialogues, encounters, and responses of our entire lives. Learning about your personality is a lifetime project. In Chapter 11, I will introduce a model of personality types and explore some specific patterns that each of you might recognize as your own personality.

Your personality was **built for survival.** If your childhood situation was quite challenging, your personality may have been warped significantly in order for you to survive those circumstances. If so, your personality might now be a bit dysfunctional – that is, not well adapted to your current living conditions. Dysfunctional personalities can be changed somewhat. And you can learn to live around your personality instead of out of your personality. In the best-case scenario, your personality may be a useful set of habits, but even then it is past-oriented. Personalities tend to be stubbornly and enduringly conservative of the past. But we do not live in the past. We live in the mysterious openendedness of NOW. Therefore, personality is never fully adequate as a guide for genuine living. Personality lacks freedom. Personality is a useful robot, programmed to do a specific pattern of things in specific ways. Freedom is a vastness beyond the personality structure.

For most people 99% of all they do is little more than act out their personality habits. They may make 2 or 3 truly free decisions in a whole lifetime and these times of decision scare them so deeply, they do not want to experience such free decisions ever again. Most people, 99% of the time, do not know what they are doing. They are just doing their social conditioning, doing their program of personality habits.

For the saint, Spirit adept, or enlightened being perhaps 50% of his or her decisions are rooted in freedom. Such persons have embraced the courage of Freedom and live from that source during a significant portion of the time. But even the most fully realized human still has a personality and still operates from that personality much of the time. For all of us, more of our behavior than we can even imagine is rooted in automatic, habituated, and mostly unconscious personality patterns.

SELF-IMAGE

In the diagram above I have also drawn inside the circle a small balloon simulating those we see in cartoons drawn over the heads of a cartoon character and filled with words the cartoonist is having that character say. This balloon in my diagram contains what we say about ourselves.

In other words, the balloon is a symbol for our self-image. Self image is who we think we are. Typically our self-image is derived from what little we know about our personality plus some exaggerations and some omissions that render that image more pleasing to us. There is some truth to our self-image or it would not work as a self-image. But my image is not me, and your self-image is not you. These images are self-created. My self-created image of me is not the same as the mysterious essence of me. Your self-created image of you is not the same as the mysterious essence of you. Not even close.

THE MYSTERIOUS ESSENCE OF YOU

The large circle in the above diagram represents the mysterious essence of you. You and I and each human being are indeed mysterious. You don't know who you are. You know a tiny bit of who you are, but the vastness of who you are is a mystery to you. The so-called "self-made man" or "self-made women" is just that, something made up. The real you is not made up by you, it is given with your birth, your genes, your human community, your place in the evolution of the planet, your aliveness and awareness within the unfolding of the cosmos.

And this mysterious you, this mysterious me is present NOW, and only NOW. In the Eternal Now is where you are, and I am. We meet NOW, mystery to mystery – your mystery to my mystery. Neither of us knows who we are. Neither of us ever will know who we are. We know little scraps of this and that about our own selves and about one another, but what we don't know vastly exceeds what we do know. We can know, however, that we do not know who we are. We can recognize the vast mysterious essences that we are. That does not mean that we comprehend who we are or can put who we are in some set of concepts. Who we are remains mysterious, surprising, overwhelmingly more than we suspect.

Nevertheless, the human mind can talk about what we do not know. We can describe this boundlessly unknown true self in sermons, talks, essays, books – indeed whole libraries of description. The key words used in the Christian description are Trust, Love and Freedom. Other words hover around these three core words: Joy, Peace, Hope, Tranquility, Courage, Affirmation, Compassion, Enchantment, and so on. But all these "holy" words are not themselves the Holy Spirit. The Holy Spirit is the mysterious essence of you that never ceases to be mysterious no matter how many words you use to point to this essence.

Trust includes trusting the mysterious essence of who you are. You don't know who you are. All your thoughts about "who you are" are just thoughts invented by you. These thoughts are not "who you are." Trust embraces not knowing who you are. Trust also embraces not knowing what Reality is.

Love includes being enchanted with the Unknown, opening into affirmation of the mysteriousness of your own person as well as being with other persons without squeezing their mysterious essence into your own categories of interpretation.

Freedom includes entering into the sheer emptiness of having no certain idea about what you can do or what you cannot do. Martin Luther had no idea that he could inspire the Reformation. Many of you have begun things that seemed beyond you and you did just fine. Many of you have started things that you thought you could do, but it turned out that they were beyond you.

Freedom means choosing to open to the truth of not knowing who you are. Freedom means not limiting yourself with: "I never do that," or "I could never do that," or "That is not in accord with my personality," or "I am not like that." Freedom means giving up any certainty you have about who you are. Freedom means not knowing. Freedom means acting beyond what you thought were your limits. Freedom also means obeying limits you may not have known you had. It is not true that "I can do everything I set out to do." And it is not true that "I am always smart enough to handle anything."

Freedom means acknowledging that my actions are never perfect. Indeed, my actions are always to a large extent wrong. Freedom means choosing which wrong thing to do. There are two kinds of wrong action. One derives from our finite nature, our lack of knowledge and wisdom about how life works. The other sort of wrong action derives from our estrangement from this omnipresent mysteriousness – from that little that we do know and from that much that we do not know. Freedom means accepting forgiveness before we act, while we act, and after we act. Freedom means creating action after action within the constant context of praying this old traditional prayer, "Lord have mercy on me a sinner." I also like crying out, "Have mercy on us all." Just "Have mercy" will do. We need not know to whom or what we are praying, and we need not know for what we are being forgiven. Freedom means launching our lives into the sheer mystery of being our mysterious self, responding to the Final Mystery.

Freedom is an act of Trust that the Final Mystery is always welcoming us home to the Final Mystery no matter what we have done or what we have not done. Freedom is an act of Love in response to a Final Mystery we freely Trust as Love toward us.

4.

Holes in Who We Think We Are

In this chapter I invite us to explore further the journey from identification with our personality to identification with our Spirit Being. This journey also means a death to our self-constructed ego.

EGO IDENTIFICATION

"Ego" is who we think we are. Ego is an image constructed by us of who we think we are. So as we move toward awareness of who we truly are, ego disappears. Ego is an illusion. When the Truth comes, illusion disappears. But as long as illusion reigns in our lives it has a powerful effect upon our behavior, our sense of reality, and our states of feeling. We cling to our ego because we think it is who we are. Our liberation into true soul (Spirit Being) entails the loss of our ego, the death of clinging to an ego, the realization that our ego is and always was an illusion. It is true that every illusion contains some truth; it could not last without some toehold in truth. But when the fullness of truth comes, the partial truth is killed and its juice is integrated into a larger wholeness. In this sense, the ego disappears when our true soul (Spirit Being) is realized.

Unlike ego, personality does not disappear as true soul (Spirit Being) is realized. Personality is a structure of habits established since childhood. It is largely unconscious. We can become more conscious of our personality, and we can become more detached from our personality. But personality never goes away. It can change to a certain degree, but it is also true that our basic personality pattern (laid down in the first years of our life) will remain. We can moderate our basic pattern, but we cannot do away with it. We can live beyond our personality, in the sense of making decisions rooted in our Spirit Freedom rather than in our personality habits, but our basic personality remains as an ongoing structure in our lives. Freedom means the ability to live beyond our personality habits. Freedom also includes the option of intentionally following our personality habits when we deem them useful.

Ego, however, is not an enduring structure. Ego is our current self-created image of who we think we are. Our ego may be an identification with our personality or with parts of our personality. Our ego-identity may involve a denial of some of our enduring habits of personality. To the extent that we identify with our personality, we identify with a past-oriented set of default patterns for living. This is not who we are. As a self-constructed identification, our ego does not encompass our entire reality. Our true self is a flow of Awe. Our true self is a here-and-now direct experience of the flowing Awesome Wholeness of Being. The ego is a substitute for this True Awe-filled Self. Our ego may have no or little awareness of being something other than the familiar ego we take ourselves to be.

The ego is a delusion, but it is a plausible delusion that is somewhat useful for navigating through the wickets of adult living. The ego-identified person may get along well enough to be totally unconscious of his or her True Nature. Such unconsciousness allows one to suppose himself or herself complete, without defect or deficiency.

SPIRIT IDENTIFCATION

A complete unconsciousness of our True Nature, our Spirit Being, seldom if ever exists; therefore, the "living soul," who views himself or herself as ego, can experience what seems to him or her to be deficiencies in that ego. When we begin to see that we are different from the person we have heretofore taken ourselves to be, this may be distressing. Discovering that we are not who we think we are can be terrifying, so terrifying that such discoveries are promptly forgotten, buried, suppressed, and avoided in the future.

The ego is an enclosed space of its own making. That enclosed space then acts as a lens through which all reality is seen. Thus, our ego's sense of reality is only a partial view of Reality; nevertheless, our sense of reality is our sense of reality. We may not want to know how partial that sense of reality is. So, as Reality breaks into our sense of reality, it is as if holes are being punctured in our sense of reality. If these holes can be promptly patched, life can continue unchanged. But such patches may tear loose, and new holes may appear that cannot be patched. Perhaps our encircling sense of reality becomes more like a sieve than an enclosure. Our box is full of holes. Our sense of reality has become unsustainable. Desperate measures can seem needed. Suicide is one of these desperate measures: "If I cannot continue seeing myself and my world as I am accustomed to seeing it, then I don't want to live at all." More often the desperate measures taken by a threatened ego are more like murder than suicide: "I want to kill every bearer of truth that challenges my sense of reality!" If killing the self or killing others seems too extreme to a particular person, more moderate measures are taken. Perhaps patterns of being unconsciousness are constructed. These might act themselves out as various forms of rationalism, moralism, or sentimentality that are strong enough and convincing enough that we believe our ego to be our true self.

Like suicide or murder the construction of stronger delusions is a desperate measure, for Reality continues being Reality. Thus, delusions are continually vulnerable to being shaken into the nothingness that they are. Living in the delusion that our ego is who we are means living in the dread of being found out, in the anxiety of having our house of cards collapse. We may be living in horror. We may feel we are entering into a full-blown despair over our hopeless project of self-construction.

Fortunately, there is another direction for us to take. We may be reluctant to take this direction, for it entails a disidentification with being the self we think we are. To give up our habit of ego-identification means a surrender of our sense of reality and a step into an unknown Reality that is beyond all that we have heretofore taken to be real.

This may be a painful process, for Reality may contain certain pains that we have been avoiding. This may also be a releasing process, for Reality may contain possibilities that we have not been noticing. In all cases, Reality is a killer of our customary self-image or ego. This ego-death includes the death of our sense of reality. This death cannot be welcomed by our ego. But such deaths can be welcomed by our deeper self, our True Nature, that here-and-now flow of Awe. Indeed, it is only our True Nature (our Spirit Being) that can welcome an expanded realization of who we truly are.

Thus the fuller realization of our True Nature means passing through experiences that we humans typically avoid. Arrogantly we cling to our false selves no matter how strong or how weak they may appear to us. A familiar self, however objectionable, can be preferred to stepping out into the sheer unknown. Even if we believe that we may thereby become happy and fulfilled, this new person is someone we have never been before. If we are to begin and continue on the journey of Spirit realization, it is necessary for us to face these painful aspects of dying to the old and venturing into the new. We have all experienced these painful times, but we tend to suppress them or mislabel them and thus miss their importance for our Spirit journey.

Here is a poem that describes having holes punctured in our sense of who we think we are. I owe thanks to A. H. Almaas for assisting me to these insights. Each word in this poem has been carefully chosen. This is a complex poem written in two parallel columns. The left column deals with sensing a hole appearing in our ego, seen from the perspective of our ego. The right column deals with sensing this same hole from the perspective of true soul or Spirit. Read the left column of the poem first. Then read the right column. Then read the poem again, reading each verse in the left column followed by its companion verse in the right column.

Some time recently a hole appeared
in who I thought I was.

I looked into that hole and I saw nothing.
I saw blackness.
I saw the darkest of all dark nights.

And I feel deficient.
There is a hole in who I thought I was.
I am not intact but fractured.

I do not know who I am anymore.
I feel strange; I feel lost.
The familiar landmarks have vanished.

I am uncentered.
I don't know what to do.
I have no motivation to do anything.

I am disoriented.
I don't know where I am.
I don't know what direction to take.

I have lost my purpose in life.
I am going nowhere.
Everything is futile.

My life has no real importance.
I am insignificant.
I don't matter.

I feel worthless.
My self-esteem is gone.
I am of no account.

Nothing has any meaning.
I am not involved in my own life.
I just don't care.

I feel scattered.
My life has no point.
I am an old eggshell, broken and useless

Some time recently a hole appeared
In who I thought I was.

I looked into that hole and I saw nothing.
I saw blackness.
I saw the darkest of all dark nights.

As I walked into that hole
I looked back and saw my deficient self.
I saw that "he" was not me.

I am larger than I thought.
I am not the me with a hole.
I am spaciousness, vastness.

Being this vast person is my focus.
This is my life.
This is my calling.

Living the here and now
of my vast actuality
is my direction.

Being my vast being
is my purpose.
I need not cling to passing purposes.

Nothing is more important than my vast being.
My self-constructed selves are but shells
that cannot contain me.

I have no need for value added to my life.
I am value.
I am filled with wonder.

Everything I touch has meaning
because it is I who touch it.
I make meaning wherever I go.

This is the point of my existence:
to shed all self-made selves and
to be the being I am being be-ed to be.

Both columns of this poem view the same moments of living, but these moments look different from the opposing perspectives. *Left column:* As long as we cling to being the ego we have hitherto taken ourselves to be, we will experience the onslaught of Reality as an enemy bringing about "deficiencies" in our familiar person. This painful, assaulting Reality typically produces profound melancholy and downright despair. *Right column:* But if we choose to be open to the fresh Reality streaming into our awareness, we will be open to experiencing levels of fascination that go along with our dread. We may experience levels of joy that accompany our sense of humiliation. And we will experience our capacity for courage to embrace the Awesomeness of Reality as well as the Awe that is bubbling up within us. This expansive Awe, blowing through our lives, is our true soul.

FREEDOM

The poem dramatizes our primal choice: ego delusion or true soul. Experiencing this choice means experiencing our profound "Freedom." When opting for Freedom, we choose to live in the continuing choices of Freedom. When living in bondage to an ego delusion, we cannot choose Freedom, for we have chosen to do what our ego-habits dictate. The poem dramatizes that becoming aware of our ego's delusory narrowness is at the same time becoming aware of our Freedom, our Freedom to choose Freedom rather than to continue in bondage. Freedom is also the freedom to choose bondage. In fact, the experience of Freedom is the awareness that our bondage came about through human choices. Freedom was our initial state. Our hiding within the box of ego identification came about through many complex instances of choosing bondage. Once we have chosen bondage, bondage endures; for bondage does not possess the capacity to choose Freedom. Only Freedom can choose either bondage or Freedom. So the rescue from bondage requires a restoration that cannot be produced by bondage. Freedom comes from beyond our ego's powers. Freedom comes as a free gift that we do not achieve but only accept through a free surrender made possible by this very Freedom.

TRUST

The choice between ego and Spirit can also be called "Trust." If we choose our true nature rather than continuing in the delusion of ego, we trust that our true nature is good for us. Indeed, Trusting our true nature includes Trusting the Whole of Reality that posits us in being this true nature. When the author of Job, Augustine, and others proclaimed that "All that is, is good," they said this from the perspective of our true nature. From the perspective of the ego some things are good and other things are bad. Whatever promotes the ego's sense of reality is good; whatever challenges the ego's sense of reality is bad. To get beyond good and bad into a Trust of Reality, we have to renounce our identification with ego. In Trust, we become who we truly are: a ramp from here to Eternity with angels moving up and down. Trust means becoming a cosmic dialogue with the Awesome, an open encounter with Awesome Overallness and a surrender to the responses of Awe. Freedom and Trust are two aspects of this responding Awe.

LOVE

The choice between ego and true soul can also be called "Love," Spirit Love, Love with a capital "L." Such Love is more than a feeling, more than an act of service, more than a commitment to do something. Such Love is a state of our true nature, a state of Awe, an angel sent by Eternity to traverse our ramp from here to Eternity. Such Love loves the Eternal; it is enchanted with Being; it is fascinated with both life and death; it is curious to explore more and more Reality – however mysterious, however horrible, however challenging. Such Love includes a thoroughgoing and forgiving affirmation of the entire self – body, mind, personality, soul, and Spirit. Such affirmation of self is the prerequisite for loving our neighbor as we love ourselves. Spirit Love includes loving the neighbor, whether friend or enemy, whether delightful or horrific, whether near or far, whether dead or alive, whether living or unborn, whether human or prehuman, whether alive or inanimate, whether earthly or extraterrestrial. Spirit Love cannot be enacted by the ego. Spirit Love is an angel. Spirit Love is not an accomplishment of our ego, but an experience of our true nature in spontaneous operation. The opposite of Spirit Love is malice – malice toward God, malice toward self, and malice toward our neighbors. Identification with the ego ensures a life of malice. Some egos may not admit this, for they call their obsessive manipulation of others "love." Or they call their delusional sentimentality "love." Or they call their dutiful codependency "love," and so on. Malice has a thousand faces, but all of them are masks covering our true face. When all the masks of malice are removed, our true face is Love. Love, like Freedom and Trust, is who we are.

* * * * * * * * * * *

So how can we be delivered from malice, mistrust, and bondage? How can we become dead to ego and alive to our true nature? How can we be restored to the humanity that identifies with Jesus, the Buddha, and other persons who symbolize human authenticity? These questions point to the underlying topic of this entire book.

5.

A Vocabulary of Inwardness

"Self," "soul," "personality," "ego," "Spirit," and "mind" – these terms point to different aspects of the flow of living within each singular human being. Different writers use these words in different ways. These terms tend to slip and slide, flowing into one another. Furthermore, descriptions of our inner being are clouded by the limitations of words. Inward processes are not nouns or verbs. These processes mock all linguistic containers. Nevertheless, I find that a careful use of words can help us notice the difference between flowing in a natural manner being our true self and defending a self-created self. In this chapter, I am going to further clarify how I am using these basic words. This will be a review of insights already stated or implied and a preparation for the more detailed explorations of later chapters. I am especially concerned to define "soul" and to underline how personality is a fixation of the flow of the true nature of the soul. Spirit with a capital "S" will be my name for the true nature of the soul. By "Spirit" and "true soul" I mean the same unachieved gift of our essential nature.

SELF

"Self" is the most general of these terms. It can mean anything and everything from our physical body to our deepest inward being. This term is associated with how we identify who we are. Are we our bodies? Are we our sensations? Are we our desires? Are we our emotions? Are we our thoughts? Or are we something deeper and more inward? What is our true self? What is our authentic self? The term "self" is more a question than an answer.

SOUL

"Soul" is a term I stopped using for a time. I needed to drop every meaning of this term that was associated with being a ghostly substance that lives on after the body dies and ends up in a terrible place called "hell" or a wonderful place called "heaven." I first consented to use the word "soul" when discussing African American soul music, but I did not explore at that time how such music was rooted in the deep flow of our authentic humanity. Nevertheless, the word "soul" in soul music did hold for me the sense of an inward core that is emotionally open and expressive, a capacity to be deeply sad and deeply happy. Such an understanding of "soul" turned out to be a good beginning for a fresh use of this word.

I have been further encouraged to reinstate the term "soul" by the teachings of A. H. Almaas in his book *The Inner Journey Home*. He uses the word "soul" to indicate the natural flow of awareness in the present moment of our living. By "awareness" I mean that consciousness of consciousness that is unique to the human species. Soul is that aware presence that we can experience in the depths of our particular solitary being. So understood, soul is a flowing and impressionable actuality. Like flowing water, it interacts with whatever it touches; the soul is influenced by whatever is being experienced. The soul is the central "me" whether that soul is in estrangement and despair or participating in a true and happy state of being. In the first two chapters I described our true soul with the image of a ramp from here to Eternity with angels moving down and up.

When the soul is being its true being it is like water that flows freely through all the situations of living, taking them in and actively engaging in them. But this flowing water can become frozen into rigid estrangements. Frozen water is water that does not flow well anymore. It moves slowly like a glacier or awkwardly like ice cubes. Rigid cubes can make it through some situations but not others. The soul, when flowing well, can flow through all situations. When rigid, it hangs up on the narrow places of living. Whether rigid or flowing, our soul is an actual presence; it is a palpable quality of our inward life at each moment of time.

When we speak of inward experience, we are speaking of experiences of "soul." This "soul" is more than emotions; it is a sensibility that includes emotions. This "soul" is more than thinking; it is an experience of life that includes thinking. This "soul" is more than the superego of internalized critical judgments, yet the soul is that sensitive flow that is affected by these superego judgments. Thus even the judgments of the superego are experiences of the soul. The soul is that core sensibility, that core presence that we can experience as the actual flow of our inner life.

There is a sense in which the non-human species also manifest soul. Though we only experience soul directly in our own being, we notice behaviors in other species that indicate some sort of "animal soul." I certainly feel that I have a soul-to-soul relationship with my animal friends. I am also aware that we humans tend to project upon our animal friends a human quality of experience that is not actually present. This is especially blatant in some animal fiction. An experience with a living dog or cat is quite different from the likes of Mickey Mouse or Bambi. So, in our observations of our animal friends, let us explore the following assumption. These friends are conscious in all the ways that we are conscious with one extremely subtle and determinative exception: they are not conscious that they are conscious. They do not lie awake nights reflecting upon their unlikely birth or upon their inevitable death.

The human soul is distinguished by its consciousness of being conscious. This enables in our species the great potential for astonishing creativity, grandeur, and saintliness, but also for the harsh feelings of anxiety, guilt, shame, and despair, as well as the great tragedies of malice, self hate, delusion, and destructiveness.

PERSONALITY

"Personality" is a term I will use to point to a pattern of habits built up by the soul over the years. Each of us "develops" a personality. The personality is developed in dialogue with the experiences we are having. Each experience of living can be summarized and remembered as a little dialogue of encounter and response. These little dialogues are stored in memory, reinforce one another, and become habitual patterns that we apply consciously or unconsciously to our ongoing perceptions of Reality. These stored dialogues also include our repertoire of responses that we can play out in our ongoing circumstances. The term "personality" points to this overall pattern of an individual's patterns of perception and response. We would not want to be without a personality, and we want our personality to be a functional personality rather than a dysfunctional one. Our personality is our default pattern for living. It is what we normally perceive, think, know, and do. Without a personality we would have no order in our lives, no repertoire of responses, no skills of living, and little or no consciousness of our consciousness. We would still be conscious in the way that an infant is conscious – totally merged with the flow of experience, but that experience would be undifferentiated and unreflected. The infant is conscious without interference from a highly structured personality, but the infant is not conscious of that consciousness and does not yet have the reflective powers to put that consciousness of consciousness into a realized form of living.

Our development as a personality is, in the optimal case, attended by the development of an expanding consciousness of consciousness. Having a personality is necessary for our human development, and it is advantageous for practical living. But our personality can also become the locus of a serious distortion: it presents us with a way of becoming estranged from our true nature. Since the personality is a product of memory, since it is a set of habits, well practiced through the past years of our living, the personality is not entirely appropriate for living in the here-and-now flow of actuality. When we identify with our personality, we limit our view of who we are to our personality. We become a restricted soul. Our true soul, our Spirit, has become trapped in the box of personality.

When we are stuck in the habits of personality, the flowing water of the soul no longer flows freely; it is restrained. The normally flowing waters of the soul have become frozen. The image of "frozen" is not an exact description, for the personality is also dynamic. The personality, like the soul, is a living process, an aliveness in ongoing motion. Awake or asleep, the personality is an ever-operating dynamic. But this operation is machinelike. It is fixated into certain repetitive patterns. It is predictable in how it responds to given situations. It can be characterized. Its patterns can be described. Various psychological systems have delineated the various ways that human beings become personalities. In Part Three of this book I am going to examine nine specific personality types. These nine types, known as the enneagram personality types, comprise a useful topology, an empirical gestalt of the personality types that human beings typically develop. It is helpful for us to discern what personality type we are, for this assists us to see the ways that we are rigid or fixated and thereby separated from the full flow of our authentic soul. Observing our personality can give us guidance for the way back from being limited by personality fixations to rejoining the flowing nature of our true soul.

EGO

"Ego" is the "me" I think I am. It is helpful to speak of "ego" in first person singular. My ego is my picture of me created by me. This picture is more than my reflection in a mirror. Usually, my picture of me takes into account the personality habits that I have noticed myself manifesting. Also, this picture of me may be elaborated with denials and additions to what I notice about myself. I may be entirely unconscious of parts of my personality. These very real factors, which are noticed by many others, may not go into my picture of myself. I may be minimally aware of my personality and primarily identify with my physical body. In whatever way I have come to picture myself, this self-constructed self-image is my ego. We could say that my ego is my image of my soul. But this image of my soul is not the same as my actual soul. The "ego" I think I am includes some of the sensibilities and powers of my actual soul, but the full reality of my soul is suppressed or naively overlooked.

For example, I can be aware that I am an aware being and still not realize the amazing awareness than I am. I can take in situations and respond to them and still not realize the depth of the Freedom that I am. My image of who I am can remain very far from the reality of who I am. I can be unaware of both my wondrous actuality and my deep estrangements from my actuality. When I think that my ego is "me," I have exchanged my real "me" for a self-picture of my own construction.

How does this "image of me" I am calling "ego" come about? Let us notice that the personality is like a building made of thousands of little dialogues that comprise my memory of my previous living. Each of these little dialogues might be pictured as a rod. One end of the rod can be labeled "I" and the other end of the rod can be labeled "other." Each rod is an "I"-to-"other" dialogue. The "other" may be my mother, a nipple, my crib, a friend, an enemy, my house, my culture, my planet, etc. My personality is a structure of habits made out of all these rods. Now, suppose that my ever-active mind asks the question "Who am I?" An answer to that question can arise through a gestalt of some of the "I" ends of these remembered rods of dialogue. The ego, being "mind-made" from these remembered dialogues, may be somewhat useful in assessing who I am. But this mental creation of me is always a misrepresentation of my entire soul. Being my ego is a substitute for being my true soul. If I believe that my ego is the true me, I have fallen away from being, in the present moment, the flowing reality of the soul that I actually am. The ego is a misrepresentation, a mere image of who I think I am. But this ego is not me in my fullness. My fullness is a ramp from here to Eternity with angels moving down and up upon it. I am a more expansive being than I think I am. When I surrender to being my true soul, I have possibilities and options that the ego does not allow itself to notice. The ego, like the personality, is stuck in its ruts. The true soul is alive in the living present as a mysterious and creative noticer and actor.

SPIRIT

"Spirit" is a word I am using for the soul that is functioning in the flow of its true nature. I am using "Spirit" and "Holy Spirit" interchangeably. This is an important theological assertion. Holy Spirit is just Spirit, the Awe responses that are natural to every human being. Such Spirit is called "Holy" because it is the Whole, Real, Awe-filled Self. Holy Spirit is a ramp from here to Eternity with angels moving down and up upon it. In other words, Awe initiated by the Presence of the Awesome is the true nature of the soul. Whenever this Awe-relatedness dawns, all the little dialogues of our lives become parts of this one Master Dialogue between the Awe-filled Self and the Awesome Other. Each specific dialogue of our lives is surrounded by this Master Dialogue. Standing behind each person and each object in our lives is that Holy Other of Complete, Inclusive, Overwhelming Reality. Living beneath each of my responses to another person or object is the Holy Self, the Awe-filled Self, the complete self, the self I actually am in all its fullness. The ordinary aspects of my life can become for me transparent to the Holy Other and this Holy Self. The Holy Other moves down the ramp encountering me as the Awesome. The Holy Self moves up the ramp as a response of Awe to the Awesome. When Christian Theology uses the term "Holy Spirit," we need to learn to associate that term with these ongoing Awe responses to the Awesome Other.

Awe is a flow. Awe is the flow of dread, fascination, and courage that characterize the soul that allows itself to stay in the Presence of the Awesome and be filled with Awe. Awe has many aspects, each difficult to describe, yet clear as day to the person experiencing the Awe. These many aspects of Awe have been pointed to with words like: "trust," "love," "freedom," "tranquility," "bliss," "joy," "strength," "autonomy," "allurement," "merging," "enlightenment," "realization," "nirvana," and so on. All the "angels" described in the earlier chapters are states of Awe emanating from the Awesome and returning to the Awesome as actions by the true "me."

"Spirit realization," in good Christian theology, means becoming more fully who we essentially are. Spirit realization means a journey through time in which we move toward identifying with our Spirit Being and thus away from identifying with who we think we are (ego) or with our fixated habits (personality). Spirit realization also entails movement from our initial experiences of Spirit toward an ever-fuller awareness and embodiment of Spirit. Spirit Realization is the core topic of this book.

MIND

Finally, I need to clarify what I am pointing to with the word "mind." Some writers are using the term "mind" to refer to the whole inner being. Others speak of "mindfulness" in a manner that implies that the mind includes attention and intention. I am assuming that attention and intention are functions of the soul. Attention and intention are aspects of our consciousness of consciousness.

I am using the term "mind" to point to the biological brain viewed from the inside by the soul. I am distinguishing the soul (our living consciousness of consciousness) from the mind. The mind is a tool of the soul. The soul is aware of mind and uses mind. Without the tool of the mind the soul would be greatly handicapped. Indeed, the mind evolved as an aid to the soul in being the grand soul that characterizes our human essence. The gift of the biological mind has given the soul its ability to communicate with others and to reflect upon its own experience.

There are two basic levels of the human mind. A description of these helps to further define the reality pointed to by the term "mind." First, there is the mind that humans share with all recently evolved animal life. I call this level "the image-using mind." By "images" I mean concrete multi-sensory reruns of previous experiences. The brain seems to act like billions of tiny recording machines that make multi-sensory recordings. Sights, sounds, smells, and pain record especially well. New smells, sights, sounds, tastes, pains, pleasures remind us of those early recordings. The brain throws up a host of somewhat organized information to interpret the current incoming sensory experiences. The brain of a cat, dog, horse, porpoise, chimpanzee, and human all work very well at organizing these memories and current experiences into useful guidelines for current conscious choices in anticipation of yet to happen futures.

The second level of mind is unique to humans. (Perhaps a few other species have intimations of this mental process or did have before they became extinct). This level of mind has to do with symbol using, where symbols are abstract mental products that *stand for* a collection of these more concrete multi-sensory images. Symbols may stand for a set of common aspects of many experiences. For example, "four" is a symbol that gathers into association four chairs, four dogs, and four clouds. Dogs to not use or notice abstractions of this nature, but for humans such abstractions or symbols are the key to describing language, mathematics, and all the arts. This mental facility in the human brain is, I believe, unique among currently living species. This mental capacity makes possible our complex cultures, language, art, and so on. The aspect of "human mind" is the biological foundation necessary for the emergence of human soul – that consciousness of being conscious that characterizes the human.

Consciousness and soul need to be distinguished from both levels of mind. Thinking is an action of the soul using the mind (the interior experience of brain) to intensify consciousness and apply that consciousness to survival needs as well as to inquiries of a heightened curiosity and projects of bold adventure.

As we have already described and will describe further in later chapters, the second level of mind is a great gift enriching the life of the human species exponentially. And at the same time, these enhanced capacities of the human mind bring into play a horror in the life of the human species. This horror begins with mistaking some self-created product of mental meaning for Reality. In Christian theology this mistaking is called "sin." In the best of Christian understanding, the body is good; the mind is good; consciousness is good; the whole of human nature is good; but humanity can confuse these Reality-established goods with a self-invented "unreality" by which Reality is then judged to be partly good and partly evil. Sin is this confusion of Reality with a human invention of reality. This confusion leads to despair, for Reality cannot be defeated. To be at odds with Reality is a losing hand. The healing of sin entails folding that losing hand and taking in a new deal that honors Reality more fully.

This challenge to live beyond the mind (seeing mind as a tool of the soul) is not to be misunderstood as a negation of the goodness of the mind. Rather, it is a negation of a common ego-delusion about the mind. Since the ego is "a picture of me" created by the soul's use of mind, it is understandable that a soul who has identified with that ego tends to view this creation of the mind as immortal. But the mind is as mortal as finger nails. It is simply the soul's interior experience of the brain, a product of biological evolution. The mind is wondrous. The human mind is one of the most wondrous developments in the whole evolutionary story, but the mind is finite, which means incapable of grasping Final Reality. Final Reality can, however, be experienced directly though those enigmatic processes of soul that we have called "intuition," "inspiration," "enlightenment," "revelation," and other "beyond-mind" experiences. Mind can reflect upon these experiences, draw inferences from them, organize life in terms of them, but the mind cannot understand them. All experiences of Final Reality are beyond the mind. Nevertheless, Final Reality is that incomprehensible Awesomeness that we all face in every moment of living. Our souls are in direct contact with this Eternal Mysteriousness, unless we have retreated into the egos we have invented by the operations of our wondrous minds.

Getting out of our mind and into our soul's direct experience is prerequisite for the journey of Spirit realization, the realization of the "true me."

PART TWO

The Ascending Angels as Spirit Aspects

6.

The Trinitarian Breakdown of Holy Spirit Aspects

In the writings of the apostle Paul we find the Holy Spirit described in many ways: Faith, Hope, Love, Freedom, Wisdom, Joy, Peace. All these words indicate aspects of Holy Spirit – various "families of angels" or "states of Awe."

The One and the Many in Christian Theology

The poetry of angels is a device used in the biblical literature to deal with the "manyness" of our experience of the One God. We might say that there are an infinite number of angels, and yet there is only One Final Reality from which each of these angels is a messenger. There is *One* Awesome Reality that occasions in humans *many* states of Awe.

In Christian heritage, Holy Spirit is said to be *One* and *one with* the Almighty and with the Christ. Nevertheless, the apostle Paul uses *many* terms to describe the Holy Spirit. Our Awe response to Awesome Eternity has many aspects. I believe that Paul's discussion of Holy Spirit can be summarized as a description of three overarching families of Spirit aspects: "Trust," "Love," and "Freedom." Faith, Peace,

Rest, and Wisdom can be shown to be aspects of his fully elaborated description of Trust. Spirit Love, as described by Paul, John, and others, can be shown to include aspects like Strength, Enchantment, Joy, and Compassion. Courage, Decisiveness, Liberation, and Hope can be viewed as aspects of a fully elaborated description of Freedom. All these and other such terms can be viewed as angels, as aspects of our Awe response to the Ultimate Awesomeness.

Three is a special number in the Christian heritage. First of all, Christian theology distinguishes three primary aspects of the experience of the One God: God, the Awesome Otherness; God, the Awe itself; and God, the Awed humanity in history. The Wind of Awe blowing through our lives is the Holy Spirit. And this wind, this Spirit, this human essence, this True Nature can be described as three families of Awe experience: Trust, Love, and Freedom. These three subparts of Awe can be show to be parallel with the master trilogy of the Awesome, the Awe, and the Awed Ones.

Trust is Awe as a relation with the Awesome. In Trust we know the All-Encompassing, Almighty Wholeness as Love for us. Through Trust, the Final Reality, in spite of its mysteriousness and severity, becomes our Friend.

Love (Spirit Love) is Awe as a relation with Awe itself. Love is the deep being of Awe. Love is the strength and delight in being with Reality. Love is enchantment with Reality. Love is compassion for all beings.

Freedom is Awe as a relation with the community of Awed Ones. Freedom is being the Awed part of the human species. Freedom is doing Awe, doing Spirit, doing Trust, doing Love, and doing Freedom in the everyday moments of living.

The following diagram shows these relationships:

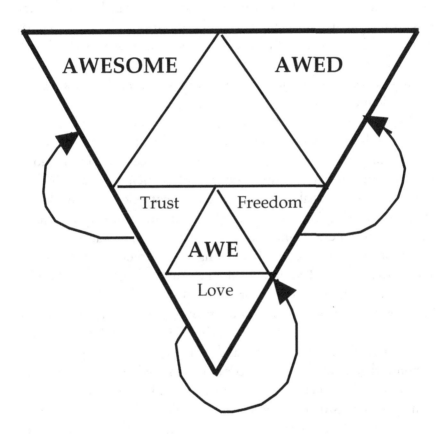

Knowing, Being, and Doing Spirit

These Trinitarian dynamics are rooted in the nature of human consciousness. Consciousness is both knowing and doing, both attention and intention, both passive and active, both sensitive and responsive. A third basic aspect of human consciousness is a style of living that holds our knowing and our doing together. I will call this "being." A style of being may be balanced or imbalanced; it may be a natural flow or a fixed pattern. Whatever be our style of being, it undergirds and informs our knowing and doing. Knowing-being-doing is a unified dynamic of consciousness. These three inseparable aspects define the functions of consciousness.

When we use the word "knowing" to indicate a third of this knowing-being-doing dynamic, "knowing" does not mean information or rational content. "Knowing," in this context, means our foundational participation in Reality. This foundational participation may include information or rational content, but this content reflects a deeper knowing. The knowing indicated in this knowing-being-doing dynamic is deeper than words. It includes the rationally unknowable as well as the rationally knowable. Such knowing means an openness to Reality, a receptiveness of Reality, a willingness to have all one's treasured rational content contradicted or upended by Reality. Consciousness begins with this passive but curious "taking in" of Reality. An amoeba differs from a rock in its ability to "take in" its surroundings and "take in" its internal genetic messages and then use this knowing to forge a response that tends toward its comfort and feeding, its survival and the survival of its species. The human species is much more inclusive in its sensitivities than the amoeba. Knowing, in the human species, is complex and profound beyond the capacities of the human mind to fathom. Furthermore, our knowing of Reality and of ourselves is occluded by the various fixations and rigidities that have become habits in our thinking and living.

Knowing, when allowed to flow naturally, flows into ever-deeper connections with our True Nature, our fullness of being, our Holy Spirit of Trust, Love, and Freedom. In this sense, being follows knowing. Progress toward more consciousness and greater authenticity takes the path of moving from an ever-more-open knowing to an ever deeper being of our True Being. This being of our True Being then becomes the foundation out of which our active living proceeds. This is the natural flow of consciousness: from knowing to being to doing.

When we enact or "do" our current state of being we expose ourselves to further Reality. This can mean an expansion of our knowing that can lead to a further deepening of our being of our True Being. Enacting that deeper level of being further enriches our doing. Knowing-being-doing-knowing-being-doing is a continuing flow toward an ever-more-open knowing to an ever-more-deep being to an ever-more-effective doing . . . as an unending process.

Delusionary living comes about by reversing this natural direction – that is, knowing-doing-being-knowing-doing-being-etc. When we jump from knowing to doing without first being some fresh aspect of our True Being, then our action proceeds from the current concepts in our minds rather than from an integrated state of our personal being. This results in moralistic, rigid, and even malicious actions.

Also, when our living is moving in reverse from our current patterns of doing to our next states of being, then our actions are functioning as a limit on the intensity with which we are being our True Being. We do not arrive at greater authenticity by willfully creating that authenticity. Rather, willfulness creates inauthenticity. We arrive at greater authenticity by allowing our True Being to flourish with its own power.

Finally, when we are moving in reverse from our current level of being toward knowing we limit our openness to know by what we are currently being. Knowing is therefore blocked: it becomes a process of justification for the style of being that we are currently being, rather than a fresh openness toward further Reality.

A visual presentation of these dynamics may help. This first diagram depicts the progression toward greater authenticity.

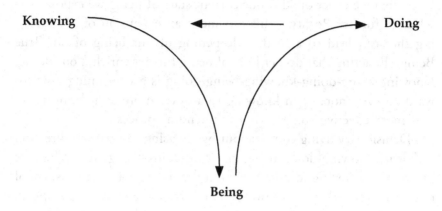

If we reverse the arrows, we have a diagram that depicts regression toward moralistic doing, delimited being, and occluded knowing.

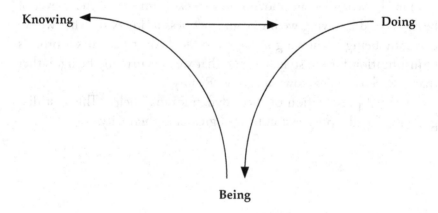

The following illustrations may help us focus our consciousness on our own experience of these dynamics.

Christian fundamentalists begin with a literal knowledge of the New Testament and move from there to an ethics of action based on precepts found in their interpretation of that book. This renders *doing* moralistic – a rigid following of mentally conceived rules. The fundamentalist then moves from this moralistic *doing* to a reduced style of *being* that supports moralistic action. The wonder and fullness of True Being is reduced to a justification for an already operating outward performance. This is the opposite of allowing True Being to flow into action. Lastly, this reduced state of being curtails further *knowing*. It renders *knowing* closed rather than curious, open, and willing to take in greater Reality.

We can illustrate movement in the positive direction by describing a progressive mode of biblical interpretation in which we seek fresh truth from the Bible about our lives rather than rational answers, religious beliefs, or ethical rules that give us a sense of security. We search the Scriptures for clues to the actual experience of our ongoing inner lives. We study the Scriptures in order to inquire into our own being. We open ourselves to see more deeply how human life actually functions. We allow truth to come into our lives from beyond our current doctrines and moralities. Then, as the *being of our true being* is deepened, we are enabled to act from our deep being rather than from our minds only. This corresponds to the biblical teachings about acting from Love rather than from law. We thereby learn what the New Testament means by Freedom and how enacting this Freedom of our True Being differs from enacting the legalisms of our rational mind, the customs of our group, or the dictates of the internal structures of our superego. When we act from our Spirit Freedom rather than from our current formulations of mind, we find that these ventures of free *doing* teach us further lessons of *knowing* how Reality truly functions. And this cycle continues – intensifying being, further freeing our action, and deepening our knowing.

The knowing-being-doing order of unfoldment is congruent with the way Final Reality functions when our life is being expanded. The Christian Trinity as a whole follows this knowing-being-doing dynamic of living. First of all, the Christian experience of God is *knowing* the Almighty, the encounter with the descending angels, the messengers from the Awesome. This leads to *being* in our deep Being the response of Awe to that Awesomeness. This response is the Holy Spirit of Trust, Love, and Freedom. And this being of our Spirit Being then leads to *doing* the life of the Awed Ones. In other words, we manifest the body of Christ in the practical processes of our life story and in the specific history of the times in which we live. Such living then brings us into deeper knowing of the Almighty, and the cycle continues.

The progression of knowing-being-doing is an endless journey in the sense that every new appropriation of being leads to further doing and further knowing and still further deepening of our appropriation of being our True Being. Knowing Spirit leads to being Spirit leads to doing Spirit leads to knowing Spirit leads to being Spirit leads to doing Spirit as an endless spiral of ever deepening movement into the Infinite abyss of pure Mystery.

For many years I have cherished these closing lines of the D. H. Lawrence poem entitled "New Heaven and New Earth":

> Sightless and strong oblivion in utter life takes
>   possession of me!
> The unknown, strong current of life supreme
> drowns me and sweeps me away and holds me down
> to the sources of mystery, in the depths,
> extinguishes there my risen resurrected life
> and kindles it further at the core of utter mystery.[4]

The Aspects of Trust, Love, and Freedom

The knowing-being-doing pattern can also be used to discern and organize the inclusive subparts of Trust, Love, and Freedom. Here is an outline of the major subparts of these three inclusive aspects of Holy Spirit. This is an abstract outline designed to plot basic differentiations. In the following chapters I will descriptively illustrate each of these aspects of Holy Spirit.

---

[4]   D. H. Lawrence, *Selected Poems* (Viking Press: 1959) page 81

Trust can be subdivided into three inclusive subparts:

1. Trust is trust in the human capacity to pay attention to the full Reality that confronts us. Trust is beyond mental belief, yet it includes trust in the discriminating capabilities of the human mind. Trust is openness to knowing Reality, however grim, satisfying, challenging, rewarding, or joyous. This aspect of Trust is a state of Awe that I will call **The Illumination of Transparent Attention**. This is the knowing aspect of Trust.

2. Trust is trust in the truth of our forgiveness and benevolent care by the Every-Thing-Ness in which all things cohere which is also the No-Thing-Ness from which all things arise and into which all things return. This Trust in the benevolence of Reality toward our awakening soul is an actual experience rather than simply a mental assent to an idea. This aspect of Trust is a state of Awe that I will call **The Absolute Truth of Universal Forgiveness.** This is the being aspect of Trust.

3. Trust is trust in the human capacity to accept our acceptance and let Reality be the Reality it is. Such trust is the surrender of all efforts to deserve or earn or cause the divine benevolence that is being extended to us. This aspect of Trust is a state of Awe that I will call **The Rest of Effortless Letting Be**. This is the doing aspect of Trust.

Love can be subdivided into three inclusive subparts:

1. Love is love as the unconditional affirmation of one's own true being. This love is experienced as confidence, as faith in oneself, as an energy of strength in the face of all circumstances, as a sense of autonomy, as a reconciliation with aloneness or singularity. This aspect of Love is a state of Awe that I will call **The Self Affirmation of Autonomous Strength**. This is the knowing aspect of Love.

2. Love is love as the unconditional affirmation of the Every-thing-ness/No-thing-ness we can lovingly call "God." This love is a felt experience, an actual state of Awe rather than simply an idea or an ideal. This aspect of Love is a state of Awe that I will call **The Joy of Enchantment with Being**. This is the being aspect of Love.

3. Love is love as the unconditional love of all one's neighboring beings. This love is experienced as an active and creative consent to do our living with whomever and among whomever we are actually living. This love

includes enemies as well as friends. Indeed, it sees God's love flowing toward us through both enemy and friend, and it responds to both enemy and friend in affirmation of their best interests. This aspect of Love is a state of Awe that I will call **The Realism of Out-flowing Compassion.** This is the doing aspect of Love.

Freedom can be subdivided into three inclusive subparts:

1. Freedom is freedom from bondage to the habits of the developed personality and its ego delusion. This Freedom is experienced as a journey beyond the appearances of the body, beyond emotions, beyond thoughts, beyond states of soul to the interior ground that supports all aspects of personhood. This aspect of Freedom is a state of Awe that I will call **The Primal Merging Beyond Self Image.** This is the knowing aspect of Freedom.

2. Freedom is freedom from bondage to all views of good and evil. This freedom entails a disidentification with one's superego, with the images of good and evil taught to us by our parents or society. This Freedom is an actual experience rather than an idea or an ideal. This aspect of Freedom is a state of Awe that I will call **The Inherent Purity Beyond Good and Evil.** This is the being aspect of Freedom.

3. Freedom is freedom from bondage to fatalistic perceptions of the surroundings. This freedom means experiencing the future as always open, that one is a co-creator with the Creative Wholeness. This aspect of Freedom is a state of Awe that I will call **The Attuned Working Beyond Fate.** This is the doing aspect of Freedom.

In the following chapters I will describe each of these nine aspects of Holy Spirit in considerable detail.

On the next page is a triangular diagram that displays these nine basic aspects of Holy Spirit in a pictorial arrangement. Within each overarching triangle, the knowing subpart is placed in the upper left, the being subpart is placed in the downward center position, and the doing subpart is placed in the upper right.

I have placed the numbers 1 though 9 with the title of each of the nine major subparts. Each number refers to one of the nine personality types in the enneagram analysis of Spirit aspects and personality types. In Part Three, I will discuss the enneagram heritage in detail. I will use the enneagram heritage to describe the many-faceted fall into false identification. But first I want to describe, in a more thorough fashion, the Angels of Trust, the Angels of Love, and the Angels of Freedom.

Consider this triangle to be a piece of contemplative art, a device that allows the mind to open to the wide range of experiences that enrich our understanding of "Holy Spirit." Obviously, this is a rational model and like all rational models it can be superseded by a better model; nevertheless, this model points beyond itself to the actuality of Holy Spirit in human life. And this perception of Holy Spirit is based upon decades of my personal experience. Nevertheless Spirit is always more than any rational model can encompass, always more than any one person has discovered. Yet, the capacities of the human mind include this strange ability to give memorable order to the Incomprehensible.

7.

The Angels of Trust

In our colloquial talk, we sometimes refer to our "higher angels." This chapter and the next two describe these angels, these states of our essential being. The angels of Trust link us to Eternity. Trust is part of our Awe response to the encounter with the Awesome Mysterious Final Reality. We do not actually experience Awe or the Awesome unless Trust is present. Without Trust the encounter with the Awesome is avoided or forgotten. Standing still for the experience of Awe before the Awesome requires Trust. As we take courage to live in Trust over a sustained period of time, our awareness can become tuned to the nature of Trust. We can discriminate its major subparts.

In this chapter I am going to describe the three major families of angels of the overall angelic clan of Trust. Assuming that I can render such a description may seem presumptuous, for who am I that I can say what Trust is, much less give names and descriptions to the three major subparts of Trust? I confess that I – in spite of being a long-term experiencer and describer of Trust – am also a beginner on this topic. We are all beginners on the boundless topic of Trust. What I will say in this chapter will not be all that could be said. It will not be all that I could say. Therefore, I ask the reader to recognize that I am playing with word symbols in order to provoke recognition of a Reality that is beyond words and beyond rational order, including the order that I will provide.

In the model I am presenting, the angels of Trust are divided into three subfamilies. Here are the names of these families: **The Illumination of Transparent Attention, The Absolute Truth of Universal Forgiveness**, and **The Rest of Effortless Letting Be**. These families of angels can go by the following shorter names: **Transparent Attention, Universal Forgiveness**, and **Effortless Letting Be**.

Transparent Attention is the **knowing** pole of Trust. Universal Forgiveness is the **being** pole of Trust. And Effortless Letting Be is the **doing** pole of Trust.

The Illumination of Transparent Attention

The following poem is a playful piece, but also a serious piece about Transparent Attention. It expresses an important point: we begin the journey toward Spirit realization by paying attention in the present moment. We notice what is happening to us within our own bodies, within our own minds, and within the waters of Reality within which we swim.

> I opened my Bible
> and found to my surprise
> that the words were gone.
>
> Every page contained the same phrase,
> "Pay Attention!"
> I searched other scriptures
> and they were all the same.
> Every page said,
> "Pay Attention!"
>
> "Pay attention to what?" I inquired.
> Every page said back,
> "The content will be provided.
> Pay attention to
> paying attention."
>
> "But where shall I look?"
> I inquired.

"Look anywhere.
Look everywhere –
pain and pleasure
death and life
failure and success
written and unwritten
nature and history.
Just pay attention!"

"Is it helpful to ask questions?"
I inquired.

"Your questions can be excuses
for not paying attention.
But paying attention can include questions–
questions that admit your ignorance
questions that are curious inquiry.
Such questions are paying attention.
So do you have any more questions?"

"Thousands," I replied.

"What are they?"

"Well, I don't know.
I want to know
what my best questions are."

"Pay attention!
and you will know."

Gene Marshall 2002

With the title "Transparent Attention" I am pointing to a knowing of Reality that precedes all attempts at rational ordering. Transparent Attention is about how our awareness participates in the Every-Thing-Ness in which all things cohere. Our awareness makes discriminations before our mind begins its work. Before an infant's mind has a name for toe, infant consciousness begins to be aware that its toe is *me* in a way that the crib slat is not. Awareness makes differentiations between *my* being and *my* mother's being before *my* mind has a name for mother or for self. As the mind learns names and learns to use them well, the self remains an aware being who can watch the mind do its work. Awareness can watch the mind make representations of what awareness already knows.

Our awareness can differentiate specific things from the enduring Every-Thing-Ness without losing the awareness that all things participate in one overarching Every-Thing-Ness. When awareness focuses only on our mental representations, it can forget that these separately named things are not actually separated in Reality. Such forgetting is most serious when we assume that the "I" who rationally knows things is separate from the things we know. It is a delusion for us to assume that "I" am "over here" and the things known by "me" are "over there." I the knower and the things I know are interlaced. So, "here and there," "them and me," are only mental discriminations. In reality, each of us is an inseparable, ongoing, flowing part of an All-encompassing Oneness. This we know, not by any rational deduction, but by paying attention.

We might say that all things are "transparent" to the Wholeness that stands behind them. An All-inclusive-Every-Thing-Ness is shining through each of the specific things our conscious experience has differentiated. Our own self and all things seen by us are expressions of this Oneness. All beings are a wave, a ripple in the one ocean of Reality. Specific "things" come and go. Things emerge, stand forth for a time, and then return to the No-Thing-Ness from which they came. This No-Thing-Ness is also the Every-Thing-Ness in which all things cohere. Awareness knows this or can know this without having to mentally think about it. But awareness can forget this when our focus of consciousness is upon the mind's representations rather than simply noticing Reality's Oneness of vast diversity.

When mentally focused, we live in our own self-created world of ideas. In this mentalization of Reality, a specific oak tree is just an instance of the enduring idea "oak tree." But that specific oak tree is not fully seen unless the conscious soul sees the enduring Every-Thing-Ness that is shining through that specific oak tree. This "shining through" gives this specific oak tree its sacredness. This shining through also honors the sacredness of the human awareness that is differentiating this oak tree. We can also notice that this Every-Thing-Ness/No-Thing-Ness of Total Reality is also shining through the human soul as this soul pays attention to this specific oak tree or to other things, processes, dynamics, or realities.

Transparent Attention also views the work of the mind and sees it as transparent to the sacred Whole. The soul of a human can know that there is no end to the mind's work – no final permanence of knowledge – nevertheless, the soul can also know that the mind's work is sacred, honored, and necessary. The mind is the soul's tool for the practical survival of the body and also a tool for the soul's curious inquiry into the Mysterious Overallness that is directly felt as an impression upon the soul's sensitivity. When the soul trusts its own Transparent Attention, the Inclusive Overallness streams through every thing, every event, every process that the mind can name.

Most important of all, Transparent Attention means trusting Reality rather than trusting one's own rational constructions. Our openness to learn more is an aspect of trusting Reality. When Reality is viewed as trustworthy, we have found an invincible type of trust, for Reality can indeed be trusted to be Reality. In this sense, Transparent Attention has a quality of paradoxical certitude, a quality of rest, a quality of knowing the Final Mystery and thereby knowing everything that can be known. Transparent Attention sees directly into "The-Way-It-Is," (or as some prefer to put it: "The-Way-It-Moves.")

Transparent Attention also sees the ways that the human soul, my human soul, backs away from paying attention, deludes itself, and sets up patterns of partial truth that become defended from the whole truth. Transparent Attention sees that this fall into delusion and defensiveness is a process that was going on before I was born. It is a process into which I was raised and within which I continue to live. I may subtract some of these illusions, but I may also add some fresh illusions of my own. Whatever be my current state of delusion, Transparent Attention sees or can see that this is the case – that I am a thinker and speaker of lies and that I dwell in the midst of an entire society of liars. The deeper I trust the angels of Transparent Attention and thus pay attention to the fullness of Reality, the deeper I see how far I and my companions have fallen away from the whole truth, the full truth, and nothing but the truth about the Reality in which we all do actually dwell.

"Confession" is a Christian name for the aspect of Transparent Attention just described. The confession of sin is often spoken about in Christian heritage, but it is frequently perverted into a mere admission of moral failings. Confession, fully understood, goes deeper than moral failings; it includes noticing that even the moral rules that we have failed to obey are themselves departures from Reality. Moral rules are guidelines created by human beings for effective living; social life could not proceed without them. But self-achieved moral goodness can be a moldy virtue that separates us from the greater reality of life; it can become a lie and even a malice that needs to be confessed. As Transparent Attention shines the light on this aspect of our living, confession takes on a deeper meaning.

Deep confession leads us into the dark nights of paying attention to the most distressing aspects of human experience: our despair over life itself, our capacity to prefer death to going on with our existing lives. Yet even in these most grueling moments of our conscious experience, Transparent Attention can see through the despair to the light that shines behind it. Despair is a doorway from our self-created worlds of delusion to the actual realm of our true being. In seeing this, we recognize that Transparent Attention is Trust in the Trustworthiness of Final Reality.

Transparent Attention is not a self-achieved virtue; it is an angel, a gift, a real presence from which we have all run away. It is part of the essential ramp of our soul, a soul that extends from our space-time coordinate to the Eternal Every-Thing-Ness. We do not have to invent Transparent Attention nor achieve it; we only need to allow ourselves to know it, be it, and do it. And this means nothing more and nothing less than allowing our soul to see directly into the Reality we actually experience and thereby into our own most personal fights with and flights from that Reality.

The Absolute Truth of Universal Forgiveness

I have just described the knowing pole of Trust. The being pole of Trust can be named "The Absolute Truth of Universal Forgiveness." Reality is not lying in wait to punish us for our departures from realistic living. The confession of our unrealism does not result in our being beaten or fined or jailed. Our unrealism is our jail; our delusions are our punishment. Confession is our readiness to leave the jail and come home to Reality. And when we arrive home, like the prodigal son in Jesus' parable, Reality runs to meet us, celebrates our return, gives us a kiss, puts new clothes on us, and throws a feast. "This, my son (or daughter), who was lost, is alive again." Reality is one big welcome mat. "Welcome home" is what forgiveness means. Here is a poem that may help us experience or recall this deep truth of forgiveness:

> There is One Truth:
> Forgiveness.
>
> And Truth is One:
> Forgiveness.
>
> The righteous and the wicked
> both vanish into one
> overall humiliation:
> Forgiveness.
>
> The friend and the enemy
> both melt into one
> all encompassing affirmation:
> Forgiveness.
>
> The best and the worst
> play their roles
> in one grand drama:
> Forgiveness.
>
> Blaming someone,
> blaming one's self,
> blaming something,
> blaming everything,
> is not the Truth.
>
> There is one Truth:
> Forgiveness.
>
> When the Truth of forgiveness dawns
> all philosophies of life crumble
> like a tall building
> into a heap of dust.

The Truth of forgiveness
is a scandal to the moralist
and sheer foolishness to the thinker.

But whoever steps off the cliff
of moral and intellectual certitude
into trusting the Truth of forgiveness
becomes mighty and golden,
becomes enlightened royalty
and dedicated servant,
dependable leader and wise follower,
seeing the whole picture
with compassion for all.

Gene Marshall 2002

A. H. Almaas uses the term "Absolute Truth" in a manner that helps me illuminate what I mean by "The Absolute Truth of Universal Forgiveness." He uses the term "Absolute Truth" as the fourth category in his description of the levels of truth.[5] Here is my abbreviated description of his four levels of truth:

1. Relative truth is our awareness of things that come and go. I know my cat. I know my sadness. Cat and sadness come and go.

2. Essential truth is our awareness of being an enduring personal presence. Awareness is consciousness of being conscious. Aware presence is the core or soul of being human.

3. Formless truth is our awareness of the mysterious, transrational, boundless, transconceptual quality of every outward or inward actuality.

4. Absolute truth is our awareness that all formless mysteries, all aspects of personal presence, and all

---

[5]   Almaas, A. H.; *Spacecruiser Inquiry* (Shambhala 2002) page 148

things that come and go are united in the Oneness in which they cohere. Absolute Truth is our awareness that relative truth, essential truth, and formless truth are inseparable aspects of one all-inclusive truth.

And this Absolute Truth is experienced as the "Living Daylight" of forgiveness. We are accepted. We are welcomed home by this Every-Thing-Ness/No-Thing-Ness that is the source and the end, the sustaining and the limiting, as well as the all-encompassing unity of all things.

The Absolute Truth has no duality, no conflicting parts. Absolute truth permits only denial or acceptance by the human soul.

The soul in denial of Absolute Truth sees "my truth" and "your strangeness"; or my "dogma" and your "heresy"; or my "vision" and your "blindness." Living, therefore, becomes conflictual. Life becomes a war against error. Life becomes a constant battle to prevail over opponents, human and cosmic. Life is a challenge to beat life into a proper shape. Life is a game to be won or lost. Life is a struggle to prevail over forces that oppose what we believe to be true.

Those who are aware and accept the Absolute Truth of Universal Forgiveness have no need for victories over anyone or anything, because the victory of Absolute Truth is always already won. The only challenge that remains is assisting others to be aware of this victory. All error has already lost. All error is already forgiven and welcomed home to the Absolute Truth. The only challenge that remains is the challenge to claim this victory, to accept the consequences of living this Truth, and to announce this Truth in the presence of those who are fleeing from it. The consequences of announcing this Truth will surely result in significant rejection by others, but this rejection is not something that has to be defeated. It is already defeated. Its defeat is already manifest in its existence as a futile opposition to the Absolute Truth. The denial of Absolute Truth and of the truthful persons who bear witness to Absolute Truth is the final judgment upon the denial. The denial of Truth melts into nothingness when awareness of Absolute Truth appears.

Those who deny Truth do not know that they do so. And this not knowing what they are doing is part of their denial of the Truth.

To know the Absolute Truth is to no longer deny it. Absolute Truth always wins. Universal Forgiveness simply IS.

This is the Absolute Truth: you are forgiven. You have always been forgiven. You always will be forgiven. Everyone is forgiven. The Muslims are forgiven. The Jews are forgiven. The Hindus are forgiven. Atheists are forgiven. The Buddhists are forgiven. The Christians are forgiven. All are forgiven. All always have been forgiven. All always will be forgiven.

This is the good news that Christians are commissioned to bring to every person on earth. The good news is not that everyone should become a Christian. The good news is that everyone is forgiven.

It is, however, necessary for each of us to accept our forgiveness. When we accept forgiveness it can be said that healing has come into our lives. In the New Testament there is a story about a man named Zacchaeus who was a tax collector for the Romans. Zacchaeus was short of stature but long on cheating. When Jesus came by, Zacchaeus climbed up a tree in order to see this unusual person. Jesus observed his energy and called out that he would have his next meal at Zacchaeus's house. This offended the moralists in the crowd, but Zacchaeus got the message of his forgiveness. He cried out, "I will give half my property to the poor. And if I have swindled anybody out of anything, I will pay him back four times as much." Jesus said to him, "Salvation (healing) has come to this house today."

Healing comes to our being when we accept our forgiveness. As Paul Tillich put it, the completion of the healing experience is the accepting of our acceptance.[6] Our acceptance is a cosmic fact. But we must accept our acceptance for healing to come into our house.

The metaphor of "forgiveness" seems to assume the literal existence of a Personal Divine Somebody who accepts us. But we need not literalize this mythic language. The meaning here is more simple. We do not live in a moral universe. At the profound level of things, everyone is welcomed home to Reality no matter how great his or her departures from Reality have been. When we, the prodigal sons and daughters that we are, return home to the actual Reality in which we live, punishment is not what we encounter. Rather, the Mysterious

---

[6] Tillich, Paul, *The Shaking of the Foundations* (Charles Scribner's Sons: 1948) page 162

Every-Thing-Ness of the actual cosmos is like an ever-loving parent who is exceedingly glad for our return.

It is true that on the temporal level of operation we reap what we sow. If we sow overeating, we reap obesity and its many health issues. If we sow ecological thoughtlessness, we reap dirty air, polluted water, and the like. If we sow greed through our national businesses, we reap hatred throughout the world. But on the profound plane, the Spirit plane, every departure from optimal living is forgiven. When we return to Reality we are not punished for our departure; the departure itself and the despair that goes with it have been our punishment. Returning to Reality is met by an open-armed Reality celebrating our return. Our guilt is relieved. Our future is opened for a fresh start. The sun shines on all aspects of our inner and outer lives. It is as if we were dead and are now alive. It is as if we were blind and now see. It is as if we were deaf and now hear. It is as if we were lame and now walk our actual lives.

There is, however, a certain cost implied in accepting our forgiveness. We have to admit that we are someone for whom forgiveness is needed. This is the real miracle of our healing. This was the miracle of healing in Zacchaeus's life. Zacchaeus acknowledged his need for forgiveness. Having the healing witness of forgiveness come to eat in his house cost him his self-righteous greed. The economic revolution in Zacchaeus's life was merely a sign that Zacchaeus had accepted his forgiveness. Zacchaeus had come home and the startling changes in his behavior signaled his celebration and gratitude for being home.

Every one of us is forgiven. We always have been forgiven. We always will be forgiven. This is the witness that Christians are commissioned to bring to every person on earth. A secondary commission of Christians is to remember Jesus, to remember him as the one who so clearly pointed out this universal truth that everyone is forgiven. Thus, there does exist in Christian heritage a beckoning to become a Christian and to help with this commission to tell all persons about their forgiveness. But if we respond to the beckon to become a Christian in order to be healed, we will be disappointed. It is only the acceptance of our specific forgiveness that heals us. Becoming a Christian is secondary. And we need not become a Christian in order to be healed. We become a Christian in order to be part of that movement that brings the good news of healing forgiveness to others. And as we do this, we need to remain clear that our gift to others is not inviting them to be Christians, but inviting them to be healed through accepting their forgiveness. This is all that is required of those to whom we take the healing witness – that they accept their forgiveness. They can remain Muslims. They can remain Buddhists. They can remain skeptical about all religion. Or they can remain or become Christians. This does not infinitely matter. What infinitely matters is that they accept their forgiveness and return home to Reality. This is the Absolute Truth. This is the being dimension of the family of Angels we call "Trust."

The Rest of Effortless Letting Be

The Rest of Effortless Letting Be is the doing dimension of Trust. Trusting is the opposite of anxiously doing works that attempt to make ourselves worthy of forgiveness. The doing of Trust can also be viewed as a nondoing. This paradoxical nature of Trust has troubled the minds of Christian theologians and religious thinkers for thousands of years. Here is how John Wesley stated this paradox: "Trust is one hundred percent God's gift, and Trust is one hundred percent my action." When Trust is misunderstood as the mind's assent to doctrinal beliefs, Trust becomes an effortful doing that a human being can do or not do. But when Trust is understood as a Spirit aspect, as an actual Trust in the trustworthiness of the Wholeness of Being, then Trust is not something that a human being can simply do whenever he or she chooses. As Christian witnesses like Paul, Augustine, Luther, and Calvin have said, a human being is initially trapped, bound, or enslaved in a lack of Trust. Trust must be given and no amount of effort on the part of the trapped person can generate that Trust. The trapped person, by all his or her own effort, can only deepen the trap. Trust is given as a free gift that springs the trap. Then the human being can do Trust not as an effort that achieves Trust but as a Letting Be of that Trust that already exists. In other words, Trust is not an accomplishment – "lest anyone should boast" (Paul). Trust is an aspect of our Spirit nature, of our personal essence. Our role as a human being who Trusts Reality is an Effortless Letting Be. It is a surrender not an accomplishment. The following poem expands on this topic.

The mightiest of all actions
is Surrender.

Surrender to the Truth.
Surrender to Forgiveness.
Surrender to being one's own essential self
        within one's own actual circumstances.
Surrender to the actual possibilities
        that lie in the offing.
Surrender to being elected by Reality
        to be the Real being I already am.

Willful achievements do not last.
Clever manipulations yield passing victories.
Surrender is the only action that matters.

Surrender joins us
with the good fortune
of our one and only life.
Surrender places us
on the wheel of time
that is our actual calling.
Surrender means being with it
rather than out of it.

Surrender joins us all
body to body and soul to soul
in an intimate love affair
with Being.

Surrender accesses
the life of the entire planet
flowing through us
in creative fruition,
rendering us the
Earth mother of all things,
living and unliving.

Surrender penetrates us,
fertilizes us,
and makes us the place
of Spirit conception.

Gene Marshall 2004

The doing of Trust is a form of Rest. It is the Rest that Augustine was indicating when he said "our hearts are restless until they rest in Thee, O God."

This paradoxical aspect of Trust has been expressed by secular as well as Christian writers. Here is a quotation on this topic from the psychologist and spirit writer A. H. Almaas:

> The most important insight needed for a student to move from the deficient lack of support to the actual state of support is the recognition that the feeling of helplessness, of not knowing what to do to be oneself, is not an actual deficiency, not a personal failing. It is rather, the recognition of a fundamental truth about the self, which is that we cannot do anything in order to be, for to be is not an activity. We can come to this understanding only through the cessation of intentional inner activity. At this point, not to know what to do is a matter of recognizing the natural state of affairs, for since there is nothing that we can do to be, then it is natural that we cannot know what to do. There is nothing to know because such knowledge is impossible. Nobody knows what to do to be, and the sooner we recognize this, the easier is our work on self-realization. In fact, feeling that we don't know what to do to be ourselves is the beginning of the insight that we don't need to do anything.[7]

In other words, Effortless Letting Be is required to be our true being. I have also met Buddhist teachers who recommend a rigorous meditation practice on the one hand and then on the other hand teach that such effort does not accomplish enlightenment. Enlightenment, they say, is an accident that happens when it happens. Meditation merely makes one more "accident-prone."

Paul Tillich, the renowned Christian theologian, tells us that "grace" is such an accident that happens or does not happen. In his sermon "You are Accepted" he tells how "grace" "strikes us when we

---

[7]   Almaas, A. H.; *The Point of Existence* (Shambhala: 2001) page 256

walk through the dark valley of an empty and meaningless life," when we are at the end of our tether, when we do not know what to do to be a true self, when "despair destroys all joy and courage." Sometimes at such a moment it dawns upon us that the helpless person we know ourselves to be is, nevertheless, being supported by something greater than our own ego strengths. Indeed, as our ego is threatened or shaken to its foundations, our true self hears or can hear the message that we are accepted, accepted by that which is greater than our own self acceptance or our lack of it, accepted by that which is greater than other people's acceptance of us or their lack of it, simply "accepted by that which is greater than you, and the name of which you do not know."

Tillich then says, "Do not ask for the name now, perhaps you will find it later. Do not try to do anything now; perhaps later you will do much. Do not seek for anything; do not perform anything; do not intend anything. Simply accept the fact that you are accepted."[8]

The "grace" Tillich describes is a universal aspect of the authentic human Spirit. The doing of Trust is the result of a cosmic doing that is done for us. When we hear ourselves saying, "I am trying hard to be myself," we need to pause and recall that those who are trying to be themselves are not being themselves but are striving to be what they are not and thus are indulging in an unwillingness to be themselves.

When we hear ourselves saying, "I am struggling to live my life in the here and now," we need to pause and recall that no effort is required to live in the here and now. Reality supports living in the here and now. Reality supports this so vigorously and so powerfully that we need not and cannot add anything to the support we already have for living in the here and now. All our efforts to live in the here and now are efforts to not live in the here and now. Living in the here and now requires no effort.

Why might it seem that our authentic life requires effort? We may be unconscious that we are actually attempting to hang on to old patterns of behavior; this does require effort. Instead of relinquishing old patterns, we are trying to live more realistically without relinquishing unrealistic habits. This requires effort, and such halfway authenticity can never succeed. Relinquishing the old patterns is the only route to

---

[8]   Tillich, Paul; The *Shaking of the Foundations* (Charles Scribner's Sons: 1948) page 162

authenticity, to self-realization, to living in the actual here and now, to being present as the Spirit being that we are.

So, the Trust of Effortless Letting Be means noticing that our false self is false and then allowing that falseness to fall away. This relinquishing of the false self becomes more viable for us when we realize that our false self is killing us, driving us to despair, perceiving life to be meaningless and empty, experiencing Reality as against us. It is our lack of Effortless Letting Be that is cutting us down to less than we are, or blowing us up into a fragile balloon of grandiosity. We are misguided when we cling to our effortful creation of an illusory self. This effort kills the true soul. Our true soul is grand, happy, lively, more than we could ever have imagined or hoped for. The "happy" and "appropriate" response is to do nothing – that is, to simply "let be" that authentic being that requires no construction by us.

Does this mean that when we are being our authentic being we never intend anything or do anything? Not at all. As Tillich suggests, "perhaps later you will do much." But this "much" that you or I may do is not done in order to become a true self. It is just an acting out of the true self we are. A true self is both attention and intention. It is the false self that does not pay full attention and does not intend realistic living. Instead, the false self intends to become something "better" than humans are constructed to be. The true self intends to be the true self and this intention manifests as an active presence among those around us, a presence that manifests the quality of being that all human beings are constructed to be. Actively being this presence is the doing that calls others out of their "safe" boats of old personality habits and encourages them to walk with us and with Jesus and with the Buddha on the wild and wondrous waters of our actual lives.

Effortless Letting Be also includes a more vital connection with nature. The Being that we are letting be is a ramp to Eternity from a space/time coordinate in the biological life of planet Earth. Being this ramp means being our natural blood-and-bone embeddedness in the biological evolution of life on this planet. It does not mean flight from life in this dismal Earth suit to some disembodied ghostliness. Our soul is the whole ramp; we are fully embodied in our specific body. At the same time, being this ramp means that we are not identified with our body as the sole definition of who we are. This detached engagement in being our body is not a far off ideal that requires a mighty effort to be realized. Engaged detachment is our natural being, our true being, our Spirit being. Our bodies and our souls are only healthy when we are both detached from our bodies and engaged in our bodies.

In a full realization of this whole-ramp essence, we lay the foundations for a Spirit-based ecological ethics. Christianity became one of the causes of the ecological crisis when it was perverted toward a depreciation of the body. Such moralistic asceticism is the opposite of Effortless Letting Be. Effortless Letting Be, as I am describing it here, is a recovery of the Earth Mother as one of the goddesses or angels moving on our ramp. This angel/goddess teaches us that our earthiness is holy and that there is no holiness without earthiness. We might say that most of the angels that constitute the family of Effortless Letting Be are motherly figures with a warm lap and warm arms for all the natural powers of the human body. Such angels support passion and delight in the pleasures of the body. At the same time the angels of Effortless Letting Be drink in death and destruction – allowing the whole range of finite life to be what it is.

Finally, Effortless Letting Be includes letting be the specific extent of Spirit restoration that is taking place in our current lives. Spirit realization is never complete. Each moment of Effortless Letting Be is a moment of letting that incompleteness be. Each of us is on a specific Spirit journey from our despair, malice, and bondage to essential Trust, Love, and Freedom. We do not manifest all of these higher angels in any one moment of Effortless Letting Be. We manifest only the specific angels that have come to visit us in that specific moment in which we are called to Effortlessly Let Be. In the next moment we may be called to manifest something else or something more. Our life is a journey, and we never arrive at the end of the Spirit journey. Effortless Letting Be includes letting our imperfections be as well as an ever-increasing manifestation of our Spirit actuality. Trust means letting be our potential for continually moving toward the full Spirit realization that never arrives.

The angels of Effortless Letting Be might be seen as lazy angels, lacking in ambition to be more than the present moment provides. When the prodigal son came home, a feast was thrown immediately. There was no waiting to celebrate until this wayward person had worked out of his system all those years of riotous living. The celebration takes place Now. Tomorrow more homecomings will happen, and they will be celebrated as well. But for Effortless Letting Be it is always and only Now. Tomorrow will be another Now. No effort is needed for that tomorrow. Effortless Letting Be is simply allowing this particular homecoming to be the homecoming it is. Let the celebration begin. Let it begin Now.

* * * * * * * * *

Transparent Attention, Universal Forgiveness, and Effortless Letting Be are three families of angels within the larger clan of angels called "Trust." We might name and describe many more angels in the Trust clan, but they would, I believe, all find their home in one of these three family groups. Trust is an infinite actuality with an infinite number of angels; yet we, with our feeble yet amazing minds, can use the rational modeling of Trinitarian analysis to organize these states of Awe. At the same time, we must take care not to use our rational modeling as a means of closing ourselves off from the boundless quality of the Infinite Reality we are pointing to with our models. The Trinitarian imagery, properly used, is not a box to live in but a tool to open us up to Boundless Actuality – in this case, to the infinity of Trust-angels that move up the ramp that is our soul – or if we prefer, along the endless highway to the horizon of Reality.

This same Trinitarian analysis will also help us probe into the mysteries of Love and Freedom, the topics of the next two chapters.

8.

The Angels of Love

Spirit Love, like Spirit Trust and Spirit Freedom, is one of the three major aspects of our Spirit Being. Spirit Love is not an emotional state, a project of thought, nor a program of action. Emotions, thoughts, and actions may attend our participation in Spirit Love, but Spirit Love itself is a deeper dimension of human experience. Spirit Love is an angel that moves up the ramp of our soul from here to Eternity. Spirit Love is a response of Awe to the Awesome. Spirit Love, as described in the Christian heritage, has three major headings: love of self, love of God, and love of others. These three can be understood as the three inclusive subparts of one overall Spirit aspect called "agape" or "Spirit Love."

Spirit Love of self, God, and others can be described as three families of angels in the overall clan of Spirit Love. Here are the names I will give these three families of angels: **The Self-Affirmation of Autonomous Strength, The Joy of Enchantment with Being,** and **The Realism of Out-flowing Compassion.** These angels can go by shorter names: **Autonomous Strength, Enchantment with Being, and Out-flowing Compassion.** These names encourage a fresh understanding of the more familiar categories: love of self, love of God, and love of others.

Autonomous Strength is the **knowing** pole of Love. Enchantment with Being is the **being** pole of Love. And Out-flowing Compassion is the **doing** pole of Love.

The Self-Affirmation of Autonomous Strength

The phrase "Autonomous Strength" gives us a clue to the nature of Spirit Love for one's own self. Spirit Love does not indulge the whims of our personality nor give license to egoism. Discovering our Autonomous Strength is being and affirming our true nature. It means finding our own deep strength of soul as we participate in and affirm all things. It means finding our own strength of soul for our own specific journey toward Spirit realization.

This love of self manifests as a vast confidence, a deep faith in ourselves, a sureness that part of our true nature is profound strength. This strength includes the strength of standing alone before the whole of living; the strength of standing forth as an autonomous being; the strength of breaking the cord with parents; the strength of seeing and living beyond our native culture; and the strength of independence from lovers, spouses, friends, and fellow workers.

"Autonomous" means alone but not alone in the sense of being withdrawn. It means alone in the sense of being our own person, making our own decisions, knowing our own wants and feelings, choosing our own values and purposes, designing our own presentation of our self to others.

This Autonomous Strength is a flow of felt energy bubbling up within the soul. This is not an idea or an ideal; it is a force, a capability, a spontaneous power to act differently than we act when our identity is rooted in being an anxious, cautious person or an anxious, reckless person, or a person who is pretending to act in a fearless manner. Autonomous Strength is the absolute assurance that we are supported completely by the invincible Ground of our actual being.

Autonomous Strength is sometimes confused with a stubborn independence that is actually a defense from accepting our weaknesses. On the finite level of consideration every human being is weak, not strong; limited, not invincible; struggling, not confident; fearful, not courageous. Courage is a Spirit quality that swims against the stream of fear, dread, anxiety, horror, and downright despair. Strength, as a

Spirit quality, is paradoxical. It begins with the admission of weakness. Spirit Strength includes the courage to admit weakness. Nevertheless, this Strength is beyond our weakness; it is an inexhaustible confidence that no finite weakness can undermine.

Here is a poem that may help us see more deeply into the nature of Autonomous Strength:

> He would not dance
> except to his own music.
> He would not read
> except his own theories.
> He would not act
> except in his own good time.
>
> Such independence may mask deep hurt.
> Perhaps some caretaker of his innocent child
> refused to celebrate his essential independence.
> Perhaps now he labors
> to defend obsolete habits of
> self-constructed independence.
>
> Though unintended,
> self-constructed independence is slavery.
> True independence
> is open to truth
> wherever, whatever, whenever
> it appears.
>
> Ah!
> Death!
> Death to all achieved and defended habits,
> How liberating is your sternness!
>
> Ah!
> Void!
> Void of boundless unachievement,
> How strengthening is your presence!
>
> Ah!
> Strength!
> Strength supplied by the Ultimate Supplier,
> How satisfying is your aliveness!

Gene Marshall 2006

The strengths we attempt to construct for ourselves all turn out to be limited. Indeed, strengths turn out to also be weaknesses of one sort or another. Are you a strong athlete? There are athletes stronger than you. Are you a strong scholar? There are scholars stronger than you. In many areas of your life and mine, we are weak compared to most people. Even our greatest strengths are fragile aspects of our passing lives.

But Spirit Strength is not fragile; it is supplied by the Invincible Ground of Being. We do not have to construct it. We simply have to access it. And no person, thing, or event can undo this Strength. It is established by the Infinite.

Spirit Strength is like a hot energy, fiery red in color, active, living, outward moving. It is rooted in the personal experience of Reality. It is a passion to slay all falsehood. It does not knuckle under to lies and misrepresentations or to intimidations and moralisms. This Strength slashes through all opposition and laughs at rejection. It does not wait nor hesitate nor postpone, it blurts out self-initiated responses without fear of consequences. This is the self we love, and the only self we can truly and fully love. This fearless, autonomous "me" is the true "Me" that exists in the very midst of all our weaknesses which we can freely admit because none of them limit our ability to be this strange, deep, wondrous Spirit strength. Indeed this Strength is an angel, a messenger sent by Final Reality to be our own actual potential.

This Strength is also the capacity to wrestle the roaring lions of our own biological nature into submission and to ride these tamed beasts into an energetic living of our lives. This Strength is the capacity to lift high and drink the chalice of blood that represents our own death – our own courage to meet whatever challenges may come. This Strength means the capacity to take the two-edged sword from the Goddess Kali and slay all the falsehood in our lives and in the world in which we live. This Strength means a type of wisdom our minds cannot encompass but which, nevertheless, guides us into confident action, action that comes from our true self. This Strength means finding that place of Infinite Stillness from which raw creativity can flow. This is the self we love with a Spirit love.

The Joy of Enchantment with Being

Curiosity may have killed a few cats, but curiosity has made the feline species one of the great survivors of mammalian life. Humans are even more curious than cats. A small child, if not beaten or shamed into rigid carefulness, is curious about everything. Such a child is open to Mystery, to the unknown, to the unexperienced, to the fuller experience of whatever has enchanted him or her. Adult humans – unless restrained by fear, rigid doctrines, lethargy, or grogginess – are also incredibly curious beings. We are curious about the structure of the cosmos, the origin of all things, the composition of matter, the dynamics of time, the origin and nature of life, the workings of the human psyche, the workings of a human society, the history and destiny of the human species, and on and on and on. We are curious about the people, animals, and plants in our daily lives. We are open to know Reality in depth – to participate, dwell, and act within the Mystery of the Wholeness in which we dwell.

This enchantment with Mystery can mature into an ever-fuller awareness that Reality is a Mystery that never goes away, a Mystery that cannot be solved, a Mystery that is unfathomable. All our ideas and solutions crash on the shore of a stubborn Reality that is infinitely beyond us. By "Reality" I do not mean a final explanation or a unifying theory. Fully experienced Reality is a wall of blackness, the unknowable unknown. This can be frightening, but our dread can also be balanced by fascination. It is like passing a serious automobile accident. We are not only repulsed by the horror of it, we are also drawn to look at it, to explore it, to experience it. Though our dread inclines us to flee from the fullness of life and the emptiness of death, we are also drawn, fascinated, enchanted with both life and death. Our dread and fascination tend to balance each other, leaving us in a state of cool, courageous curiosity.

And our Spirit Love of Being is more than being curious. In the depths of our Being we are enchanted by joy. We sometimes speak of finding our bliss. We can speak of adoring Mysterious Reality as our God. We can make Ultimate Reality our touchstone for appropriate living, the ongoing joy of our lives. Here is a poem that may assist us to notice this state of Spirit:

Seers advise: "Find your bliss,"
as if bliss were a far way off –
at the top of some mountain,
at the end of some arduous journey.

True bliss is, indeed, a lofty destination.
And it takes a journey to get there.
Yet "there" is not a far way off;
it is here and now.

The long, hard journey takes us
through our reluctance
to be here and to be now
what we always were, still are, and will be.

Bliss is not adding something
to my ordinary life.
It is taking something away:
my flight, my rebellion.

Who is the real me?
Underneath all the dross, I am:
Awesome liberty, compassion,
trust, tranquility, and joy.

This real me is my bliss,
and this bliss is not far away,
though I may be far away
from my bliss.

Yet my case is not hopeless.
I can return to my bliss.
I can admit my waywardness.
I can accept my Welcome Home.

I can celebrate.
I can feast,
here and now,
at the table of forgiveness.

Gene Marshall 2002

Bliss, joy, rapture, and other such words are found in every religious heritage. Yet the deepest meaning of these words remains hidden from us by our preoccupation with lesser states. We have become absorbed with not having something we want, or with having something that we do not want. Such preoccupation with passing realities eclipses our true bliss. We have somehow unlearned the simple truth that joy is given with life itself. Our true joy comes not from changing something but from simply noticing that life is joy in the same ordinary way that life is breathing. We have simply lost contact with that joy. We have perhaps sought substitutes for it in some shallow peace or unconscious fogginess. Or perhaps we have sought substitutes for it in pleasures that we can more effectively control and understand. Perhaps we hide our joy in some habitual funk, about which we complain, but with which we are also comfortable. Our true joy is a deep awareness but also a deep intention by means of which we rise from our fogginess and grogginess and jump up and down in some fashion. Here is a poem that challenges us in that direction. This poem needs to be read aloud, slowly, and with vigor.

> Happiness is vigorous:
> not one, not two,
> but three hallelujahs.
>
> Don't hold back!
> Take the whole moment!
> Let it fill with life!
>
> Hallelujah!
> Hallelujah!
>
> HAL
>
> LE
>
> LU
>
> JAH!

Gene Marshall 2006

Such emphasis on joy may strike us as odd, even offensive and un-realistic. If we have lived beyond the naiveté of adolescence, we know that life is at least half death, suffering, and destruction. For every star that is born, another explodes into billions of fragments. For every great tree that magically grows from a small nut or seed, there are other trees that are burned to ash in some great forest fire. In our daily lives, there may be as much pain as pleasure, as much sadness as gladness, as much grief as relief, as much death as life.

Enchantment with Being takes place at a deeper level than these considerations. We are exploring a human potential for joy that can exist in the midst of both halves of life: birthing and dying, security and insecurity, pleasure and pain, affection and loneliness, knowledge and ignorance, success and failure, and all other such pairs of opposites that express the wholeness of our lives. A joyous sunlight can be seen to shine on everything. To notice it and appropriate it, we have only to sweep away the dark clouds that we ourselves have created.

When we are established in this joy, we are aware that the course of events not only kills our old selves, it also promotes perpetual rebirth. Reality is an unending launch into a new era of living. Every death of the last moment is the birth of the next moment. Every old ledge of living becomes a stepping-stone for the next adventure. Perhaps we can feel (however vaguely or keenly) our potential to be curious about this next adventure; perhaps we can sense some openness to whatever may be next for us. Perhaps we can take joy in shedding what must be shed and accepting the new birth that lies ahead. Surely, we can each remember times when we have been enchanted by the overwhelming Mystery that embraces us. Perhaps we can imagine living in this "place" always. Perhaps it is not so strange that our bliss, our joy, our fulfillment are here already waiting for us to simply surrender to them. Though it may seem at times that we must go very far to arrive at our bliss, we can take joy in simply realizing that joy is already here, characterizing the deepest aspect of the deepest aspect of our Spirit being. Spirit Love, as the Joy of Enchantment with Being, is an angel sent by Ultimate Mysterious Reality to move up our ramp of soul from here to Eternity. This Enchantment, this Joy, this Bliss is our true soul, our essential being.

The Realism of Out-flowing Compassion

The word compassion is composed of two parts: "com," meaning with, and "passion," meaning an out-flowing energy. We can be with others energetically. Being with someone is something more than merely filling the next chair. Being with someone means finding resonance with the vital self that lives behind the eyes, the smile, the frown of the other. Being with someone requires the courage to be with ourselves, with those feelings in ourselves that allow us to notice the feelings of the other. Being with the suffering of another means being willing to be with our own suffering. It means being willing for suffering to be part of human living.

Being with someone is much more than an exchange of thoughts, though thoughts may be included. Being with someone in Spirit love is an exchange of soul; it means noticing that our separate ramps from here to Eternity are also the same ramp with all the same angels. If the person we are with is in despair, we do not have to be in despair to be with them, but as persons who have moved through despair to Spirit Love, we know that despair results from a refusal to be some aspect of this ramp that is the soul of each of us.

Being with someone in true compassion means being and living beyond the facades and roles we pretend to be in order to be acceptable to others or to ourselves. Being with someone means allowing honesty and truthfulness to move through or around our customary lies. Being with someone means making contact, connection, resonance with that person, with his or her humanity. This we can do only if we are willing to make contact, connection, resonance with the humanity that exists within ourselves.

Being with others in their pain, their dread, their anxiety, their despair is challenging, but equally challenging is being with others in their pleasure, their fascination, their lightness, their joy. These more desirable states can bring up responses of envy that distract us from enjoying with others their joy, pleasure, fascination. The more somber states can engender within us an aversion to such tragedy or a compulsion to fix something. Compassion means simply being with others in full harmony with them, in full resonance with them, in effective mirroring of their actual experience. Such compassion is an inclusive Realism that includes a union with our own depth of being.

Out-flowing Compassion includes finding the creative balance between being with others where they are now and yet at the same time assisting them to understand how they might more fully be themselves and actualize the potential of their lives. On the one hand, we tend to hold others in contempt by not being willing to be with them, not honoring them with attention, and not forgiving them for being exactly where they are on their journey of living. And on the other hand, we tend to indulge people and disrespect them by not challenging them to move beyond their current blockages and take those appropriate next steps on their journey. No one can tell another how to hold this delicate balance, but Out-flowing Compassion includes the wisdom to operate within this balance. And this creative balance is needed in each situation. Furthermore, each situation is different. Spirit Love requires creativity, creation out of nothing. Continually, we face challenges that cannot be minimized by thinking we know what usually works. The habit-addicted mind will not be able to make appropriate decisions toward the lives of specific others. Each moment is a fresh challenge. We cannot lean on mental certainties. And we cannot focus on how we are coming off or how good we may or may not be. The Realism of Out-flowing Compassion focuses on the other person and responds to that person without distractions.

Out-flowing Compassion encompasses enemies as well as friends. Both Buddhist and Christian teachings have strongly witnessed to the existence of this strange quality of Spirit Love. Both traditions call for loving kindness toward both enemies and friends, intimates and strangers, both pleasing and appalling persons. With whomever we might be living, the Realism of Out-flowing Compassion is called for. The specific actions with enemies may be different from those with friends, but we can be with our enemies with the same intensity that we are with our friends. We can see in our enemies the same humanity that we see in our friends and in ourselves. We do not have to demonize an enemy in order to be firm with him or her. We do not have to demonize an enemy in order to resist and even kill that person. Our being with the enemy may even make it easier to realistically defeat him or her. Our being with an enemy also makes it possible to learn from that enemy what we need to learn. And the experience of being with both friends and enemies will teach us that every enemy is also a friend and every friend is also an enemy.

Some have erroneously taught that we do not have enemies, but we do. Anyone who is actively opposing us, resisting what we are doing with our lives, is our enemy. And the more deeply we embody our Spirit Being, the more enemies we will have. The challenge of Spirit Love is not to avoid having enemies or to deny that we have enemies. The challenge of Spirit Love is to love the enemy with the same intensity that we love the friend, and to love them both with the same intensity that we love ourselves. This does not mean, however, going along with our enemies or doing what they wish us to do. It means being ourselves even during genuine conflict with persons who are at this time opposed to us.

The Realism of Out-flowing Compassion relates us to social structures as well as to individual persons. Social structures are necessary creations by human beings for the benefit of human beings. This is a different orientation than relating to social structures as definitions of rational duty or manifestations of ideological views. Social structures are carriers of Spirit Love to the extent that social structures sustain, protect, and enable real persons – our own self, friends, enemies, strangers, and those not yet born. Our compassion with regard to social structures can express itself as peaceful political action, vigorous social reform, thoroughgoing revolution, or even warfare. The test of genuineness for this Love is not the form of the action but the underlying Spirit. Are we promoting social ideas for the sake of being right or patriotic or noble, or are we genuinely concerned with the well-being of all those among whom we dwell? A program of social action that is based in Spirit Love will differ in vision, strategy, and means of action from programs of social action that are based differently. The full elaboration of a Spirit-based social ethics is beyond the scope of this chapter. My aim in this chapter is to describe briefly some of the essential qualities of this family of angels that I am calling "The Realism of Out-flowing Compassion." These angels enrich our actions both in our interpersonal relations and in our sociological activism.

Spirit Love, especially in its love-of-others aspect, is often confused with other types of "love." For example, sexual desire or union is often called "love." Spirit Love can exist simultaneously with the sexual arousals of the body, but sexual experience, no matter how grand, is not the same thing as Spirit Love. Similarly, we must distinguish Spirit Love from those emotional bondings that we call "love." Emotional attachments, feelings, longings, satisfactions are an important part of human living, but we need to recognize that they are finite operations each of which has a polar opposite. Our desire for pleasure when denied becomes a sort of pain. Our emotional bonding with others, when broken, becomes sadness or grief. Our feelings of satisfaction are matched by disappointments and fears of disappointment. For every delight there exists an aversion. For every hope there is a fear. For every appreciation there is a resentment. Our popular love songs bear witness that our emotional loving is matched by emotional blues. All these feelings are wholesome dynamics of human life, but they are not Spirit Love. Spirit Love transcends our emotional feelings. When we make emotional love our ultimate definition of loving, we condemn ourselves to hatred toward those who disappoint us. And since everyone disappoints us from time to time, we end up hating everyone and life itself.

Spirit love may be attended by feelings, for each living moment includes feelings. But Spirit love is not those feelings. Spirit Love is an affirmation of all feelings and all situations and persons who occasion those feelings. Spirit Love affirms self and others in a manner that is infinitely deeper than the feelings involved.

Spirit love must also be distinguished from mental and moral actions. Spirit Love is not a noble action of the mind, and Spirit Love is not proved or disproved by whether its results are measured "moral" by our moral standards. The results of Spirit Love may violate our most prized principles and all our "moldy virtues." And Spirit Love is not a mental ideal, goal, or aim. We use our minds in Spirit Loving, but Spirit Love is more than mind. Spirit Love is an action of soul; it is our deep affirmation of Reality put into action with help from the mind. Spirit Love is visible in the outward world to those who have eyes to see it, but Spirit Love cannot be contained in our mental and moral boxes.

The Realism of Out-flowing Compassion, like all the aspects of Spirit Love, is not a quality that we need to achieve. It is not an ideal that can be realized through hard work. Like all the other angels, this angel is part of our True Nature.

* * * * * * * * *

Spirit Love in all its dimensions is not a hard climb up some craggy hill; it is a surrender to the true nature of our own Being as that Being is being given to us by the Wholeness of Reality in this here and now of actual living.

9.

The Angels of Freedom

Like Spirit Trust and Spirit Love, Spirit Freedom is one of the three major aspects of our True Self. Spirit Freedom is part of our True Being. Spirit Freedom is a family of angels that moves up the ramp of our soul from here to Eternity. Spirit Freedom is an Awe response to the Awesome Otherness that is encountering us. Spirit Freedom is an aspect of Holy Spirit.

Spirit Freedom is not an emotional state, a process of thought, nor a program of action. Emotions, thoughts, and actions attend our participation in Spirit Freedom, but Spirit Freedom itself is a deeper aspect of human experience. Spirit Freedom is the opposite of bondage: bondage to our self image, bondage to our conscience about good and evil, and bondage to our images of outward fatedness.

The Angels of Freedom can be assembled into three families. These three families can be distinguished by the form of bondage that they overcome.

(1) Spirit Freedom means overcoming the bondage to our self-image: this includes becoming aware of the difference between free will and freedom.

(2) Spirit Freedom means overcoming the bondage to our conscience: this includes being creative action rather than obedience to any form of moralism or any pretense of possessing an ultimately valid knowledge of good and evil.

(3) Spirit Freedom means overcoming the bondage to images of outward fatedness: this includes taking charge of the course of history rather than railing against or resigning ourselves to some supposed inevitability or futility.

Here are the names I will give these three families of angels: **The Primal Merging beyond Self Image**, **The Inherent Purity beyond Good and Evil**, and **The Attuned Working beyond Fate**. These families of angels can go by these shorter names: **Primal Merging**, **Inherent Purity**, and **Attuned Working**.

Primal Merging is the **knowing** pole of Freedom. Inherent Purity is the **being** pole of Freedom. And Attuned Working is the **doing** pole of Freedom.

The Primal Merging Beyond Self Image

Robert Fritz, in his book *The Path of Least Resistance*, makes a convincing case for the importance of "choice" in our psychological health and in our potential to be creative human beings. He describes three levels of choice: secondary choices, primary choices, and fundamental choices. Secondary choices are the choices we make to carry out our primary choices. Primary choices are the choices we make for their own sake not for the sake of something else. For example, we might choose to be an artist not for the sake of the money it might bring, not for the sake of winning the heart of some person, but simply for the sake of expressing our lives through painting pictures. Then we might make secondary choices like buying paint, attending painting classes, studying the great painters of the world, and so on.

Fundamental choices are choices that are even more basic to us than our primary choices. Here are two illustrations of what Fritz means by fundamental choices: (1) the choice to be the predominant creative force in your life and (2) the choice to be true to yourself.[9] The choice to be "the predominant creative force in my life" is an aspect of the choice to be Spirit Freedom. The choice to be "true to myself" is also a choice for Spirit Freedom if we understand Spirit Freedom as who we essentially are. So this is the fundamental choice: the choice to be Freedom.

The choice to be Freedom is a choice made with that very Freedom we are choosing to be. The choice to be Freedom is not the creation of Freedom, but a surrender to being the Freedom that is already the essence of our being. This is why we can speak of "A Primal Merging Beyond Self Image." Spirit Freedom is a Self Realization, a merging with who we essentially are.

Further, this Spirit Freedom is not the same thing as the so-called "free will" that is so often written about. The ego (as I have defined it) has free will, but the ego's free will is limited by the ego's definition of itself. The ego is a construction of the human mind. This construction may allow for the presence of some elements of our essential Freedom. But because it is a human construction, the ego also restricts the full expression of our Spirit Freedom.

Freud spoke of the ego as a choice maker, as a regulator of the conflicts between the id and the superego. Most of us can see these dynamics operating within ourselves. The id is our basic biology with all its genetically rooted desires, dreams, and symbol-using capacities. The superego is our internalized social conditioning with all its moralities, definitions of good and evil, guidelines for successful living, customs, taboos, and other teachings on how to live within the society that brought us into our uniquely human lives. The id and the superego conflict with one another. Our biology sometimes desires what our society forbids. Our society sometimes demands what our biology resists. These conflicts can be somewhat resolved by the ego, if the ego is willing to be conscious of these conflicts and make choices about them. One of the factors that makes these resolutions by the ego difficult is that much of our id and much of our superego are unconscious to our somewhat conscious ego. So the ego has to find the means

---

[9]   Fritz, Robert; *The Path of Least Resistance* (Ballantine Books, 1989) page 197

and the courage to face these unconscious conflicts in order to make choices about them.

In this Freudian description, a measure of freedom in the life of the ego is assumed. But the Freudian description also calls our attention to the fact that the ego can be unconscious to such a degree that it is not actually free to make many of the available choices. In other words, the ego can be bound as well as free. The ego is bound by its lack of consciousness. It may also be bound by its lack of courage to become conscious. Because of this partly conscious and partly unconscious abdication of full Freedom, the ego is not in control of the overall person. Therefore, our lives are being driven by the unconscious forces of our id and superego and by the conflicts between these two forces. Some egos may be more enslaved to their id and thus experience some sort of addiction to sex, love, comfort, escape, food, states of feeling, etc. Some egos may be more enslaved to their superego and thus experience some sort of overriding automatic obedience to specific patterns of politeness, reserve, safety, carefulness, moralism, righteousness, certitude, status, success, or some form of rebellion against such norms. The Freudian description of the ego makes clear that the ego can grow in its consciousness and thus grow in its freedom.

If with the help of Freud and other psychologists we see that the ego is both free and unfree, we see a basic issue in realizing our essential Spirit Freedom. The ego has free will within the boundary of some overarching bondage. At the same time, the ego is a slave to that overarching bondage that is restricting full Freedom. To realize an undiluted experience of our Spirit Freedom entails the death of our identification with our ego. To experience our Spirit Freedom entails the merger with a far deeper and more profound "me" than being the ego with which we are familiar and with which we are (or perhaps are not) comfortable.

The stories about Jesus in the first three books of the New Testament often probe beyond the "free will" of the ego toward the Freedom that Jesus asks of his followers. Here is an example:

> But he said to another man, "Follow me." And he replied, "Let me go and bury my father first." But Jesus told him, "Leave the dead to bury their own dead. You must come away and preach the Kingdom of God."

(Luke 9:59-60; J. B. Phillips translation)

Jesus sees that this man's Freedom is bounded by his attachment to family obligations. Spirit Freedom for this man means turning loose of that attachment. Here is another example:

> Another man said to him, "I am going to follow you, Lord, but first let me bid farewell to my people at home." But Jesus told him, "Anyone who puts his hand to the plow and then looks behind him is useless for the kingdom of God." (Luke 9:61-62; J. B. Phillips translation)

In this case, the man wants to make everybody he loves feel good about his decision to be a Spirit person. But this is not the whole-hearted Freedom required in the kingdom of Spirit Realization that Jesus represents. Here is a third example:

> And while he was still saying this, a woman in the crowd called out and said, "Oh, what a blessing for a woman to have brought you into the world and nursed you!" But Jesus replied, "Yes, but a far greater blessing to hear the word of God and obey it."
> (Luke 11:27-28; J. B. Phillips translation)

In this story Jesus does not deny the truth of what the woman says nor reject her enthusiasm. But he cuts through this woman's images of subservience, her contentment with less than full discipleship. He challenges her to be a Spirit woman herself and not simply an enabler of someone else. She sees the greatness of Jesus' Freedom, but she is reluctant to see herself as the very same greatness waiting to be enacted. Her ego has its small measure of "free will," but her ego is also limiting her Freedom.

Full Spirit Freedom may appear to us as a frightening and demanding challenge. In his play *A Sleep of Prisoners* Christopher Fry has one of his characters pronouncing the word "freedom" as FREE DOOM. The experience of Freedom is DOOM to the comfortable ego. The experience of Freedom is an awakening of the prisoners from their sleep. Free will is something with which we can be comfortable or even proud. We can be proud to be in control of certain outcomes or to be capable of choosing between our current understandings of good and evil. But full Spirit Freedom is a DOOM that we, in our ego identifications, deeply fear. And such FREE DOOM never becomes something of which we can be proud. Spirit Freedom is not an accomplishment but a response to the Total Demand to surrender who we think we are and thus let loose who we truly are. Freedom is a DOOM that is freely given to us. Indeed, we are determined to be Free and there is nothing we can do about it. Even though we try in every possible way to escape our Freedom, it is inescapable. It tags along on all our attempts at escape and mocks us for choosing to be a slave of our own self-constructed ego.

We might say that this inescapable Freedom laughs at us as we persist in using our Freedom to escape a Freedom that we cannot escape. This Freedom is experienced as DOOM only because we are intent on escaping it. And toward what alternative are we trying to escape? We are trying to escape to an identification with our fragile self-constructed ego that is content with being a bit of free will, but is resistant to being the vast Freedom that we essentially are.

Freedom may also enter our lives as an experience of judgment, shame, or guilt. The arrival of Freedom confronts the ego with the need to admit that it is not free, that its petty little free will is living within a larger context of slavery. When Freedom appears in our lives, we begin to realize that we do not do what we say. We say one thing and do another. We say we want to lose weight, but our hands open the refrigerator door looking for some more ice cream. We say we want to have more friends in our lives, but our bodies sit in our solitary rooms doing busywork to forget that we are lonely. We say we want to be a musician, but we do not do the study and practice required to make that dream a reality.

The arrival of Freedom may also reveal to us that we have allowed our minds and bodies to buy into some cruelly addictive pattern of temporary exhilaration. Rather than working through our suppressed pains to an experience of the quiet joy, wonder, and the strength of true Freedom, we have opted for an artificial pleasantness that is leading us into an ever-deeper pit of shame and despair. The arrival of Freedom will disclose to us how we are inventing excuses with our lying mind. When we are identifying with our ego, the arrival of Freedom can be the very last gift we want to see.

Yet Spirit Freedom is not in itself gloomy. Freedom is jocular, light, and fun. Freedom laughs at us and invites us to laugh too. It is with our ego identifications that we create seriousness by clinging to our bondage. As ego-identified persons, we experience Freedom's demands as "no laughing matter." When we do not identify with our Freedom, Freedom looks like DOOM to the imagination of that delimited self-image or ego that we have constructed.

The direct experience of truly knowing our Freedom means dying to our ego. And it means merging with our primal actuality. We do not have to struggle to be free. We only have to merge with the Freedom we already are. The cost of this merger is giving up the person we think we are. In fact, the cost of being Free may mean giving up most of our customary thinking. Thinking will be returned to us later. But Spirit Freedom is infinitely beyond thinking. Only when Freedom is fully established as our self-identification, can thinking be given back to us as a useful tool in the hands of Freedom. Freedom in and of itself is entirely irrational, entirely transrational, entirely prior to all reasoning. We cannot think our way to Freedom. We have to unthink our way to Freedom. Freedom does not make sense. Freedom is just an irrational, inescapable part of the nonsense of overall Reality. As we learn to know the absolute nonsense of Freedom, we can also learn the usefulness of the mind to aid us in making whatever fragile sense we can of our experience for the practical living of our life of Freedom.

The gigantic capacities of the human mind provide a subtle trap that leads us again and again into bondage. We create some sense for our lives and then forget that we have created it and let that self-created sense create us. But Reality is always more, and we are always more, infinitely more, than the petty little sense that we have created. We are Freedom and with that Freedom we have created our own personality, a personality that we often mistake for our true person. As we merge with our Spirit Freedom, we no longer know who we are, for we are experiencing ourselves as pure responsibility to create our fundamental choices, the choices that will determine how our life will be manifest in the situations we are given.

Here is a poem that points to the strange wonder of this Primal
Merging:

> I am an alert deer.
> Dread gets my attention
> and I can move quickly
> in many directions.
> I am a surprise
> and hard to predict.
>
> A fear of real enemies
> is the alertness of a deer,
> While my alertness is
> dread of a mysteriousness
> no deer can know.
>
> And I am unpredictable
> in a manner
> no deer can match.
>
> Dread of the Unfathomable
> is my essence.
>
> Surprise
> is my being.

Gene Marshall 1992

The Inherent Purity beyond Good and Evil

The being aspect of Freedom has to do with overcoming a primal
illusion, that living by our humanly created values is the best way to
live. Strange as it may seem to many, the story of Adam and Eve
is about entering into this primal illusion. This story is not about
the first upright-walking primates, nor is it about the first ensouled
humans. This story is just a story. It is poetry, poetry about the fall
from humanity's inherent purity into an illusory knowledge of good
and evil. Adam and Eve are symbolic of us all. We are all Adam and
Eve. We eat every day from the tree of which humanity in this story
was forbidden to eat. We destroy our authentic lives by eating this
forbidden fruit, by eating the knowledge of good and evil.

Why is the knowledge of good and evil a forbidden food? It might seem that knowing good and evil is a very good thing. Our parents taught us good and evil. Our religious community taught us good and evil. Our public school taught us good and evil. Our whole culture is filled with ideas of right and wrong and good and evil. What is wrong with that? How can knowing good and evil be viewed as the most basic violation of human authenticity?

Having ethical guidelines to follow is not a problem if we are using those guidelines creatively – if we are employing our essential Freedom, if we are lord over our guidelines and not letting our guidelines be lord over us.

The evil fruit is the illusion that we can know good and evil in some absolute sense. We crave certainty. We want to know that we are doing the right thing. Knowing good and evil in that way has to do with making sense out of life – of knowing with certainty what to do and what not to do. But this is not our real situation. We don't know anything for sure. Life does not make sense. Life has never made sense. And life will never make sense.

REALITY is Mystery. We humans know a lot, but in the final analysis Reality is nonsense to human intelligence. As the good scientist says, "The more we know about nature the more we know we don't know." Theology does not have absolute answers either. Good theology bears witness to the Mysteriousness of Reality.

We theologians sometimes say that life "makes sense only to God." But to say that life "makes sense only to God" is saying that it does not make sense to us. Life is beyond comprehension by the human mind.

Clearly we have partial knowledge. We need some knowledge to survive. A dog needs some knowledge to survive. But in the final analysis Reality is Mysterious to the human being as well as to the dog. And Reality is not less Mysterious to twenty-first century human beings than it was to those who lived three thousand years ago.

According to the second and third chapters of the book of Genesis, ignorance of good and evil is our true state; it is life as it should be. Indeed, an ultimate valid knowledge of good and evil is forbidden to the human species. It was always forbidden; it is still forbidden; it always will be forbidden.

But often you and I do not believe this. We have already eaten from the forbidden tree. We believe that cuddly kittens are good and wild wolf packs are evil. We believe that gentle breezes are good and that hurricanes and tornadoes are evil. We believe that capitalism is good and communism is evil. Or we believe that communism is good and capitalism is evil. We believe that Judaism or Christianity is good and Islam is evil. Or that Islam is good and Hinduism is evil. Or that Hinduism is good and Islam is evil. At the very least we think that sickness, suffering, and death are evil and that health, pleasure, and life are good.

In some way or another we think we know what we actually do not know. We have gotten "lost" in our pretense that we know good and evil. We do not accept our state of essential ignorance. We want to know. We want to be the judge of what is good and what is evil. And we judge everything. We applaud part of life, and we reject part of life. We profoundly hate some aspects of life. We no longer live in the Garden of Eden. We live somewhere to the East in the land of Nod.

Let's go back to the biblical story, remembering that it is a story about us. It is a story about our lives today. The snake said something like this to Eve:

> "The knowledge of good and evil is sweet to eat and it will make you wise like God. Take some. Why would you want to go on living in a land of sheer Mystery when you could make sense of life? You could know how to live. You could have some certainty about things. God did not have your best interests in mind when he forbid you to have this wonderful thing."

> So she ate some certainty and gave some certainty to her husband and he ate some certainty too.

> Then their eyes were opened. They saw life in terms of good and evil.

> Oops, they noticed that they were naked. Ooooh, this was bad. So they hid their shame behind some fig leaves.

"Naked" is a symbol for being exposed in our basic decision making. To be naked in this way means to be without certainty that what we are doing is correct. Naked is our true state. We do not have an absolute certainty of good and evil in which to clothe ourselves. In order to be certain we have to lie; we have to hide. We have to hide ourselves from our selves and our neighbors. And most basic of all, we have to hide from Reality.

Our mode of hiding might be a state of shame for being so uncertain. Shame can be an indication that we have eaten the forbidden fruit. After eating false certainty, Adam and Eve entered into a life of shame about who they were. That is, WE enter into a life of shame about who WE are.

Here is a poem about that shame:

> When, in the distant Garden of our past,
> human beings desired to be Eternal,
> shame entered the cosmos.
>
> Sensuality became shameful.
> Ugliness became shameful.
> Weakness became shameful.
> Ignorance became shameful.
> Our crummy childhoods became shameful.
> Our lopsided cultures became shameful.
> Our deaths became shameful.
> Our desires became shameful.
> Our feelings became shameful.
> Our thoughts became shameful.
>
> Yes, when we chose to be wise, like God,
> everything that was not Godlike
> became shameful.
>
> My cat knows no shame.
>
> Gene Marshall 1996

In the Genesis story, Adam and Eve are ashamed of their actual lives. They are hiding their delusory living behind the fig leaves of their denials, lies, and suppressions. Then Reality comes walking through the garden in the cool of the day. I love this story.

> "Where are you?" says Reality, "Who told you that you were naked? Did you eat from the forbidden tree?"

> "Well," says Adam, "Eve said blah blah blah."

> "Well," says Eve, "the snake said blah blah blah."

> "NO EXCUSES," says God, "OUT!   Out of the Garden."

And what is the garden? The garden is the land of Mystery. It is a land of WONDER, of "Wonderstanding." But we humans want a land of understanding. We want to know. We want certainty. We want to judge one another. We want to be prigs and bigots and dogmatists and arrogant know-it-alls. There is no place for such persons in the Garden of Innocence.

Not only Adam and Eve but all of us tend to prefer being "certain" to being a fragile bit of finitude in a land of Wonder. We prefer understanding to "wonderstanding." Rather than our actual wonder-filled life, we prefer to be "smart," hoping for a life we do not have. The Genesis stories that follow the Adam an Eve story suggest that this fall into false certainty results in (1) killing those whom we envy (Cain and Abel), (2) corruption so widespread that humanity as a whole is threatened (The Flood), and (3) social projects that foolishly try for divinity (The Tower of Babel).

We are asked by these stories to "wonderstand" that the choice to eat the knowledge of good and evil is the foundational delusion. Humans in all eras of history have rejected Reality in favor of some humanly invented culture of certainty. In our personal lives we also reject the vast Mystery of our actual existence in order to have answers in our hip pockets. Both personally and socially these choices have dire consequences.

The Bible also contains an ever-expanding story about recovering our Freedom. Moses left behind the answers of Egypt in order to lead a community of Freedom in the desert. The Prophets called Israel beyond the limits of a national self-worship. Jesus spent his entire ministry fighting against the moral certainties of the scribes and Pharisees. Paul made freedom from legalism the cornerstone of his preaching. The whole Bible witnesses against worshiping the so-called "moral certainties" of any religious tradition. Nevertheless, we have all eaten from the tree of the knowledge of good and evil.

Our parents taught us good and evil and expected us to live by it.

Our Jewish synagogue taught us good and evil and expected us to live by it.

Our Catholic catechism class taught us good and evil and expected us to live by it.

Our Protestant Sunday school taught us good and evil and expected us to live by it.

Our atheistic uncle taught us good and evil and expected us to live by it.

Our entire culture taught us good and evil and expected us to live by it.

The knowledge of good and evil is sometimes called "moralism." Moralism is an oppressive ruler that rules our lives. Jesus, you may recall, fought against moralism in most of his teachings. It is a disease from which none of us have fully recovered.

This poem likens moralism to a king, an oppressive king who must be dethroned in our lives:

> Kill the King, I say.
> Let anarchy reign.
> Kill all moral principles.
> Bury them in the Earth
>   and let them rot.
>
> If you feel grief
> for any kingly principle
> or any principled king,
> EXPRESS it emotionally &
> honestly & passionately.
>
> EXAMINE your loss carefully
> to see what feelings

these principles have been suppressing,
to see what spiritual freedom
they have encrusted.

In place of the King,
assemble a COUNCIL,
a council in your mind.
Seat men & women --
the best five or twelve you know
-- best at expressing their feelings
and thinking clearly.

Place yourself in the circle with them.
Ask them each to speak
on your agenda,
on what you shall do with your life,
on how you shall become wiser,
on how you shall find & express
        your heart,
on how you shall commit yourself
        to action.

LISTEN!
Let their words sink into your heart.
Say no words in response.
Think no critical thoughts.
LISTEN
for what you have never heard before.
Ask the next to speak
and the next.

When all have spoken,
now you may speak.
Do not begin with evaluation
of what the others have said.
Say what wisdom you have heard.
Say what feelings rise in your heart
        or chill your bones.
When this is thoroughly done,
then allow yourself to sort out
the best your council said
from the dross.

If any kingly principle rises
to frustrate this process,

command it to return to the abyss.
Let fresh and fragile principles,
guidelines really,
be formed by you
to order your practical living.

Do not take your guidelines seriously.
Live from your heart.
Let Spirit Freedom reign.
Principles are your servants,
not your masters.

The King is dead.
Long live LIBERTY
your COUNCIL
and YOU.

Gene Marshall 1994

Inherent Purity means that the cosmos is working perfectly. Gravity is working like it is supposed to be working. Evolution is working like it is supposed to be working. Human processes are working like they are supposed to be working. Living is working like it is supposed to be working. Dying is working like it is supposed to be working. Human essence is working like it is supposed to be working. The fall from human essence into futility and despair is working like it is supposed to be working. Recovering from despair is working like it is supposed to be working. Realization of our true nature is working like it is supposed to be working. Everything is working perfectly. In the metaphor of biblical talk, "God does not goof."

And this Inherent Purity beyond good and evil is given to us, not achieved. It is one of the angels on our ramp from here to Eternity. And this ramp, with all its angels, is constituted by Eternity, not by human effort. Our true Purity, our true righteousness, our true Perfection, our Freedom is not something for which we have to strive. Freedom is a gift of our true being to which we have only to surrender.

The Attuned Working beyond Fate

Finally, I will describe the doing pole of our essential Spirit Freedom. This is the ninth and last family of angels in the pantheon of angels that move "up" the ramp of our soul in response to our ongoing encounter with the Eternal. "Attuned" means being aligned with the way the cosmos works, with the way human nature unfolds, with the way interactions among human beings operate. In our colloquial speech we sometimes speak of being "with it." The opposite of being "with it" is being "out of it." In casual speech we seldom say what "it" is. But if we suppose that "it" refers to our Personal Essence, to a conscious participation in the Ground of our Being, then being "with it" is a promising expression of what I mean by "Attuned Working."

Attuned Working is both obedience to the The-Way-It-Is and creativity as self-initiated action. Freedom as Attuned Working is both obedient and creative. Freedom is obedient creativity and creative obedience. Attuned Working is a totally different understanding from the one we associate with "fate" or "fatalism." We are indeed fated to be a part of this cosmos, this humanity, this era of history, this individual person. Nevertheless, being "with it" (being attuned to the Final "IT") does not mean being stuck in a groove on an already recorded record of fate. The symphony of our life has not yet been written. It is unfolding measure by measure. And our creativity is contributing to this unfolding. The author of the Gospel of John has Jesus say, "My Father is working and I am working." This gives us a sense of what Attuned Working is like. Our working is indeed creative, but if our working is "with it," then it is also obedient to that Master Working within which we are also working.

We can be unattuned in two different ways. We can suppose that our destiny is already set and that we can do nothing about it. Or we can suppose that our destiny is entirely up to us and that we must design our purpose and plan our lives in opposition to the powers that be. Indeed, so popular are these two ways of not being attuned, it is difficult to even understand the notion that there is such a thing as obedient freedom or free obedience. We easily assume that if our life is free, it is not obedient – and that if our life is obedient, it is not free.

One of the ways that Attuned Working comes into view is fully grasping that Freedom is part of The-Way-It-Is. Being obedient to The-Way-It-Is includes being Freedom. This means that there is no specific purpose to which each of us is called. It is not in accord with The-Way-It-Is to say that the cosmos or nature or God has a plan for our lives. The purpose of our lives has not yet been chosen. This openendedness is part of the The-Way-It-Is. Being obedient to The-Way-It-Is means participation in choosing our specific purpose and working out our specific plans. And this choosing continues throughout our lives.

At the same time, such choosing is Spirit Freedom only if it is done in obedience to the Master Working. The cosmos works the way it works, human nature unfolds the way it unfolds, and human interactions interact the way they interact. Our Essence is what our Essence is. Freedom is what Freedom is. The Joy of being "with it" is what the Joy of being "with it" is. If our choosing chooses to fight with or to ignore the Master Working, then our working is not attuned, our Freedom is not free, our obedience is not obedient, and our joy is not the joy for which we are constituted.

Here is a poem that may help us feel our way toward an experience of Attuned Working:

"The purpose of life,"
some theologian said,
"is to trust the Mystery
and to enjoy Mystery forever."

Some sage in the East put it this way,
"Those who say what the purpose of life is, don't know,
And those who know what the purpose of life is, don't say."

The Infinite seems to be silent on the subject.

So I say, "The purpose of life is to ask
what the purpose of life is continually,
but to never know or expect to know –
indeed to know
that the purpose of life is
not to know
what the purpose of life is."

So let us choose in freedom

some finite purpose for our lives,
knowing that we have chosen it
and that we can choose again
when its limitations appear.

Gene Marshall 2000

What does "when its limitations appear" mean? How do we know when our creations meet limitations? One might suppose that if Freedom were our essence, no limitations would exist. While it is true that our Freedom is unlimited in the sense of being a raw cause that is uncaused by any other cause, it is also true that the specific temporal creations of our Freedom meet with limitations. Our life is a dialogue with Reality, not a monologue in which we create the whole story of history. We are co-creators with an "Infinite Creator" who each moment sustains us in being as a co-creator. Our choices make a difference. The outcomes of the future are not already settled; nevertheless, we are not in full charge of those outcomes. In fact, we are powerless to even know, much less determine, what the outcomes of our choices will be. Nevertheless, because we choose, the future unfolds differently. I once wrote a poem that contained this key verse:

God waits to decide what the future will be
until you decide who you will be now.

Gene Marshall 1960

An eternal weight of significance is placed on each decision we make. "God" is a devotional word for Reality, for Infinite Mysterious Reality. This Reality responds to each choice we make. Life is a dialogue in which we are challenged to choose again and again. Our Attuned Working is an ongoing dialogue: Thou–I–Thou–I–Thou–I–Thou. God has the first and last word of this master dialogue, but our attunement to being in this dialogue with the Thou of Reality co-creates the course of history. This attunement includes attunement with our encounters with Reality and attunement with our own Freedom to respond to those encounters.

When I was studying the life of Martin Luther and the whole history of the Protestant Reformation, an image appeared to my mind that I have never forgotten. I saw Martin Luther as a hard rock that stood up in his time and place. I envisioned God using this rock as a pivot upon which the entire history of that era was turned. Martin Luther made history, yet he never knew what history he was making. We could also say that God made history in response to God's loyal player, Martin.

Attuned Working is more than a blind surrender to the mysterious wall of darkness that Reality always presents. The person in this state of Spirit embraces the full power of human reason to know what can be known in an inclusive and future oriented way. He or she may build instructive models of the past and use them to build inclusive visions of possible futures and the means to moving toward those chosen visions. In other words, Attuned Working is something more than spontaneous response to each passing situation. Attuned Working means being attuned to the whole sweep of cosmic and human history. As Attuned Workers we seek to be attuned to the whole sweep of our particular life as that life interfaces with the whole sweep of Reality. In Attuned Working we inquire about the appropriate purpose for our life and build that purpose in the full knowledge that it is we who build it and that all our constructions are fragile. Nevertheless, if we live in the Spirit quality of Attuned Working, the building of our life purpose is not simply arbitrary. It is an act of obedience to the whole sweep of cosmic and human history.

Such Obedience to the Whole is the back side of the coin of Freedom. Freedom is Obedience to the whole sweep of Reality. Obedience to the whole sweep of Reality is Freedom. Further, we can glimpse how both of these things are true when we see that obedience to anything less than the whole sweep of Reality is a form of bondage. If we are obedient only to the well-being of our family, we are not free to act creatively on behalf of all families. If we are obedient only to the well-being of our nation, we are not free to act creatively on behalf of all nations. But if we are obedient to the whole sweep of Reality, then we are truly and fully free. To wonderstand this paradox is to wonderstand Freedom as Attuned Working beyond Fate.

Like all the other angels, the angel of Attuned Working is an aspect of our essential soul. Attuned Working is an angel (a family of angels) moving up the ramp of our essential soul in response to that Eternal

Reality that constitutes the whole ramp and all the angels upon it. Freedom, like Love, like Trust, is not a human achievement but a gift of our essential being.

PART THREE

The Fall into Personality Identification

10.

The Myth and Truth of the Fall

In Part Two I described Trust, Love, and Freedom as three hosts of angels (Awe-figures) that constitute our true being. But typically we human beings are not being (or are not entirely being) our true being. We have fallen away from Trust, Love, and Freedom into despair, malice, and bondage. We often avoid applying such negative words to our condition. We confuse our fallen states with some "nature" that we cannot change. We may even view our fallen states as an advance rather than a fall. Or perhaps we grieve our fallen states. Perhaps we see the chamber of horrors that our fallen states truly are, but see no possibility of an alternative. And some of us are simply unconscious of this entire dynamic of our essential self and our fallen states. Indeed, all of us experience some unconsciousness of these dynamics. Becoming more aware of our fallenness is an aspect of our restoration to being our true being of Trust, Love, and Freedom.

ADAM AND EVE

The second and third chapters of the Bible begin telling us about the entrance of evil into a good "creation." In Genesis 2:7 to 3:24 we find this strange myth about the first humans who eat from the tree of the knowledge of good and evil.

We must underline the fact, introduced in chapter 9, that the Adam and Eve passage is a myth, a story created by ancient people. It is not a historical exploration of the origin of evil. It is not a speculation about the origin of evil. It is just a story that attempts to describe the dynamic of "fallenness" in you and me and every human being. When we understand this story deeply, we can see that it is, indeed, true to life. It is our story. Adam and Eve are you and I. So what does this story say about us?

It tells us that an absolute knowledge of good and evil is forbidden to the human species, and that we are in a state of alienation (a fallen state) because we have crossed this line (We have eaten this forbidden fruit). The story does not imply that knowledge is bad or that having guidelines for decision-making is bad. It tells us that our sense of value, our knowledge of good and evil, is not absolute. It tells us that in spite of all our schooling and all our moral training, we remain fundamentally uncertain beings. We are ignorant. We are not wise like God. Our knowing is not infinite. Furthermore, this story implies that any pretense to be absolutely wise like God is the root cause of our fallenness, of our chamber of horrors, of our estrangement from our true being. On the day that we eat from this forbidden tree of moral certainty, we do not become wise; we enter into illusion. This illusory sense of reality is in mortal combat with Reality, and Reality always wins. Hence, living in an illusory state includes experiencing states of despair, malice, and bondage rather than manifesting our higher angels of Trust, Love, and Freedom. In the words of the Genesis myth, we experience ejection from the Garden of Innocence and now live somewhere to the East of Eden in the Land of Nod.

The truth of this story is profound, so profound that it may seem amazing that people living about 3000 years ago wrote this story, understood it, and put it in their holy scriptures. In our modern arrogance, it is difficult for us to take in the ways that ancient people were wise. Our exaggerated view of modern wisdom is one of the ways that we have fallen into illusion: we think we are so wise that people living long ago have nothing to teach us. We tend to believe that people who lived 3000 years ago lived in what we call "superstition" compared with our wondrous scientific and psychological accomplishments. It is true that we do know more about electricity, gravity, air travel, and nuclear energy, as well as many dynamics of the human psyche. But in all ways we are not wiser than many of our ancient ancestors. And certainly, we are not absolutely wise. Our knowledge falls infinitely short of a complete grasp of Reality. Our scientific knowledge and our awareness of human consciousness is such that we can never go back to those earlier eras of our species; nevertheless, we are still ignorant as we stand before the Absolute Mystery. Indeed, we are as ignorant as those who wrote the Adam and Eve story. When compared with the Infinite, finite knowledge is always zero, no matter how advanced our finite knowledge may become.

The myth of Adam and Eve assumes that primal humanity, before eating from this forbidden tree, was entirely ignorant of good and evil. Apparently, we who are living today have already eaten from this forbidden tree. Our parents taught us good and evil; our culture taught us good and evil; our religious bodies taught us good and evil. Our superegos are filled with teachings of good and evil. And without even thinking about it, we believe our superegos. Even after thinking about it, we may still take seriously the teachings lodged in our superegos. We eat these teachings and obey them every day. We expect others to also eat and obey the teachings of our superegos. We may be somewhat generous and allow others to eat and obey the teachings of their own superegos, but we actually feel it would be better if they ate and obeyed the teachings of our superegos. When Western superegos first went to visit primitive tribal groups in out of the way places, they found the superegos of those people appalling. We still do. Moderns find primitives appalling. Christians find Muslims appalling. Muslims find Christians appalling. New Yorkers find Texans appalling. Texans find New Yorkers appalling. The more tolerant among us find the intolerant appalling. The more intolerant among us find the tolerant appalling.

At some point in our life journey we may awaken to the realization that every person's superego is stupid. Indeed, all of us have become stupid by eating from the tree of the knowledge of good and evil. The snake in our Genesis myth promised that we would become wise like God, but the Genesis myth is quite clear that the snake lied. The truth was spoken by the Infinite Silence, who walked in the garden in the cool of the day and asked Adam and Eve why they were hiding behind their fig leaves. The answer was that they were hiding from Reality (God) because they had committed an unreality. They had chosen to believe that they had a knowledge of good and evil that made them wise. Actually, their knowledge of good and evil made them stupid. It killed their true beings. It exiled them from the Garden of Innocence and condemned them to live in an alien land East of Eden. This consequence was "good" because this is how Reality works: those who choose illusion instead of truth receive a life of estrangement from Reality. Any knowledge of good and evil viewed as ultimately valid by a human mind is an illusion. This includes all the teachings of the Bible, the Koran, or any other book written by human beings, however inspired that book is supposed to be. The knowledge of good and evil is forbidden to the human species, forbidden by Reality. This is the way the cosmos is put together. Ignorance about good and evil is the natural and holy state for a human being.

DID ADAM AND EVE TAKE A STEP UP?

Some have argued that the myth of Adam and Eve tells about a step up in evolution rather than a fall from our created goodness. Here is a quotation from a prominent contemporary Christian theologian, Lloyd Geering.

> Let us take the biblical myth of Adam and Eve. It can be read at different levels. It contains a remarkable number of insights, some of which have been lost sight of or ignored because of the way traditional Christian doctrine interpreted the myth as the fall. It has been too little noticed, for example, that it depicts God as telling an untruth. The myth relates how God solemnly warned the couple not to eat of the tree of the knowledge of good and evil because on the day they did so they would die. It was the wily serpent that revealed the truth. He said they would not die but their eyes would be opened and they would "be like God, knowing

good and evil." As the story proceeds we are left to realize for ourselves that it was not God but the serpent that was speaking the truth. They did not die on the day they ate the fruit – and their eyes were certainly opened! The serpent implied that it was out of divine self-interest that God had placed the prohibition, not wishing his human creatures to become like himself. This implication is even confirmed by the narrator who, at the end of the story, rather surprisingly interprets the divine plan as unfolding something like this. It was bad enough for humans to have become like God by having gained the knowledge of good and evil: it would be even worse if they were to eat from the tree of life and become immortal like God. So God found it necessary to expel them from the Garden of Eden to protect the uniqueness of his own immortality![10]

In the next paragraph Geering points out that the philosopher Hegel understood the Adam and Eve myth to be about the transition from the animal state to the human state and that Hegel thought the myth should be referred to as a "rise" not a "fall."

But neither Hegel nor Geering understands the biblical myth. Their misunderstanding of the myth is an indication of the depth of the issue we are exploring.

In the context of the Bible, this myth is about a fall. And the God figure is telling the truth. An ultimate valid knowledge of good and evil is a forbidden fruit (not morally forbidden, but factually forbidden.) It has always been forbidden; it is still forbidden; and it always will be forbidden. The human being is finite. The human being is not like God, knowing good and evil. Our knowledge is fragmentary, temporal, passing. Humanity is not "like God" if the word "God" points to the Infinite Reality.

Furthermore, this story is not about the transition from the animal state to the human state. Adam and Eve are already human beings who talk and think and even dialogue with one another, God, and snakes. This myth is about the fall from human authenticity into a lie. And

---

[10]   Lloyd Geering, *Tomorrow's God* (Polebridge Press: 2000) page 60

what is this lie? The great and primal lie told by the snake is that we can have certainty, lasting certainty, a meaning for our lives that lasts, a definite knowledge of what is good and what is evil. Such meaning may be the longing of every anxious self, but its possibility is not the truth. To eat this lie is to crawl into a box of our own making. To eat this lie is to identify with our own invention rather than with our true nature. To eat this lie is to die to who we are and become a sham person. To eat this lie is to worship human creations of meaning instead of the "meaningless," mysterious, unknown and unknowable Infinite Reality that the Bible names "God."

So why do intelligent, thoughtful people like Geering and Hegel choose to see this myth completely backwards? They, like most of humanity, identify with the human mind's quest for meaning. They value the creations of the human mind more than participation in realism before that Final Reality that provides us with human minds and the limitations of those minds.

Though the mind cannot know Final Reality (that Finally Unknowable God of the Bible), in another sense God is *known* by the soul. The soul, our consciousness of being conscious, knows God as the far end of our own being. The soul we explored with Jacob in Chapter 1 is a ramp from Awesome Eternity to the Awe-filled core or our being. Angels (Awe figures) flow toward and away from our finite space/time coordinate. The soul knows itself receiving Awe and responding in Awe. The soul can directly know itself, and in knowing itself knows God. But this is a different sort of knowing than the knowing of the mind. The soul knows itself and God as a direct experience, the sort of experience that precedes thinking about it.

And this knowing of self and God adds nothing to our quest for meaning. It is even a kind of frustration of our quest for meaning in that it is an acknowledgment that Reality is meaningless to the human mind. Yet this awareness does not negate the quest for meaning, it merely puts this valid quest in its place. The place for our quest for meaning is right alongside our quest for security, for pleasure, for love, for achievement, for power, for righteousness, and for any other temporal drive of our finite existence. These drives are not evil. And their frustration is not evil. Evil or sin, according to this ancient Genesis myth, is something else entirely. Sin is human consciousness lying about the state of things, lying about our finitude, confusing ourselves about our ability to possess truth with our minds. A primary aspect of our finite lives is this: an ultimately valid knowledge of good and evil is forbidden to us. We live our lives with fragmentary knowledge of what is valuable and what is not. All our modes of evaluation are subject to upending. All our decisions are made in the twilight of ambiguity that is spread over all real world choices. Whenever we think otherwise, we have fallen into delusion, into estrangement from Reality, into sin against God.

If we embrace this way of understanding the fall, it is safe to say that we have all fallen. We have all eaten a bite of humanly created certainty that is not certain and then pretended that it was certain. The Adam and Eve story is not only a myth about the first fall in the life of humanity; it is also a myth about falling as a dynamic in every age of history and in every human life.

ALL THAT IS REAL IS GOOD

The biblical context for the myth of the fall is spelled out in the first chapter of the Bible. The opening chapter of the Bible makes the point that all nature, including human nature, is good. This identification of the real with the good is present in the theologies of Augustine, Aquinas, Luther, Bonhoeffer, H. Richard Niebuhr, and many other Christian theologians. What does it mean for us to honestly affirm that all that is real is good?

Death is certainly real enough; is death good? Pain in my cramped leg is real; is it also good? There is much suffering of body and psyche; is all this suffering good? A vast ecological catastrophe of the entire planet may be forthcoming. Is this also good? If so, what do we mean by "good"? Good with respect to what? Good from what perspective?

And if all that is real is good, what then is evil? Augustine and others answer that question: evil is the absence of Reality; evil is a departure from Reality; evil is our illusions about Reality.

But are not our illusions real? At least, do not our illusions have real consequences in our living? Illusions are not real, but they do have real consequences in our living. Therefore, if the real is good, then the consequences of illusory living are good. Such consequences are the way the cosmos is constructed to work. It is good that illusions are followed by their consequences. Illusions destroy our close relationships with others. That is good. Illusions lead to needless violence and warfare. That is good. Since Reality cannot be defeated, illusions are futile. That is good. Illusions can never win in the end. That is good. Illusions are a hopeless way to live. That is good. Illusions lead to despair, perhaps suicide, perhaps murder, perhaps raging against the whole of life and everyone in it. Such despair is good. It is the way illusory living is constructed to work out. In fact, when we are willing to openly experience the despair in our lives, we are not far from understanding what it means to say, "All that is real is good."

But how do we decide what is real and therefore what is good? No human perspective will do, for no human can ever see the whole of Reality. No human sees Reality whole. Reality is unknown. So we must say that it is only from the perspective of Reality itself that all that is real is good.

So how can we humans experience the perspective of Reality? Directly, we can't. We experience Reality as a Mystery, as the Unknown Unknown, as the Infinite Silence that says nothing, as the No-Thing-Ness from which all things come and to which all things return, as the Every-Thing-Ness in which all things cohere. Nevertheless, when this Reality, this Infinite Silence speaks to us, this is what it says, "All that is real is good." That is the message of the first chapter of the Bible, "It is good; it is all good."

But to believe this, just because the Bible says those words, is not enough. We have to see for ourselves that what the Bible says is so. We have to hear the Infinite Silence speaking to us with our own "Spirit" ears. We have to take in personally this message: "All that is real is good."

MORALISM

The moral principles we possess are no more than useful guidelines. As Jesus said about the Sabbath laws, "The Sabbath was made for humans, not humans for the Sabbath." All rules and principles are created to be useful for the living of human life. But humans are not made to be imprisoned by the rules and principles humans have created or learned. This understanding applies to all evaluations rendered through any mode of value assessment. After even our most careful thinking about values has been done, we are still ignorant about what actions are best. Those who think they know for sure what to do are in illusion and turn out to be the most destructive forces in human life. Moralism and perfectionism are sin – estrangement from Reality. Ethical ignorance is our natural and holy state.

Why are statements like these so hotly opposed? Because we humans do not believe that all that is real is good. We believe that we know what things are good and what things are evil. We arrogate our puny knowledge to the status of absolute truth. Therefore, we humans do not trust Reality or see it as good. We presume to judge parts of Reality as good and other parts of Reality as evil. This presumption is the foundational estrangement from God described in the opening chapters of the Bible.

In order to experience the good of Reality and Reality as good, we have to give up our right to be the judge of what is good. We have to be content with being ignorant about good and evil. We have to renounce our own superego, our own cultural mores and principles, our own bodies' wants and desires, our own feelings of comfort and discomfort. We have to stop fleeing from Reality, stop suppressing Reality, stop hating Reality. We have to be open to living the fullness of Reality in each and every situation. This is what it means to embrace the assertion that all that is real is good.

Embracing Reality as good means being open to Mystery, for Reality is Mysterious. We do not know Reality. All that we know is merely a scratch on the great rock of Unknown Reality. All that we know is only a drop in the great ocean of Reality. Being open to Reality and its Mystery means being open to knowing more. Curiosity is an aspect of loving Reality. Love of Reality means being willing to change our minds regularly, perpetually, our whole life long. We never arrive at what we can finally believe. We never learn the final doctrine. We never meet our final teacher. We never become "wise like God." If what is real is good, then we must be reconciled to being ignorant, to never expecting our lives to become without ignorance. Even if we are the most accomplished scholars on earth, we are still ignorant with regard to Reality. A life that affirms that all that is real is good is a life of utmost humility. Humility is the good life, the realistic life – the life that believes that all that is real is good.

We have just described what it means to trust Reality, to apply the devotional word "God" to Reality. This is the saving faith described by Luther. This is the ethical context for all our living spelled out by Bonhoeffer. This is the foundational trust elaborated by H. Richard Niebuhr in his contextual ethics. This healing Trust is the gift of God (Reality) proclaimed by the ex-Pharisee Paul.

STOIC RESIGNATION

Rudolf Bultmann distinguishes trust of Reality from Stoic resignation. Being resigned to Reality is not the same as trusting Reality. Resignation is an act of human will, a calculated choice to go along with Reality rather than fight Reality. Such resignation is a type of courage. It means taking the pain and suffering of our lives into ourselves without complaint, without protest. It means suppressing our frustration, disappointment, resentment, and rage toward Reality. It means counting such feelings and attitudes unworthy of us. It means making the best of our lives in spite of the difficulties. It means handling tough situations and grim feelings with the courage of resignation. The stoic says, "This is the way life is, and I can handle it."

Christian Trust of Reality can seem similar to Stoic resignation, but it is very different. Christian Trust is not a calculated choice, not an act of human will. Trust of Reality means opening to Reality. It means being open to the reality of our own feelings. It means being open to flow with the flow of Reality. It means embracing the courage to be vulnerable. And most important, trusting Reality means being willing to be healed by Reality, surrendering all hope that we can heal ourselves. Trusting Reality means allowing all our frustration, disappointment, resentment, and rage toward Reality to be experienced, to be confessed, to be brought out into the open as our sin, as our estrangement from that Final Reality that we do not trust as our God. The journey of Trust is a journey into the dark nights of our own deep fears of Reality, of our rages against Reality, and of Reality's humiliations of our self-constructed programs of living. When we open in this way, Reality does the healing. We only accept the healing. We do not accomplish it.

And what do we mean by healing? We mean overcoming our estrangement from Reality. Stoic courage merely sweeps estrangement under the rug; or more accurately, it exiles despairing estrangement to a hidden dungeon in the deep unconsciousness. Trust opens the dungeons and allows the sick soul to enter the hospital that Reality provides.

THE HOSPITAL OF REALITY

And what is the hospital of Reality like? It is like a father who sees his wayward son heading home from a life of admitted estrangement. This father sees his son coming, runs to meet him, embraces him, welcomes him back into the family, gives him a robe in place of his rags, puts a ring on his finger, and throws a feast.

The elder son does not think that Reality ought to function in this manner. He feels that doing good should be rewarded and doing bad should be punished. The returning son should at least endure a period of probation. A feast is certainly out of order. He feels that "A good guy like me has not been given a feast, why this bad boy?" And he goes into a huge pout. The father explains that it is appropriate to make merry, "For my son was lost and is found – was dead and is alive again."

Reality welcomes home those who experience the tragedy of their being away. Being away is the punishment. Coming home is the feast. No amends are required. No undoing is necessary. No admission fee of goodness is required. No promises. No intentions. No beliefs. Nothing whatsoever is required except accepting the welcome.

If we don't take the welcome, we collapse in a pool of shame or some other foolish thinking, and we don't make it to the feast. This whole story is a comedy. It is like a big joke. The joke is on all the serious people who have tried so hard to be good by whatever standards they thought were expected. And now it turns out that there are no standards. There are no requirements at all. There is just the humiliation of returning home. There is just the acknowledgment that we have been away. There is just the humility of accepting the huge gift of full membership in the divine family of realistic living without bringing one ounce of acceptability for that membership.

This unconditional forgiveness is the quintessential expression of the goodness of Reality. Each of us is welcome home to Reality. A Universal Pardon extends to all humans. Though we have all eaten from the deadly tree of the knowledge of good and evil, Reality embraces us anyway. And as Reality embraces us, illusions fall away. The goodness of Reality engulfs us. The illusion that we must know good and evil, do the good, and avoid the evil falls away. Trust in Reality's goodness is all that is required. And this is a strange requirement, for it asks for nothing except surrender to the goodness of Reality. We don't have to know what all that means. We don't have to know what foods will be served at the feast. We don't have to know what the future will bring. We only have to trust that Reality is a hospital for sin-sick souls and that Reality will continue to heal us. As our remaining illusions bubble up to the surface, they will be burned to ash by the fires of Reality. Our fears of Reality will be revealed to be needless, silly, and comical. Our rages toward Reality will be revealed to be idiotic and self-punishing. Our monsters of humiliation will evaporate like ice on a hot skillet, for the "self" being humiliated never existed at all. Our true self is the self at home with Reality, trusting in the goodness of Reality, seeing with our own Spirit eyes and hearing with our own Spirit ears that all that is real is good. This is the joy unspeakable, for the goodness of Reality cannot be taken away from us.

11.

Nine Ways to Fall from Spirit

At each step of our Spirit journey, seeing our specific states of fallenness is a doorway back to our true being. Enabling the reader to see his or her own fallenness is one of the aims of Part Three of this book. Another aim is helping us to see our companions in their full chamber of horrors as well as in their potential for recovering their higher angels of Trust, Love, and Freedom. Such vision of ourselves and of our companions enables us to be a healing presence. The following chapters may seem negative in content, but an awareness of these negative states is a positive step forward.

In our infancy we began developing a personality. This development was necessary for our survival. In dialogue with our caretakers and our society, each of us built a personality that includes a sense of reality. That sense of reality is composed of multi-sensory memory reruns of our early and recent experiences. It is also composed of our uniquely human intellectual reflections on these raw memories of our experiences. It is composed of a whole complexity of default patterns for the living of our lives. These default patterns are our personality. The personality we have built makes possible our survival and our ability to maneuver within our society.

But this personality (with its sense of reality and its sense of self) is also a cocoon that protects us from greater Reality, including the Reality of our essential self, our dynamic soul flowing with Freedom, Love, and Trust.   When we identify with our personality or with the self-image produced by the reasoning of our personality, we are misidentifying with who we deeply and truly are.

Therefore, our personality tempts us to fall into delusion. And the core of that delusion is that our particular personality knows reality, knows who we are, knows good and evil, and is certain about how to live. Such misidentification with our personality and its delusory certainties is a fall away from our true being. It is a reenactment of the Adam and Eve story.

In other words, our personality is the snake of the Eden story; our personality is our temptation to fall into a deadly misidentification. Misidentification is the issue, not having a personality. Having a personality is unavoidable. Our personality is a product of our attempts to hold together enough sense of reality to survive. But since the personality provides a substitute reality for Reality, it can tempt us away from knowing and living our true life.

Yet, paradoxically, when we are keenly aware of our personality, it can be a guide for us – showing us our path of return to Reality. When carefully observed, our personality can act as a map that can lead us back from the substitute reality of personality to the actual Reality for which the personality became a substitute. Strange as this may seem, learning the particulars of our own personality and how we have fallen into identification with that personality can help us move from our fallen states to our essential Trust, Love, and Freedom.

Various schools of psychology have built models of the different personality types. Even though it is true that every personality is unique, it is also true that human personalities can be grouped together into broad types.   For me, the most helpful analysis of personality types is found in the enneagram heritage. The word "enneagram" means "ninefold diagram." The enneagram model describes nine personality types and the relationships among them. This typology is especially helpful for our Spirit journey because these nine types of personality can be shown to correspond, one to one, with the nine major families of angels described in Part Two of this book (the three major aspects of

Trust, the three major aspects of Love, and the three major aspects of Freedom). Each personality type is a portrait of what it looks like to fall away from one of these nine major aspects of our true Being. But before we explore these nine "falls" in detail, here is a brief overview of the enneagram heritage.

The Enneagram Heritage and the Nine Types of Personality

I became acquainted with the enneagram through the early writings of Don Richard Riso. He helped me see more clearly how the people around me operate with different default patterns than I do. I found it helpful and humbling to know that there were at least eight other basic ways to be a human personality. I saw more clearly how it is erroneous to project my own personality's way of seeing and living onto others.

The enneagram heritage uses a diagram that has ancient and enigmatic roots in the Sufi tradition. The Armenian philosopher and teacher George Ivanovitch Gurdjieff introduced this diagram to modern thought. It was used very powerfully by the Bolivian mystic Oscar Ichazo and by his student Chilean psychiatrist Claudio Naranjo. These creative pioneers saw that the types of human personality were related to aspects of human authenticity. These nine personality types were later popularized by Helen Palmer, Don Richard Riso, Russ Hudson, and others. David Daniels and Virginia Price pulled together a short helpful book entitled *The Essential Enneagram*. Their book provides some condensed empirical data and some effective tests for discerning one's personality type, but it does not provide help for using the enneagram for mapping the aspects of human essence or Spirit. The more recent book by Riso and Hudson, *The Wisdom of the Enneagram,* does provide commentary on the topic of human essence as well as a vast collection of carefully organized empirical data on human personalities.

The enneagram as an exploration of human essence was more thoroughly examined by Ichazo and Naranjo and has been still further explored by A. H. Almaas in his classic book *The Facets of Unity*. I also recommend *The Spiritual Dimension of the Enneagram: Nine Faces of the Soul* by Sandra Maitri. In addition to her own study with Naranjo and her experience as a teacher of the enneagram, Maitri uses key insights worked through by Almaas, a long-term friend and colleague. Both

Almaas and Maitri focus on the enneagram heritage as a means of mapping what they call our "human "essence" or "true nature." They are not using the enneagram model as a means of assisting us in choosing a mate or hiring an employee. Some have found Maitri's book threatening or heavy because she is intent on showing the ways in which all the personality types are a form of estrangement from our human essence. But I find her work, and Almaas's work as well, profoundly helpful in clarifying the various ways we stray from our glorious essence. And their analysis also shows us how our straying ways can be seen as threads that can lead us back to our true nature.

The discussion of the enneagram that follows is not a substitute for reading the books cited above. The enneagram is a rich and deep system, a heritage that can open almost endlessly into still further insight.

The following diagram contains the names for the nine personality types used by Riso and Hudson. Other names for these nine types are used by other authors, but I like these because they seem to me to be an accurate, uncritical summation of the behaviors that characterize each type.

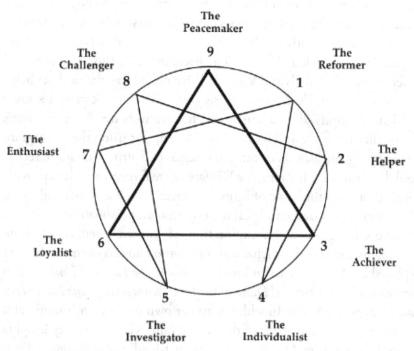

Though each personality is unique, each of us, in the early years of our lives, began building a personality in one of these nine basic ways. We may be curious to know which type we are. We may also be curious to determine the personality types of our friends and relatives, bosses, students, and acquaintances. But we must take care not to type ourselves or others too quickly. This is a profound and subtle system. Some of the types can seem similar to others. Many characteristics appear in almost all of them. And each type includes differences within that type, ranging from personalities that are wildly dysfunctional to those that are highly functional.

The reader who is new to enneagram typing might gain a hint toward discovering his or her personality type by answering the following question:

Which **one** of the following nine statements **most** applies to you?

> I seek to enjoy emotional appreciation from my intimate others.
>
> I seek to enjoy external achievements of success or perhaps beauty.
>
> I seek to enjoy inward qualities that are recognized and celebrated.
>
> I want to have the answers in an understandable form.
>
> I want to have a secure role and perhaps a daring role in the structure of things.
>
> I want to have satisfying, meaningful, and hopefully pleasant activities to do.
>
> I have a passion to be in charge of things and to exercise leadership.
>
> I have a passion to fit into things and to avoid conflict.
>
> I have a passion to be basically correct in my actions in life.

Choose a second statement that also applies to you in a major way. Then choose a third statement that applies to you. Make these three selections before you read further.

Now, having made your answers, number the set of nine statements:

2 3 4 5 6 7 8 9 and 1.

Your personality type may be one of the three choices you made.
In order to help you discern which of these three choices it might be,
answer the following question:

Which of the following three statements is most true for you?

> I am more preoccupied with outer results than with
> safety or self-image.
> I am more preoccupied with self-image than with outer
> results or safety.
> I am more preoccupied with safety than with self-image
> or outer results.

Select one of these three statements before your read further.

If you chose outer results, you are most likely an 8, 9, or 1. (You
may be a 3 or 7.)
If you chose self image, you are most likely a 2, 3, or 4.
If you chose safety, you are most likely a 5, 6, or 7.

These simple indicators may or may not reveal to you your per-
sonality type. For a more accurate indication of your personality type
I suggest the following: (1) take the simple tests that are in the small
but empirically careful book *The Essential Enneagram* by David Daniels
and Virginia Price. (2) Take the more extensive tests that are in *The
Wisdom of the Enneagram* by Don Richard Riso and Russ Hudson. (3)
And then read the thorough descriptions of each type contained in
Sandra Maitri's book, *The Spiritual Dimension of the Enneagram*. (4)
Also helpful to me have been the colorful descriptions by Eli Jaxon-
Bear in his book *The Enneagram of Liberation*.

The Enneagram of Trust, Love, and Freedom

My interest in the enneagram goes deeper than learning personality types and thereby understanding myself and my acquaintances more clearly. In this book I am exploring the enneagram types because they provide clues for understanding our Spirit nature and how we fall away from that Spirit nature.

A. H. Almaas associated each personality type with an aspect of our Spirit nature. One of his images lodged in my mind. Our Spirit Being is like a single jewel with many faces. As we approach one of these faces of the jewel we approach the whole jewel. The whole jewel is the common unity, the universal Spirit Being that characterizes the true nature of each and every human being. The faces of the jewel are the various approaches that humanity makes to this central core of Spirit essence. Each personality type of the enneagram tradition is a description of a set of flight patterns from one of the nine faces of this core jewel.

Almaas illuminated for me how each personality type is a past-oriented set of habits that obstructs the full experience and expression of the here-and-now wonder of the Spirit aspect from which that personality is in flight. In other words, each personality type is a facsimile or an imitation (and thus a falsification) of one of the major Spirit aspects.

The following chart contains the names I am using for the nine facets of Spirit Being that associate with the nine enneagram personality types. Almaas uses different language, but he is pointing, I believe, to the same states of Spirit. In the Appendix, I compare and contrast Almaas's language with the language I am using. I will associate each of the nine personality types with one of the nine major facets of Spirit that I described in Part Two – three aspects of Trust, three aspects of Love, and three aspects of Freedom. Here are those nine aspects of our Spirit Being arranged in their associations with the nine points on the enneagram model:

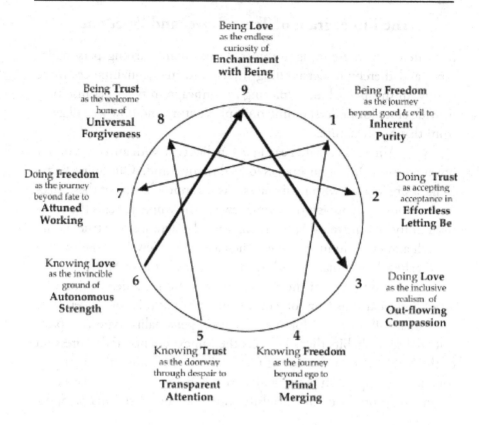

All the arrows on the above chart move from knowing to being to doing. This is the positive flow: first to know or participate in an actuality, then to be identified with being that actuality, and finally to do or manifest that actuality in the full round of our living.

Notice that points 6, 9, and 3 deal with those aspects of Holy Spirit that the Christian heritage points to with the term "agape" or "Spirit Love." Spirit love includes love of self, love of others, and love of the Ground of our Being. I am suggesting that point 6 is about love of self; point 9 is about love of the Ground of our Being, and point 3 is about love of others. As spelled out in Part Two, **Autonomous Strength** provides a description of the Spirit Love of self, **Enchantment with Being** provides a description of the Spirit Love of God, and **Out-flowing Compassion** provides a description of the Spirit Love of others. Point 6 is the knowing aspect of Love, point 9 the being aspect of Love, and point 3 the doing aspect of Love.

Points 5, 8, and 2 associate with the three major facets of the master category of "Trust." Point 5 can be depicted as the foundational or knowing aspect of Trust. Open curiosity about the multiplicity of Being is a state of Trust. I call this **Transparent Attention**. To flee from such knowing would be distrust. Point 8 can be depicted as the being aspect of Trust. Realizing the Truth of the benevolence of Being is the primary essence of Spirit Trust. I call this **Universal Forgiveness**. Point 2 can be depicted as the doing aspect of Trust. Trust is a free gift that entails the surrender of our typical willfulness and thus letting Actuality be what it is. I call this **Effortless Letting Be**.

Finally, points 4, 1, and 7 associate with the three major facets of the master category of "Freedom." Point 4 can be depicted as the foundational or knowing aspect of Freedom. Knowing our Freedom begins with liberation from our ego enabling a merging with our essence. I call this **Primal Merging**. Point 1 can be depicted as the being aspect of Freedom. The deepest essence of Freedom is a liberation from the superego, from the entire cultural consensus on good and evil. Living beyond good and evil is the heart of what Christian heritage at its best (Paul, Luther, Bonhoeffer) has meant by Spirit Freedom. I call this **Inherent Purity**. Point 7 can be depicted as the doing aspect of Freedom: Freedom experienced as an alignment with the flow of Reality rather than fighting with Reality or knuckling under to Reality as if Reality were a fixed fate. I call this **Attuned Working**.

Describing Personality Patterns as Modes of Estrangement

The nine points on the enneagram chart not only associate with the nine aspects of Holy Spirit, but also with the nine personality types, each of which is a falsification or a humanly invented substitute for one of the Holy Spirit aspects. Hence, the nine types of personality represent nine ways to fall from Spirit. The next chart provides a first impression of the ways that these various personalities become falsifications.

Persons in the left group, the mind-centered group of personalities, are *paranoid* about everything that cannot be contained within their finite minds. This fear is especially overwhelming when facing The Awesome Mysterious Otherness that is beyond all comprehension. These personalities can be characterized as dread-based or fear-based. They are preoccupied with safety.

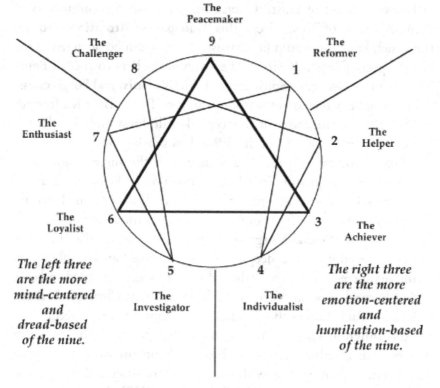

The top three are the more body centered and rage-based of the nine.

The Peacemaker
9

The Challenger
8

The Reformer
1

The Enthusiast
7

The Helper
2

The Loyalist
6

The Achiever
3

The left three are the more mind-centered and dread-based of the nine.

5
The Investigator

4
The Individualist

The right three are the more emotion-centered and humiliation-based of the nine.

Persons in the top group, the body-centered group of personalities, are *rebellious* toward the intense aspects of human inwardness. This rebellion is especially strong when relating to states of Awe. These personalities can be characterized as rage-based or anger-based. They are preoccupied with outward results that express, suppress, or channel that anger.

Persons in the right group, the emotion-centered group of personalities, are *hysterical* about maintaining their self-image. This preoccupation is especially present when being challenged to transcend ego and answer the call to be an Awed One. These personalities can be characterized as humiliation-based, for their personality patterns operate to avoid experiencing threats to their self image.

Following is a chart that spells out these basic patterns as they apply to each type:

PERSONALITY QUALITIES

		more **mind** centered	more **body** centered	more **emotion** centered
THE DIMENSIONS OF AWE	**GENERAL QUALITIES**	**paranoid** about everything esp. facing The Awesome **dread based**	**rebellious** toward inwardness esp. being The Awe **rage based**	**hysterical** about self-image esp. embodying The Awed One **humiliation based**
	THE AWE OF TRUST	dread of ignorance **5** open to unknown Transparent Attention	open anger **8** accepting defeat Universal Forgiveness	proud manipulation **2** losing control Effortless Letting-Be
	THE AWE OF LOVE	dread of being real **6** love of self Autonomous Strength	suppressed rage **9** love of Being Enchantment with Being	vain shell-building **3** love of others Out-flowing Compassion
	THE AWE OF FREEDOM	dread of missing out **7** freely with it Attuned Working	righteous resentment **1** free from good and evil Inherent Purity	envious of specialness **4** free to be ordinary Primal Merging

In the space immediately above each personality number is a more specific aspect of the more general characteristic summarized at the top of each column. In the space immediately below each personality number is a description of the aspect of Trust, Love, or Freedom that this personality type warps into a falsification.

Here is a simple chart for holding in our minds the relationship of the nine personality types to Trust, Love, and Freedom and to the knowing-being-doing dynamics.

	Knowing	Being	Doing
Trust	5	8	2
Love	6	9	3
Freedom	4	1	7

For example, this chart indicates that personality type 5 is a departure from the knowing dimension of Trust. Type 9 is a departure from the being dimension of Love. Type 7 is a departure from the doing dimension of Freedom. And so on. Each departure from Trust is some form of despair. Each departure from Love is some form of malice. Each departure from Freedom is some form of bondage. Here is a prose poem about these forms of despair, malice, and bondage:

Hiding Trust in a pattern of Despair
5. Hiding the gift of Transparent Attention in a despair over ignorance
8. Hiding the gift of Universal Forgiveness in a despair over powerlessness
2. Hiding the gift of Effortless Letting Be in a despair over abandonment

Masking Love in a pattern of Malice
6. Masking the gift of Autonomous Strength in a malice toward self
9. Masking the gift of Enchantment with Being in a malice toward Being
3. Masking the gift of Out-flowing Compassion in a malice toward others

Fleeing Freedom in a pattern of Bondage
4. Fleeing the gift of Primal Merging for a bondage to self image
1. Fleeing the gift of Inherent Purity for a bondage to good and evil judgments
7. Fleeing the gift of Attuned Working for a bondage to a fixed fate

All of us participate to some degree in all of these gifts and in all of these patterns of departure; nevertheless, each of us in our particular early development adopted as our core pattern one of these ways of not being our Spirit Being. If we view one of these personality patterns as better than another, such a judgment is simply a bias that is formed from one of the personality types. A truer view is seeing that each of these nine patterns characterizes a particular departure and a particular journey back to being our Spirit Being. It is a distraction to either rebel against the journey in which we are placed or to glory in it. How we show up is how we show up. No judgments of depreciation or praise need to be made.

Finally, like all rational typologies about Reality, the enneagram typology is not Reality itself but merely a pointer to the Reality that infinitely transcends every typology. The enneagram system is just a poetic model that may help people see for themselves something they might not otherwise see.

This next chart introduces categories of description that will be used in the next three chapters.

The far left column of this chart lists the three master categories of Holy Spirit and the nine enneagram numbers. The section entitled **"Nine Aspects of Spirit Being"** provides my naming of these nine facets of Spirit and a brief statement about each. The section entitled **"Nine Personality Patterns"** is broken down into five columns, each of which contains a way of describing these personality patterns. The following paragraphs define the categories that head each of these five columns:

The Enneagram of Spirit Aspects and Personality Patterns

No.	Nine Aspects of Spirit Being		Nine Personality Patterns				
	Spirit Aspect	Spirit Aspect Described	Characteristic Delusion	Recurring Despair	Defensive Reaction	Classical Estrangement	Behavioral Pattern
The Awe of Trust							
5	*knowing, trust* Transparent Attention	Trusting Reality means curious openness to the presence of everything.	Separate Self: I need to be informed.	Feeling Isolated	Withdrawing or Hiding	Greed Avarice	The Investigator
8	*being, trust* Universal Forgiveness	There is no evil Reality to blame. All things are One Goodness.	Duality: My life is a battle.	Feeling Guilty	Blaming Others	Pushiness Lust	The Challenger
2	*doing, trust* Effortless Letting Be	Trust is a free gift to be lived in surrender of normal willfulness.	Separate Will: I need to be needed.	Feeling Humiliated	Manipulating to be Useful	Vainglory Pride	The Helper
The Awe of Love							
3	*doing, love* Out-flowing Intimacy	Doing loving living is the natural connection with all beings.	Separate Doer: I need to be significant.	Feeling Helpless	Striving to Make it	Vanity Deceit	The Achiever
9	*being, love* Enchantment with Being	Reality is benevolent & nothing can separate us from that love.	Reduced Love: I need to resolve conflict.	Feeling Unlovable	Falling Asleep	Sloth Indolence	The Peacemaker
6	*knowing, love* Autonomous Strength	The soul knows that life is already an abundant invincible presence.	No True Nature: I need support from others.	Feeling Insecure	Suspiciously Defending the ego	Anxiety Fear	The Loyalist
The Awe of Freedom							
4	*knowing, freedom* Primal Merging	Living beyond self-image means joining All Reality.	Separate Identity: I am on my own.	Feeling Abandoned	Controlling Outcomes	Deprivation Envy	The Individualist
1	*Being, freedom* Inherent Purity	Living beyond good & evil uncovers inherent Perfection and Beauty.	Reduced Rightness: Our lives must be changed.	Feeling Wrong	Improving Conditions	Resentment Rage	The Reformer
7	*Doing Freedom* Attuned Working	Living beyond fatalism means being aligned with the flow of Reality.	Separate Unfoldment: I must find my own way.	Feeling Lost	Planning a better life	Scatteredness Gluttony	The Enthusiast

Characteristic Delusion – Each personality type tells itself a story that is not true. This story is somewhat true in the sense that it refers to a valid component of our essential nature or Spirit Being. But it distorts this essential truth into a mistaken understanding of life. This false view determines the basic fabric and tendencies of this particular personality type. A brief summation of these false views is listed in this first column.

Recurring Despair – Because each personality is founded on a specific false premise, a specific form of frustration occurs in the course of actual living. Over and over again life reveals itself as more than, less than, or different from the false truth that has seemed self-evident to this personality. Such moments can be called "despair," because despair means trying to believe what is not true, trying to escape what cannot be escaped, trying to do what cannot be done, trying to change what cannot be changed, trying to defeat what cannot be defeated. When such patterns of hopeless living arise in our consciousness, strong feelings are commonly felt. So the personality descriptions in this column are feeling names, used to provide an emotional description to the quality of despair that most typifies each personality type.

Defensive Reaction – Since despair is not something we typically want to experience or face or deal with, we react to the arising of despair with defenses that enable us to avoid experiencing despair and its implications. This third column lists the ways that each type of personality typically defends itself against despair. Understanding these defensive patterns helps us to be ourselves – to interrupt our defensiveness so we can experience our despair and dig into its implications. Despair need not be viewed as a grievous tragedy; it is simply the frustration of our familiar falsity. To experience our despair is a step forward – a doorway to our true being.

Classical Estrangement – This fourth column names with Christian vocabulary the "deadly sin" that most characterizes each personality type. All these estrangements can pertain to every person, but each personality type has been found to specialize in one of them. In each case I have used two names instead of one in order to widen our view of these nine basic states of human falsification or fall.

Behavioral Pattern – In this last column are the titles or names that Riso and Hudson have given for each of the personality types.

These titles are helpful because they describe in brief the behavioral patterns that characterize each type. These behaviors are not in themselves negative or positive. But they have negative meaning for this particular personality because of the context in which they are performed. At the same time these behaviors can be seen as gifts of effective living that each personality type develops. As a person begins to access Spirit and thus soften his or her personality identification, these same behaviors become specializations that this person has for the positive tasks of living.

In the next three chapters I will explore how these five categories apply to each of the nine personality types.

12.

The Fall into Despair

Trusting Reality is a quality of our essential being. Fleeing Reality or fighting Reality is falling away from Trusting Reality. When we fall from Trust we fall into despair. Despair is the state of realizing our hopelessness relative to avoiding or defeating Reality. Despair is part of the experience of all persons, but three of the nine personality types of the enneagram model typically manifest their escape from Reality in a fall from Trust into despair. In this chapter I will describe these three personality types: the five, the eight, and the two.

I have given these personality types names that link their characteristic behavior pattern with one of the "deadly sins." Type 5 is the Greedy Investigator. Type 8 is the Lustful Challenger. And type 2 is the Vainglorious Helper.

The basic characteristic of each of these behavior patterns is not inherently bad. We need people who investigate, challenge, and help. These characteristics can be gifts of creative living. Yet the gifts of each of these personality types are typically used to form a cocoon in which a person hides from his or her essential being. In doing so, each personality type manifests a particular quality of estrangement from his or her true self. In this chapter we will explore the Greed or Avarice of type 5, the Pushiness or Lust of type 8, and the Vainglory or Pride of type 2.

People of the same personality type vary widely in their ability to function – in their mastery, consciousness, intellectual astuteness, emotional sensibilities, or any other way that human beings can differ. I will not be focusing on this wide variety. I will be focusing on the underlying dynamics of the fall from essential being that characterizes persons of each of these three personality types.

Type 5: The Greedy Investigator

Don Richard Riso calls enneagram personality type five "The Investigator." The Investigator is a behavioral pattern that may appear in any life, but some lives are especially characterized by this pattern. The Investigator has a very strong need to be informed, a need to know, to understand, to have a grasp on things, to be intellectually correct, to believe the right beliefs. He tends to be a withdrawn person who lives in his head. He tends to get lost in his thoughts. She tends to be paranoid about the challenge that others are to her thinking. She feels a deep need to put her inner view of things in order. He tends to talk in treatises. He wants to be a person who knows. She tends to withdraw into her thoughts whether those thoughts be grand or silly. These tendencies describe a pattern of falling away from that aspect of Spirit Trust I am calling "Transparent Attention."

The five may be well informed and do well in school, but tends to be a hermit, a recluse, even a dork in the judgment of most of his peers. A man as brilliant and successful as Howard Hughes was also a recluse, often self destructively so. Less talented fives tend to become entirely invisible on the social scene. Other fives may find a way to become significant contributors to the ongoing thought of their field. Albert Einstein and Rudolf Bultmann may have been fives. A. H. Almaas identifies himself as a five. I view him as a five who has profoundly accessed his Transparent Attention to the fullness of Reality and then uses his gifted mind as a tool in the service of that realism. There are also women who are fives. Susan K. Langer, the philosopher of reason, symbols, and art, seems like a five to me. Perhaps Georgia O'Keeffe and Marie Currie illustrate this type. Unless we know these individuals personally, we are just guessing their type. There are also quite ordinary women who are fives. A five might be a conservatively dressed high school student who is almost always off to herself reading a book. If a guy seeks to know her, he has to make an effort to do so, and he has to get past his misinterpretations that she is a dull or quirky person.

The *characteristic delusion* of the Investigator is that Reality is intelligible, or ought to be intelligible, or will some day be intelligible. Even if the Investigator is an accomplished scientist who knows that the more we know about nature the more we know we don't know, he still makes knowing things the key to living successfully, safely, and realizing his other values as they come into play.

The Investigator commonly believes that she can stand apart from Reality as a separate witness and thus know Reality as something "other-than-I." The thinking "I" stands apart and seeks to grasp Reality with the mind. The sensations of the body tend to become ideas about the sensations of the body. The emotions of the body tend to become ideas about the emotions. The soul, the core of consciousness, tends to become an idea about the soul. In other words, the Investigator obsesses on mental knowledge and is thereby estranged from living feelingly and actually in the here and now of ongoing experience.

The five falls away from Transparent Attention by misperceiving that the "things" the mind distinguishes are separate entities interacting in the mind's picture of space and time. The Investigator assumes that the patterns of the mind are the patterns of actuality. This is an understandable mistake and easily made, for there is usually significant correspondence between the mind's work and the actuality of human experience. If there were no such correspondence, the mind would be useless; and the human organism would not have survived. But the five is mistaken when he views the constructs of the mind as the actual patterns of Reality. Most importantly, when a person operates within this mistake, she sees herself as a separate thing, an entity of some sort, a separate substance that is not entirely part of the coming and going processes of nature. This mistake means that the inner core of the person has backed away from the fullness of being in Reality. The five has withdrawn from his own real life experiences in the ongoing here and now. The five is hiding in the woods of her own mental creations.

When this delusion is in operation, the five can only feel secure within his own thoughts. The five is paranoid about the wider Reality and about other people's views of Reality. The five feels fragile, feels her view of things to be fragile. So, the five retreats to her own thoughts, lives in her own head, becomes greedy to possess knowledge that has lasting, security-creating significance.

The *recurring despair* of the Investigator is a feeling of abject isolation, a sense of being lost in some ivory tower, some mental prison. Challenges requiring action can be frightening when they don't fit neatly into the Investigator's mental convictions. Conversations with other persons often become difficult, because real people are not mere minds sharing ideas; they are whole people connecting intimately. As long as the Investigator can focus on ideas and his excitement about ideas, his isolation can seem tolerable or even nonexistent. But as it becomes clear that all ideas are less than Reality, a life lived in the isolation of mental ideas tends to become dry. Ideas that have no real living juice to go with them become a desert. So the Investigator can feel trapped between life in a lonely desert of ideas and his dread of full engagement in actual situations that continually challenge his ordered and controlled ivory tower of ideas. Caught between these two alternatives, the Investigator experiences despair. Reality can seem totally untrustworthy.

The Investigator may also despair over her ignorance. Temporary ignorance may be tolerated, for the Investigator hopes that knowledge will soon be forthcoming. But when it becomes clear that ignorance is a permanent condition of the human species, that even the most brilliant among us simply do not know, the investigator finds hope disappearing. When it become clear that we all face the unfathomable, the Mystery that never goes away – when these sorts of experiences come to pass, the Investigator may experience a profound uneasiness. If life does not make sense, what is the use of living?

Human beings don't like despair, so they tend to flee from it or suppress it. Typically, people do not pause to discover how despair can be a doorway through which one might pass into a land of greater awareness and aliveness. So human beings defend themselves from their own despair. The Investigator's typical *defensive reaction* is to withdraw even further from other persons, from uncomfortable challenges, and from jarring situations. In so doing he avoids feeling the full tragedy of his experiences of isolation and his despair over his isolation. The Investigator can become quite skilled in avoiding situations in which this profound isolation becomes obvious. He hides in the inner workings of his own mind and becomes mildly or strongly paranoid about the actual surrounding world.

Nevertheless, the Investigator may be successful in investigating many things. She may be a storehouse of information on many subjects. We can say that she is greedy for information. She is obsessive for moments of security and for recognition in being someone who knows something. She may see her information or knowledge as her dearest possession. Her other possessions may also become an obsession, but her core motive for having things is her need to possess security in understanding, in knowing, in possessing certainty.

In these ways the Investigator withdraws from paying attention to the mysterious fullness of Reality. Instead, he puts in the place of such "Transparent Attention" his own self-constructed intellectual worlds. He becomes a *greedy* person, greedy most of all for security within his own ideas about living. He may become an argumentative person who feels threatened whenever even a single cherished idea is challenged or ignored. In the worst-case scenario, he becomes a dysfunctional recluse totally immersed in his own thoughts, forbidding others to enter.

Economically, a five tends to be a miser. He makes security his most important economic consideration. Politically, he may have strongly held ideas, but he may be slow to act upon them. He tends to be an outsider who thinks radical thoughts, yet lives in a passive way. He tends not to rock the boat. She tends to avoid conflict, especially conflict in which her ideas might be tested and challenged. When her ideas are challenged, she tends to overreact. Perhaps she argues unnecessarily or runs away to the safety of her own thoughts, her own books, her own ivory tower of mental familiarity. This is the core quality of the five's greediness, safety in a thought world of his own making.

But when the five sees his own thinking as the limited and often silly thing that it is, he can find his way back to Transparent Attention to the actual flow of experience. This releases the mind to be the wonderful tool that it is. Such released fives may then become the significant thinkers, writers, and artists of their era, or perhaps unspectacular but clear-thinking participants in the ordinary situations of life.

Type 8: The Lustful Challenger

Don Richard Riso calls the enneagram personality type eight "The Challenger." The Challenger is a behavioral pattern that may appear in any life, but some lives are especially characterized by this pattern. The Challenger sees life as a battle that needs to be won. He feels a need to get what he wants, to act on his truth, to challenge all laziness and shoddiness in himself and others. She seeks to make things happen, and she usually does. He has little or no capacity for regret. If he fails or hurts someone, he denies it or he simply corrects the failing and moves on. He seldom acknowledges mistakes. Her talking style is "laying trips" on people, provoking people. She gives great emphasis to being competent. She is willing to act forcefully even if that competence is questionable. These tendencies describe a pattern of falling away from that aspect of Spirit Trust I am calling "Universal Forgiveness."

Some of our most terrorizing dictators and criminal gang leaders have been eights. But eights also appear in businesses and homes. We have all met eight-mothers or eight-fathers who rule their families with an iron hand. Eights who have accessed their Spirit depths, their forgiveness and patience with others, have been some of our greatest religious and political leaders. My own mentor, Joe Mathews, was a clear example of this quality. Chogyam Trungpa was probably another eight-type religious leader. Franklin D. Roosevelt and Lyndon Johnson may be examples in the political realm. Jack Nickolson and Al Pacino play eight roles very well. Eights can also be women. Perhaps Roseanne Barr, Hillary Clinton, Susan Sarandon illustrate this type. Meryl Streep showed us eight quality in her role as the boss of a fashion company in her movie, "The Devil Wears Prada."

The *characteristic delusion* of the Challenger is that there is a basic duality in life between "my truth" and "some enemy's untruth." At first, this belief may seem completely true, for no matter what a person believes to be true, someone else can be found who believes otherwise. There is indeed a war going on between systems of beliefs. Whatever we believe, we find others who resist our beliefs. The Challenger takes this war seriously. The Challenger believes that it is important for his beliefs to triumph in the war of beliefs. In this sense, the Challenger is committed to being in control. He wishes to shape the world in terms of his beliefs. She typically believes that she is in control of her own life, perhaps in control of her own family or religious community. He may seek to expand his control to his company, town, city, or nation. In extreme cases the Challenger entertains fantasies of ruling the world. If more modest, he may merely believe that his beliefs ought to rule the world.

What is the delusion here? No human being or group of human beings ever rules the world. No human being is fully in control of his own family or even his own life. We are all out of control. We are swept along by the vast course of events over which we have only moderate control. We are even controlled by our own mind's fixation with mental beliefs. Furthermore, those beliefs are never the whole truth, never that Absolute Truth that always wins. Our beliefs are partial truths at best, and they may even be passionately held fantasies.

If the Challenger were to realize that all his beliefs are partial truths and choose them intentionally, he would immediately be more humble and less controlling. If the Challenger were to realize that his "truth" need not conquer the entire world, he would experience a great relaxation of his fanatic need to control. And if the Challenger were to realize that human beings are perpetually ignorant, devoid of any possession of permanent Truth, whether from so-called revealed religion or so-called objective science, he would be restored to the actual Truth. The actual or absolute Truth is that we are ignorant of any final Truth but, nevertheless, Universally Forgiven for our perpetual stupidities.

Universal Forgiveness is the key Truth about which the Challenger is in delusion. He may not believe that all atheists are forgiven. She may not believe that all religious fanatics are forgiven. He may not believe that all sentimentalists are forgiven. She may not believe that all moralists are forgiven. He may not believe that all criminals are forgiven. She may not believe that all tyrants are forgiven. The Challenger does not believe in forgiveness for everyone. The Challenger believes that her truth must win. There is a war going on and the opponents must be defeated. But within the Truth of Universal Forgiveness, there is no war. All are welcomed home to the same Reality. There are no enemies that must be defeated. Universal Forgiveness has already defeated us all. We are all members of one Reality that perpetually accepts us home from our far countries of delusory fanaticism.

The Challenger may not be conscious that he is at war with this Final Reality of Universal Forgiveness. He tends to see this war in terms of his own completely temporal beliefs. The Challenger is aware and active in challenging other human beings. Some of those challenges may be useful. People who want a strong leader tend to follow this person. This personality type is comfortable with being a leader; he relishes it. She seeks it. She finds situations where she can be a leader. But because of her alienation from Universal Forgiveness, she tends to be a needlessly bossy leader, as well as needlessly inflexible in her directions of leadership. The Challenger feels that his sense of truth needs to win, and that there are enemies that must be overcome in order for his truth to win. In other words, he believes that he must impose his truth on others.

The Challenger's "truth" may be so obviously illusory that this person can be easily dismissed by others. Or the Challenger's "truth" may in large measure be in accord with Reality and thus relatively valid in its impacts on others. But even the most truthful Challenger tends to be in illusion about the Absolute Truth of Universal Forgiveness. Universal Forgiveness needs no battle to be fought for it. That battle is already won. Universal Forgiveness simply *is*. Every human being can discover it within his or her own experience. But the Challenger, rather than humbly assisting others to find their own path to this releasing truth, imposes his truth, assumes that he knows how others need to live. Further, the Challenger feels he knows how others need to be challenged. The Challenger counts on her efforts to make happen whatever it is that she believes needs to happen.

The *recurring despair* of the Challenger is a feeling of guilt over having missed the mark, over having led falsely or challenged others toward some untruth. Such guilt may be very strongly felt, for the Challenger is an overconfident personality type, someone who commonly acts boldly and even brashly. Therefore, he tends to find any admission of acting wrongly deeply humiliating. He cannot be nonchalant about his actual guilt, because his life is obsessing about achieving victory for his specific beliefs. All actions in the service of his beliefs seem permitted and justified. Fully experiencing an accurate guilt over this entire pattern of living is felt to be intolerable.

So the Challenger persists in defending against her experiences of guilt. The Challenger's *defensive reaction* is to blame others for the untoward outcomes. The Challenger does sometimes make reversals, but typically without admission that they were needed. The Challenger seems able to proceed in the same or in some new and better direction without even taking time to notice the full guilt of her past errors. This can sometimes appear to be a gift, for the Challenger is difficult to intimidate, stop, or slow down in her pursuit of her chosen projects. But on the negative side, the Challenger tends to learn slowly or not at all from her poorly admitted mistakes.

At the deepest level, the Challenger becomes a *lustful* bully for his own projects of living. This lust may manifest itself sexually, but lust is a broader category than sexual behavior. The deadly sin of lust is a *pushiness* that does not honor the reality of other persons. Others become mere chess pieces in his game of conquest. The Challenger becomes an unforgiving person because she ignores the forgiving, welcoming quality of Final Reality. She becomes rigid and needlessly defensive. In the worst-case scenario, he becomes a vicious tyrant violently imposing his own blatantly crazy truth. Consciously or unconsciously, he lusts to rule the world. Let Idi Amin be our example.

But a type 8 personality who accesses the Spirit aspect found at point 8 on the enneagram overview discovers Universal Forgiveness for himself and others. This grounding can result in him or her becoming the sort of effective leader that we so often need, someone who has no qualms about challenging foolishness and starting in motion something outlandishly fresh.

Type 2: The Vainglorious Helper

Don Richard Riso calls enneagram personality type two "The Helper." The Helper is a behavioral pattern that may appear in any life, but some lives are especially characterized by this pattern. The Helper is focused on the needs of others and has a deeply felt need to be needed by others. The Helper is quite often actually helpful, truly generous with time and money and attention. Yet there is also a manipulative quality about this helpfulness. Offering advice is a way this personality type talks with others. And the belief that her advice or actions are helpful is very important to her. The Helper expects to be appreciated and even reciprocated for being so helpful. And when such appreciation is missing, the Helper can become vindictive, sarcastic, or downright mean. These tendencies describe a pattern of falling away from that aspect of Spirit Trust I am calling "Effortless Letting Be."

In general, this personality type is a warm, emotionally enthusiastic person. Most of us have an aunt, a mother, a grandmother, or perhaps a male relative who embodies this type. Among well-known figures the following suggest qualities of this type: Magic Johnson, Mr. Rogers, Mia Farrow, Liv Ulmann, Elizabeth Taylor. Sandra Maitri, author of *The Spirit Dimension of the Enneagram*, claims to be a two.

The *characteristic delusion* of the Helper is her need to be needed by others. The Helper views herself as an outgoing, active, giving person, and she is. But she is also deluded about her ability to help others live their lives in a deeply satisfying manner. The Helper has advice to offer, as well as affection and acceptance, but she does not trust others to help themselves and, more importantly, she does not trust others to access the help they need from the depths of their own Being. The Helper is, therefore, arrogant in a subtle and often charming way. The Helper assumes that other people's happiness is something she can affect and needs to affect and that the juiciness of her own life is to be found in being helpful to others.

The Helper tends to bind people to himself rather than assist them in finding their own autonomy. The Helper believes that he is needed and mistakes his own obsession with being helpful with the true needs of others. The Helper tends to treat himself in a similar manner. He feels that his own self needs his own help in order to become fulfilled. So, for him, it seems to be a huge challenge to leave himself alone and access Effortless Letting Be. It is likewise a huge challenge for him to leave others alone or to support them in their Effortless Letting Be. He tends to advise and manipulate rather than patiently assisting others to find their own way.

The *recurring despair* of the Helper appears in feelings of being humiliated by others, disappointed by others, abandoned by others. Perhaps she finds that her help is not helping. Perhaps she finds that those whom she is trying to help are refusing her help. Perhaps it happens that even when her help seems to be helping, the help is not appreciated or reciprocated. Perhaps she feels humiliated by the very confusions that life brings over how to be helpful or over what is truly needed. These experiences occasion despair rather than self-evaluation because being helpful and being needed is the core commitment of this particular type of personality.

The Helper attempts to overcome the pain of humiliation by the *defensive reaction* of manipulating the situation to conform to her role as helper. She can be a bold, imaginative, and skilled arranger and manipulator of other people's lives. Some of this work may even have positive outcomes, but underneath, this manipulation is driven by an obsession with being needed. This obsession leads her into serious mistakes. She tends to neglect providing the deeper help of assisting people to discover their own true nature. She tends to create directives or advice by which others are expected to live and to count herself a failure when they do not follow them.

At the deepest level the Helper becomes a *proud, vainglorious* person masked in the charming garments of care for others. He also becomes an unforgiving person, because he is actually less interested in being helpful than in being a Helper – and perhaps also in being a Helper who is appreciated by those he helps. In the worst-case scenario, he becomes a vindictive person toward those who resist and criticize his help. In all these obsessive processes he loses touch with his own interior journey and with accepting his own opportunities to Effortlessly Let Be his own true nature. Because of this lack of self-realization, she is not prepared to truly assist others in accessing the glory and happiness of their lives. So, instead of drawing people to her, she pushes them away. She occasions resentments rather than appreciation. This results in more despair. To handle the recurring despair, she becomes ever more vainglorious in her confidence that she is only trying to help these ungrateful people.

Perhaps others allow the Helper to settle into her patterns of being helpful and simply use her to do things for them. We see alcoholic husbands making this kind of compact with a Helper wife. We see sons and daughters making this kind of compact with a Helper mother. They let her run her helpfulness pattern on their terms while holding her in an unspoken contempt and seeing her almost as their ever-ready slave. Such entanglements may become conscious to the Helper and bring her to such a profound level of despair that she is ready to see her despair as a doorway from her self-defeating pattern into the glorious quality of Effortless Letting Be – letting be her own true life and letting be the true life of others. But to do this, the type 2 personality must cease clinging to the vainglorious assumption that she is needed to make the lives of other people work out the way they "need" to work out.

A Spirit-mature two has the courage to leave people alone, forgive them, or perhaps treat them with firmness and move on. The Spirit quality of Effortless Letting Be is not a withdrawal but an outgoing, emotionally genuine action providing space for others to accept or not accept the gift that is being given. The Spirit-mature two transforms her strong emotional presence into an enduring service and a symbol of the ongoing acceptance of Being.

* * * * * * * * * *

Everyone falls from Trust, but these three personality types specialize in this aspect of falling away from their true nature. Type 5 specializes in falling away from living at attention to the deep knowing of the Unknown Unknown. Type 8 specializes in falling away from embracing the Great Dawning that self and others are always forgiven. Type 2 specializes in falling away from the Effortless Letting Be of that essential being that all human beings essentially be. These three personality types illustrate for all of us what it looks like to fall from our essential Trust of Reality into despair, and how recognizing our despair can become a doorway back to the Trust from which we have fallen.

The descriptions of these three personality types have been brief. It has not been my aim to paint an exhaustive portrait, but to illustrate the interface between the wisdom of the enneagram heritage and the wisdom of the Christian heritage of fall, redemption, and Holy Spirit. For further description of these three personality types, I recommend Chapters 7, 8, and 9 of *The Spiritual Dimension of the Enneagram: Nine Faces of the Soul* by Sandra Maitri. (Jeremy P. Tarcher/Putnam: 2000).

13.

The Fall into Malice

Spirit Love is a quality of our essential being. When we fall from Love we fall into malice. "Malice" will be my general term for the absence of Spirit Love. Malice is part of the experience of all persons, but three of the nine personality types of the enneagram model typically manifest their escape from Reality in a fall from Love into malice. In this chapter I will describe these three personality types: six, nine, and three.

I have given these personality types names that link their characteristic behavior pattern with one of the "deadly sins." Type 6 is the Anxious Loyalist. Type 9 is the Slothful Peacemaker. And type 3 is the Vain Achiever.

Type 6: The Anxious Loyalist

Don Richard Riso calls enneagram personality type six "The Loyalist." The Loyalist is a behavioral pattern that may appear in any life, but some lives are especially characterized by this pattern. The Loyalist suppresses autonomy and strength in order to fit in, to be safe, to be well received by others. Though this takes the outward form of dependability, it is actually an expression of fear, the fear of being one's whole power, of voicing one's true wants, of making waves, of rocking the boat. This personality type may also become what some call "counter-phobic." The counter-phobic moves into outward activities that prove to himself that he is not afraid. He may be one who drives fast cars, climbs mountains, jumps out of airplanes, joins a violent gang, or engages in inappropriate relations. The counter-phobic six constructs false strengths that are a step farther away from realizing Autonomous Strength. Counter-phobic behaviors are another way of fitting in as well as avoiding deep self-awareness. Whether counter-phobic or huddling in safe roles, the six is covering over an underlying fear of being one's full self. The Loyalist tends to talk in ways that limit the discussion to safe topics. The Loyalist believes he is loyal to others even though the hidden motive for this loyalty is fear. She also is prone to reject any authority or peer group that does not provide safety and seek another group in which loyalty is better rewarded. These tendencies describe a pattern of falling away from that aspect of Spirit Love I am calling "Autonomous Strength."

Woody Allen and the characters he usually plays in his movies give us an impression of this personality type. Perhaps Evel Knievel shows us a counter-phobic six. Bill Moyers and Marilyn Monroe may be sixes. As is true for all personality types, some manifest the more tragic elements of their type and some live beyond and through their personality type. A six who is living beyond his personality can transform his fear of deep selfhood into a form of sensitivity. In the personality types, a perceived weakness can become a strength when Spirit rather than personality is the source of the perceptions and actions. This is especially important for understanding the six. The six is the quintessential fear-based person who suppresses fear and tries to appear regular. At the same time, the six is a person who is sensitive enough of the deep aspects of life to be fearful of them.

The *characteristic delusion* of the Loyalist is that life is too much for a fragile human being to manage. This can be described as a deep doubt of one's own self. The internal talk of the Loyalist might be, "I need support from others. I need to be careful to merit and preserve the supports I have. I need to be loyal to those who support me lest I rock my safe boats and fall out into the wild sea of a much too stormy life." Aloneness, especially fear-filled aloneness, is not viewed as a doorway to courage, but as a disaster to be avoided. The Spirit journey of the Loyalist will begin by uncovering this mostly hidden fear. And this fear needs to be fully experienced in order to move through it toward the discovery of that True Self that has courage and strength sufficient for all challenges.

The *recurring despair* of the Loyalist appears as feelings of insecurity, perhaps a sense of deep inadequacy for dealing with things in general. Such feelings might surface when some counted-upon friend or business partner lets her down. Rejection, neglect, or opposition can become the occasion for a surge of insecure feelings and an uncomfortable amount of anger. Among safe friends the Loyalist may complain and express these strong feelings, but in many contexts where these feelings arise, they are suppressed. The suppression may result in even stronger resentments that make being a loyal worker, mate, or friend more difficult. The Loyalist does not express resentments easily, she does not wish to feel the full power of her anger or fear and thus she also avoids a thoroughgoing affirmation of her true self.

The Loyalist's *defensive reaction* is to avoid these deep insecurities by marshaling once more the false strengths she has constructed. He becomes ever more suspicious of other people, for others tend to smoke out these insecurities. He tends to see others as persons who are out to discover how weak his strengths are and then withdraw their support. A counter-phobic six might take up some new semi-dangerous challenge, the fearless doing of which would provide some further cover for his unacknowledged insecurities.

At the deepest level, the Loyalist is almost entirely out of touch with his Autonomous Strength: he feels swamped in an *anxiety* that knows no relief. This may manifest in being a too-careful person who because of this carefulness lets down those to whom he professes to be loyal. He may also become rigid and needlessly defensive of his false ego strengths. In the worst-case scenario, he becomes a frightened "yes-man" to whatever tyrannizing forces are willing to reward him with fragments of safety. Underneath these covering efforts, the six remains an anxious, fear-driven person. This fear of being himself is his core estrangement, his deadly sin.

The patterns of the six may not seem like a form of malice, but they are. They are malice toward the true self and its essential strengths. And malice toward the self will also entail malice toward others, as well as malice toward Reality in general. It may seem paradoxical to the type six personality that facing up to fears, resentments, and expressions of malice is the doorway back to the essential strengths of the true human soul. Nevertheless, experiencing the fear of being one's true self is the pathway back to that deep essential courage to be one's true self.

Sixes who embrace the wisdom of accessing the full range of their sensitivities can become effective guides for others. A Spirit-mature six is someone who relates well with others as teacher, companion, and enduring friend. The Loyalist's other-directed qualities can be transformed from strategies of finding safety to a means of enabling others to find courage to be their own Autonomous Strength.

Type 9: The Slothful Peacemaker

Don Richard Riso calls enneagram personality type nine "The Peacemaker." The Peacemaker is a behavioral pattern that may appear in any life, but some lives are especially characterized by this pattern. The Peacemaker is so named because she seeks to avoid conflict. She may actively take responsibility for resolving conflict between her parents or among her friends. The Peacemaker is not operating out of fear but out of a deeply hidden rage. She rebels against the unavoidable conflicts of living. She does so out of a desire for peace and comfort. Often the Peacemaker simply sees peace where there is no peace. He avoids noticing the real conflicts. He creates a kind of fog in which peace prevails and the real world of ongoing conflicts is masked. The Peacemaker tends to talk in sagas of avoidance. She views herself as a comfortable person. She does not notice that this comfort has been bought through a laziness that refuses to deeply view the uncomfortable aspects of living a human life. These tendencies describe a pattern of falling away from that aspect of Spirit Love I am calling "Enchantment with Being."

The peace-loving play-it-cool nines are all around us. They may not engage us strongly, but they may see our perspectives and tend to be likable persons. Nines are the most other-directed personality type. Sometimes they are famous people like Dwight D. Eisenhower who was great at helping diverse generals and politicians work together. Hubert Humphrey and Abraham Lincoln may also have been nines. Perhaps Barack Obama also illustrates this type. Actors Karl Malden and Jessica Lange probably depict this type.

The *characteristic delusion* of the Peacemaker is that life needs to be toned down. This is especially true when life manifests as deeply painful conflicts. The Peacemaker works to make conflicts go away. This can provide a type of service in some instances, but more often it is simply a rejection of the intensities of reality. Conflict usually happens because some intense value is challenging some other intense value. The fullness of Reality is reached not by toning down conflict but by inquiring into conflict until the rich values involved are clearly seen and perhaps find their own mutually enhancing resolutions. But the Peacemaker wants to avoid both the intensity of conflict and the intensity of realistic resolution. The Peacemaker wants intensity to go away. The Peacemaker wants his customary blandness to remain unchallenged. The Peacemaker is a personality fixation dedicated to the avoidance of any intensity that feels uncomfortable.

Thus the Peacemaker lives in a sort of fog. When facing unchallenging matters, she may be a clear thinker; but when huge problems or intense conflicts arise, the fog rolls in. The Peacemaker tends to sleepwalk through these tough times and not learn from them what he needs to learn. He may be very sensitive to other people and their perspectives on things. He may have an unusual ability to be understanding of other people, but intense engagement with others frightens him into a panicky form of peacemaking. He cannot face his own rage, so he is uncomfortable with the rage of others.

The *recurring despair* of the Peacemaker is a feeling of being unlovable. Conflict with others means to her that she is not loved by them, not loved by Being. She expects love to mean being understood and peacefully handled as she tends to do with others. She cannot grasp that true love can include challenging other people to wake up and experience the intensity of true living. When living becomes too intense, she panics, she despairs, she flees.

The Peacemaker's *defensive reaction* for avoiding the experience of despair is to fall asleep. His eyes close. His clarity fogs up. Despair is an experience that is too intense to experience fully, so sleep is the option taken. Some personality types might be curious about despair, inquiring into how painful it can be and how strangely it functions, but not the Peacemaker. The Peacemaker falls asleep rather than wrestling through the long nights of despair. His waking life also becomes a kind of sleep in which he tones down human living to a bearable intensity.

And at the deepest level, the Peacemaker becomes trapped in a subtle passivity, in an ever-deepening *sloth* with regard to the truly serious issues of living. This is a Spirit sloth; the Peacemaker may be quite functional within the ordinary levels of living, but she neglects to do the aggressive things required to move ahead in accessing her intense dreads, fascinations, and courage. She opts out when confronting opportunities to become more adult, to be more mature in her basic Spirit living. She meets her challenges to awaken by choosing further modes of sleep. She becomes skilled at fogging up her challenges with confusions and postponements. Only extreme happenings can rock her awake enough to move forward. And how ironic this sloth is, for it is an escape from a deep enchantment with Reality, from an endless curiosity, from the joyous dance of the cosmos, from the happiness of perpetual rebirth. Spirit sloth is an escape from the very happiness, rest, and peace that the Peacemaker may sense is missing and for which he harbors a deep longing.

The Peacemaker seldom recognizes his pattern as malice. Malice seems to imply anger and the Peacemaker has suppressed anger. When this hidden rage begins to surface, the Peacemaker tends to fog out. This very fogging out is malice toward Reality. When effectively challenged to own up to his rage, the Peacemaker may become strongly defensive and surprise himself with his intensity about avoiding intensity. Also, malice toward living the full intensities of Being results in a quiet but nevertheless destructive malice toward self and others.

But the Peacemaker who lives beyond his personality discovers the intensity of an awakening, joy, and aliveness that can make his other-directed skills channels of service rather than ways of avoiding intensity. The quality of Enchantment with Being makes the Spirit mature nine a powerful presence.

Type 3: The Vain Achiever

Don Richard Riso calls enneagram personality type three "The Achiever." The Achiever is a behavioral pattern that may appear in any life, but some lives are especially characterized by this pattern. The Achiever is focused on the outer shells of living, on personal success, fame, acknowledgment, or on being beautiful in physical presence as well as personality. The Achiever appears to make waves among her companions. She makes her presence felt. She often exaggerates her presence, her feelings, her wisdom, her competence. She is not a wallflower, but she can appear to be a shell without a center to some of her more perceptive friends. The Achiever may confuse and wear out his more intimate companions. He seems to make contact with them, but his vulnerable, true, and actual self is not presented. The Achiever tends to talk in propaganda or advertisements about his roles in the world. He views himself as successful even if his success is a grand pretense. These tendencies describe a pattern of falling away from that aspect of Spirit Love I am calling "Out-flowing Compassion."

We tend to notice the threes in our lives, for they work at being noticed and may be good at it. Here are some probable threes that we may have noticed: Shirley McClain, Bill Clinton, Sharon Stone, Arnold Schwarzenegger, Brooke Shields, Tiger Woods, Paul Newman. The threes in our daily lives may be those persons who dress well or at least provocatively, talk well or at least louder, and present themselves as somebody important.

The *characteristic delusion* of the Achiever is that she needs to do something to be significant. And "significant" means achieving an outward presentation that others can respect, honor, enjoy, appreciate, and be drawn to. In fact, the Achiever strives to create an outward presentation that she herself is drawn to, that she respects, honors, enjoys, and appreciates. Emphasizing this preoccupation with the outward wrappers of living, the Achiever typically neglects paying adequate attention to her own inwardness, especially its darker aspects. The Achiever typically distrusts his essential human nature. When he looks inward, he tends to see only a deep emptiness that frightens him. So he believes he must turn outward and create for himself a life that matters, that counts, that is worthy of him. But in truth he has substituted for his genuine greatness a self-constructed outward shell. Even in his realms of genuine personal achievement, he often substitutes outward appearances for his deeper potential for significant contribution. He has become focused on his presentation of success (and perhaps beauty) rather than on making the contribution that truly expresses his authentic life.

Rather than living in a profound surrender to an Out-flowing Compassion toward neighboring beings, the Achiever views life as a self-constructed project that she alone must achieve. When the Achiever shows up in religious communities in which love for others is emphasized, she is preoccupied with being a loving person. But instead of truly loving others, she uses others in a self-centered project of becoming a loving person. Being a loving person is not the same thing as being that essential compassion for others that is given with our true nature.

Being a loving person is not the outward goal of all Achievers. The goal of some threes may be more obviously self-serving, such as being a successful person no matter what the cost to competitors. It may be being a beautiful person, a heroic person, a noble person, an emotionally genuine person, a lively person, a sensual person, a sexy person, a leadership person, an intelligent person, a family person, a business person, and even a violent person, perhaps a competent killer. A three may play several of these roles at once. Many threes tend to be chameleons, taking on the roles and colorings that are given honor or recognition in the specific communities of people chosen by that three.

Persons of all the personality types can get lost in the outward trappings of life, but Achievers are those who have made this the central drive of their life. They then mistake these constructions of outward appearance for their true selves.

The *recurring despair* of the Achiever happens when the mask she has constructed is torn loose, and others see that the mask is not who she really is. More profoundly, she herself despairs over her own awareness that the mask she has created is not her true self. She knows at such moments that she is a liar, a pretender, a fraud, a deceiver. Even when she has succeeded in constructing the life she has always desired for herself, she can, nevertheless, despair over seeing that the whole glorious thing is a fraud. And when she has not succeeded with constructing the life she has always desired, she can despair over seeing that the quest to do so has been a waste of effort, a fraudulent enterprise to become a person that she is not now nor will she ever be. This despair may include disappointment over her real person. The facsimile she has built can appear more exciting or ennobling. Her real person can seem drab, unexceptional, empty of grandeur, less than expected, less than others will celebrate. Also, the Achiever can despair over the realization that his whole life has been a lie, a pretense, a deceit, a striving to be something other than his true humanity. The Achiever can also despair over discovering that he does not trust in the goodness of his true nature. He doubts that his essential being is a true and good person. He fears that if he does not do something that achieves some sort of goodness, that no goodness will be forthcoming.

The Achiever's *defensive reaction* to these recurring despairs is to find yet another achievement that has self-importance. Perhaps being an accomplished meditator will appear tempting. Perhaps being an accomplished teacher of emotional and spiritual subjects will appear tempting. Perhaps these programs of pretense are too closely related to an actual experience of true nature, so the Achiever moves farther away into achievements that better distract him from an inward journey. Whatever the outward form of the defensive reaction, its motive is the same – to avoid the challenge of simply admitting real despairs and surrendering to being that ordinary glorious nature that requires no effort whatsoever.

But rather than be a normal, grand, real, and loving persons, the Achiever falls into the deadly sin of *vanity*, overlaying the glory of the real with superficial achievements. He seeks status rather than Out-flowing Compassion toward all beings. Doing loving living in the ever-present here-and-now has a calm, quiet, satisfying richness. This richness manifests only in the present moment, and it requires no struggle, no effort, no achievement. Spirit Love simply flows. But the Achiever, in his worst-case scenario, is too *vain* to be a mode of being that he himself has not achieved, so he vainly tries once again to prove to himself and to others that he is the master of his own glory. No free gifts are accepted. This deceptive vanity is widespread in our success-oriented culture. We see it in the *prima donna* who makes life so difficult for those who work with her. We see it in the status climber who has no qualms about stepping on others in the process of achieving the desired status. We see it in the morbidly despairing person whose beauty or power to achieve has faded, but who is still trapped in viewing these lost outward trappings as her true self. A type 3 personality who has persistently failed in his projects may still view these outward failures as inordinately important.

These patterns of shell making are expressions of malice, but the Achiever is so preoccupied with outwardness and self-image that she does not stop to notice the destructive consequences that this obsession has on others, as well as herself. Nevertheless, here is the doorway to a true Out-flowing Compassion: turning inward and experiencing the malice, experiencing this lack of love toward others, self, and the Wholeness of Being. Beyond this self-constructed lovelessness exists the true Love for others given with our Spirit Being.

In the Spirit maturity of Out-flowing Compassion, the three finds that her abilities to live outwardly in the real world are transformed into a tool for service rather than a shell for status. She may now do much not because she needs to be somebody, but because she is the Body of Christ walking, eating, teaching, working in the everyday world.

* * * * * * * *

Everyone falls from Spirit Love, but these three personality types specialize in falling away from the Spirit Love aspects of their true nature. Type 6 specializes in falling away from Love of self into a malice of fear over being the Autonomous Strength given with solitary existence. Type 9 specializes in falling away from the Love of Being into a malice of sloth and sleepiness that hides rage toward the true conflicts, paradoxes, and enigmas of profound living. Type 3 specializes in falling away from the Love of others into a malice of outward shells that block a genuine Out-flowing Compassion for others.

These descriptions have not been exhaustive. My aim has been to show the interface between the wisdom of the enneagram heritage and the wisdom of the Christian heritage of fall, redemption, and Holy Spirit. For further description of these three personality types, I recommend Chapters 2, 3, and 4 of *The Spiritual Dimension of the Enneagram: Nine Faces of the Soul* by Sandra Maitri. (Jeremy P. Tarcher/Putnam: 2000).

14.

The Fall into Bondage

Spirit Freedom is a quality of our essential being. When we fall from Freedom we fall into bondage. "Bondage" will be my general term for the absence of Spirit Freedom. Bondage is part of the experience of all persons, but three of the nine personality types of the enneagram model typically manifest their escape from Reality in a fall from Freedom into bondage. In this chapter I will describe these three personality types: four, one, and seven.

I have given these personality types names that link their characteristic behavior pattern with one of the "deadly sins." Type four is the Envious Individualist. Type one is the Resentful Reformer. And type seven is the Gluttonous Enthusiast.

Type 4: The Envious Individualist

Don Richard Riso calls enneagram personality type four "The Individualist." The Individualist is a behavioral pattern that may appear in any life, but some lives are especially characterized by this pattern. The Individualist has an aversion to being ordinary and an attachment to being special. She is more captivated by her interior quality than by her external success and beauty. She is often a disciplined person, a meticulous person, a person loyal to her own values, and stubborn to make her own way. She is a person who pays attention to inward feelings and inward qualities. Typically she is very sensitive to the feelings of others, sometimes mistaking them for her own. She is a more inward person than the often-gushy two, but this reserve does not take away from her emotional depth. She may have wide swings of feeling – ecstatic in some moments, deeply gloomy in others. Deep feeling is her special gift as well as her special suffering. The tendency to obsess over this specialness describes a pattern of falling away from Spirit Freedom, that aspect of Freedom I am calling "Primal Merging."

Many of our well-known performers, actors, and playwrights are fours. Judy Garland, Marlon Brando, Ingmar Bergman, Tennessee Williams, Bob Dylan, Betty Davis, may all be fours. They certainly have qualities that suggest the four personality. This personality type is sometimes called "The Artist," for this type is often devoted to finding a way to express his inner quality and specialness to the world and be acknowledged for it. But not all artists are fours, and not all fours are artists. The fours in our lives will appear in all the ordinary roles: mother, father, teacher, therapist. A four may simply be that person, who when she looks at us, make us know that we are being looked at.

There is a certain toughness about this personality type, but there is also a certain melancholy. Being preoccupied with interior qualities tends to make one a hermit or at least make relationships problematical. The four personality may feel abandoned by others, may feel misunderstood by others, may long for a relatedness with others that is more intimate. This may lead into inappropriate relationships or to dissatisfactions with even good relationships. The four may long for something better and envy the more gregarious persons who seem to be doing better. Nevertheless, the four clings to his independence and individualism; she typically values independence more highly than the intimacies she also desires. The melancholy and longing for intimacy tend to be preferred to giving up independence. The Individualist tends to talk in lamentations about the various aspects of her living; nevertheless, she views herself as special, as an elite sort of human being.

Even though the four values freedom, her pattern is an escape from Spirit Freedom. The Individualist assumes that he must make his own way, be his own person in a manner that resists merging with essential Freedom. Indeed this deep Freedom that characterizes the life of every person may be viewed as too ordinary, not special enough. The Individualist may even view this deep Freedom as a void, as an emptiness that spells the death of her unique and special self. Though Spirit Freedom is a vital part of what makes humanity special, the Individualist has taken pains to become special through extensive personal effort to be an aware, creative, bold, artistic, deep, warm, or, in some other way, remarkable person. These qualities seem to be threatened by a Freedom that is a free gift to everyone.

The *characteristic delusion* of the Individualist is that she is on her own as a separate identity. Since there may be little or no outward support for this identity, the Individualist feels she must personally defend her identity and integrity. She also may seek the recognition from others she feels she deserves. The Individualist, being a sensitive person, may also notice his longing for a lost merger with some deeper reality. He may long for some basic support that he feels is missing. Indeed, this longing may be all that is left of a lost merger with the fullness of Spirit Freedom; so he clings to the longing, enjoys the longing, develops it. He becomes a melancholy person longing for what is lost with little hope of ever finding it. When the pain of this predicament is too deep, he may blast to the outside as an exaggerated dramatization of deep feelings. When this drama becomes too risky and clearly counterproductive, he moves inward again and becomes a person who fastidiously follows the good etiquette of the surrounding society. Traditional Japanese society is a picture of this pattern: strong emotions ready to blast forth and yet contained in a fastidious set of customs and face-saving politeness. This tension may produce great artists, but it may also produce fragile personalities.

Like personality types 3 and 2, type 4 is preoccupied with self-image. Twos seek to fashion a self that draws emotional appreciation from intimate others. Threes seek to fashion a self that basks in external achievements of success and beauty. Fours seek to fashion a quality interior person, and they may also hope to receive from others the recognition that these fabulous qualities deserve. The irony is that each of us is already a quality interior person. In our true nature each of us has fabulous qualities that deserve recognition and celebration. Spirit Freedom is one of those qualities. But instead of celebrating this essential quality of Freedom, the four seeks unsuccessfully to celebrate and find celebration from others for a facsimile of Spirit Freedom. The four feels herself to be a deep inner person with strong emotional sensitivities and creativities. But these inner qualities are rooted in an effort to feel good about self-constructed inner qualities.

The *recurring despair* of the Individualist is feeling abandoned. This may show up in relation to real abandonments, but the Individualist tends to exaggerate them, mixing them with deeper feelings of having been abandoned earlier on. The Individualist may be distressed about being on her own. She seeks mergers with others, but these mergers never work out to be the merger that is felt to be missing. So unpromising mergers are dropped and others are taken up only later to be found unsatisfying as well. At the heart of the matter is a feeling of having been abandoned by the cosmos as a whole. For some personality types, "I am on my own" might be an expression of Freedom, but for the Individualist, "I am on my own" has the meaning of being abandoned, of lacking love and support.

The Individualist's *defensive reaction* to such despairing moments is to attempt to control the outcomes of life around him so that support is given. He hopes that he may be able to do something to get his wife or children to love him better. He hopes to create something that his society will appreciate appropriately. But controlling life, especially the responses of other people, can prove very frustrating. In fact, such control is impossible. It is a deep delusion to believe that one has the power to control others. Nevertheless, the type four personality swings from abject hopelessness to being seduced again by some new and seemingly promising hope that will also turn out to be hopeless. Beyond the hopelessness that accompanies trying to control outcomes lies the hope that will not disappoint, the hope of Spirit Freedom. When this Freedom is present there is always hope, the hope that a creative response in the here and now of living is possible, and always will be possible. And this Freedom is also the support that the four has been seeking. This Freedom is a release from a preoccupation with self and with the experience of abandonment. Freedom comes as a joy in outwardly focused self-forgetful doing. This Freedom from ego is the Primal Merging that is missing in the life of the Individualist. The Individualist is obsessed with clinging to a self-made self-image and therefore continually avoids this merger with Freedom.

At the deepest levels of this estrangement, the Individualist feels fundamentally deprived. People do not appear to support her as she wants and feels she deserves to be supported. Life as a whole seems to deprive her. She misconstrues this supposed deprivation as a problem that might be resolved, perhaps by becoming like someone else, or having what someone else has. These characteristics of the Individualist illustrate the classical deadly sin called *envy*. This envy can take the form of withdrawing into deep depression or it can take the form of active malice toward those who are envied. In either case, this envy turns out to be self-destructive. It is a bondage to self-image that has taken the place of Spirit Freedom.

Healing for the four has to do with going deeper than self-image. It means merging with the essential soul. One of the qualities of the essential soul is Freedom from self-image. The Spirit mature four does not lose her capacity for intense feelings, but finds her distance from these feelings. She finds it possible to be objective about herself and others and make sounder choices. She finds her true capacities for courage and creativity.

Type 1: The Resentful Reformer

Don Richard Riso calls enneagram personality type one "The Reformer." The Reformer is a behavioral pattern that may appear in any life, but some lives are especially characterized by this pattern. The Reformer wants most of all to be right, to say and do the right things. Unlike the more withdrawn fives or fours, the Reformer tends to jump into life situations and attempt to make them right. He may be a defender of outcasts and the oppressed. Or he may be a defender of establishment morals from the corrosions of modern times. The Reformer may have little awareness of the relativity of his moral truths. He tends to be inflexible, though flexibility might also be one of his moral values.

The Reformer may have little awareness of the pettiness of many of her complaints against the people who surround her. Nevertheless, a Reformer may do many useful things, make waves where waves are useful. But if the Reformer does not become aware of her excessive need to be right, she will at some point become resentful of the people and situations that do not move in accord with her righteous fervor. The Reformer's style of talking tends to be preachy, telling others and herself how to think and act. The Reformer tends to have an unexamined conviction that he is among the righteous in the ongoing dramas of life. These tendencies describe a pattern of falling away from that aspect of Spirit Freedom I am calling "Inherent Purity."

Ralph Nader is a strong example of this type of personality. In his case, he is a successful leader and forceful spokesman for justice and change. Other type one personalities may be more domestically focused – doing their jobs well; keeping their house clean, their beds made, their children in line, the toilet seats down or up, and so on. The character Monica in the *Friends* TV sitcom provides a good impression of this picky yet forceful person. Here are some other well-known persons who may be ones: George Washington, Barbara Jordan, Katherine Hepburn.

The *characteristic delusion* of the Reformer is that life is a challenge to make things better, and that he knows what better is – that his standards, his traditions are the correct ones. The scribes and Pharisees whom Jesus battled on the pages of the New Testament illustrate this delusion. The Reformer is driven to action by his standards of good and evil rather than by his inherent Joy in being Freedom. The Reformer may experience resentment that the cosmos does not run in accord with the Reformer's standards of good and evil. The Reformer avoids learning that his own conscience is flawed, that his superego is an enemy of abundant living rather than a guide to be followed. The Reformer tends to believe that his views of good and evil have been derived from valid sources. This type of personality tends to be the last to admit that a human being never has an ultimately valid criterion of good and evil.

The Reformer may be a picky person, a perfectionist who irritates people with her insistence that everything must function in accord with her standards. The Reformer may also be a successful social reformer who at the same time resents the conditions of life in which these reforms must take place, resents the people with whom she must work, resents the slowness of change in people's lives and in social structures, resents her enemies, resents her friends, resents the pressure of having to do so much, resents herself that she does so little. All this anger and resentment tend to build up into stress and discomfort.

The *recurring despair* of the Reformer is a feeling of being wrong, wrong by her own standards, having the wrong standards, showing up in the wrong world at the wrong time. The Reformer is typically unconscious of his deepest wrong, the wrong of living by standards of good and evil, the wrong of fleeing essential Freedom. Instead of finding the essential Purity of being Free in a Freedom that can do no wrong, this personality type is consumed with a need to be right by standards she understands and wishes to apply to herself and others. Despair comes up when the lie in this project of living becomes apparent. When this supposed "moral truth" collapses into a heap of meaninglessness and ambiguity, the Reformer experiences despair.

The Reformer's *defensive reaction* to experiencing despair is to work all the harder to improve this or that. If society cannot be improved, self-improvement can become the goal. If self-improvement becomes discouraging, improving others can become the goal. The Reformer defends herself against despair by assuming that her despair is caused by something outside rather than inside herself.

And at the deepest level, the Reformer becomes paralyzed in patterns of *resentment* and perhaps rage. His imperatives to change things and his difficulties in doing so become a deep pit of hopelessness. He "burns out." He comes to experience his life as without joy, without oasis, without refreshment, without fun, just a never-ending hard job of struggling to change things. Resentment can arise over changes that do not happen or toward people who do not help. Resentment can become rage toward the entire cosmos that seems not to cooperate. Rage against life in general is the *classical deadly sin* many associate with type one. The Reformer is estranged from the realization that each one of us is boundless Freedom in an inherently perfect cosmos that requires nothing more of us than the Inherent Purity of living our own essential Freedom. This awareness transforms rage and resentment into simple forcefulness.

Once the joy and refreshment of this Freedom is experienced, the ethical seriousness of this personality type can be a gift used in the service of Freedom. A Spirit-mature one is a forceful and decisive person. But as long as being right by his own standards persists as his core drive, bondage remains and rage endures.

Type 7: The Gluttonous Enthusiast

Don Richard Riso calls enneagram personality type seven "The Enthusiast." The Enthusiast is a behavioral pattern that may appear in any life, but some lives are especially characterized by this pattern. Like the eight, the Enthusiast is not withdrawn. She is into many experiences, often of surprising variety. I met a woman in a therapy group who was working on a relationship with her third husband. She was the mother of two daughters, worked in psychology, religion, peace work, feminism, and ecology. She was an accomplished artist making silver jewelry. In spite of my knowledge of her as a person of many activities, I was surprised when she ran for the Governor of her state. I, being a rather withdrawn and narrowly focused person, cannot imagine where sevens find such energy. These tendencies describe a pattern of falling away from that aspect of Spirit Freedom I am calling "Attuned Working."

Whenever we see an athlete who is a top player in both professional football and professional baseball, we see a person who is probably a seven. Few others would even try such a thing. Another likely seven might be Jesse Ventura who was a Navy seal, a professional wrestler, and a Governor of Minnesota. Not all sevens are good at the things they do, but those who are may shock us with the many things they master. Albert Schweitzer, for example, was a major New Testament scholar, an excellent organist, a naturalist, a medical doctor, a missionary to Africa, and a man who answered mailbags full of letters from people all over the world. This is the sort of appearance that can be made by a personality type seven who is also a genius. The fictitious character Peter

Pan also pictures a seven personality. Robin Williams, Mozart, and Liza Minnelli may be sevens. Sevens may manifest their love of variety in less noble enterprises: alcohol, cocaine, heroine, crime, debauchery, and other enhancements. And sevens can also be quite ordinary persons whose variety of activities may not seem particularly astonishing. They just love their church, their political party, their skiing, their jogging, their ocean fishing, their pistol shooting, their peace protests, and their ecological projects.

Other personality types may also have variety in their lives; it is not simply variety that makes a person a seven. The key to the seven personality is an inward compulsion to find their own way through experiencing as much of life as they can. This personality type is restless; he is a seeker, a rather dissatisfied person, a person who hopes that the next adventure will be the one that brings fullness of life. But since all temporal experiences are passing realities, fullness of a truly satisfying sort is not found in these passing experiences. The seven tends to be scattered, lacking inward inquiry, depth, unity, and focus. In his style of talking the seven tends to be the teller of stories, stories about his adventures or plans for adventures or someone else's adventures that have intrigued him. The Enthusiast is an upbeat person who assumes that his life is okay, fine, wonderful, going great.

The *characteristic delusion* of the Enthusiast is that he must take things into his own hands, that he must plan his life, control his life, fill his life with good things, find good things with which to fill his life, make everything work out well. And this planning is done in order to counter an opposing force, a force that we might call "The-Way-It-Is" or "The-Way-It-Moves." The seven believes that if left unaltered The-Way-It-Moves will be boring, unsatisfying, less exciting than the life the Enthusiast is planning. The Enthusiast feels that it is necessary to jazz life up, to add excitement to life, to go somewhere else, to find a more fulfilling situation, more novel experiences, a new set of people, a better place, a better world. In his planning and doing the Enthusiast has lost sight of being attuned to The-Way-It-Moves. The Enthusiast is not aware that his own life must unfold the way it must unfold, go through the journeys it must go through, deal with the blocks with which it must deal, find the true humanity laid down for it in the foundations of the cosmos. So the Enthusiast creates his own separate unfoldment. She finds her own way. She indeed forces her own way upon Reality. And precisely because she is doing so, she fears that The-Way-It-Moves is opposed to the way she needs to live.

The Enthusiast is not a fatalist in the sense of being passive to the flow of events, but he is a fatalist in the sense that he assumes that an unplanned life will work out badly. Effort must be made to avoid an unfortunate fate. Good fortune depends on actively planning and injecting life with added enthusiasm and meaning. And this belief may seem to be validated by his many accomplishments, many exciting vacations, many activities, many hopes and plans for the future. But this seemingly successful frenzy of living typically avoids life's deepest joy and peace and fulfillment. The life of the Enthusiast tends to proceed more or less on the surface. The deeper potentialities may appear boring, and the slow inward changes needed to reach them may seem too painful. Pain is an experience the Enthusiast is most anxious to avoid.

Ironically, the Enthusiast thinks he is free, while he is actually fleeing from full Freedom into a superficial rat race. He is a slave to his own constantly created visions that he hopes will bring him a satisfying life. He avoids the depth of life where true satisfaction can be found. His joys may be real, but they are substitutes for the Joy that comes from being truly "with it." Herein is his delusion.

The *recurring despair* of the Enthusiast is feeling out of it, feeling lost in the woods of her own array of constructions. Over time, surface satisfactions reveal themselves as merely surface satisfactions. Over time, plans for the future do not work out to be the full and final solutions that were sought. Over time, joys that at first seemed to be worth the time become boring. At such moments the Enthusiast feels lost, feels that she is somehow not "with it," is somehow "out of it." All sorts of self-critical thoughts may arise. Resignation may set in. Hopelessness may overcome enthusiasm. Emptiness may reign.

The Enthusiast's *defensive reaction* to these occurrences of despair is to do something else, find yet another activity that will fill the void that has appeared. Rather than inquiring into these tough feelings to see what they mean and where they might lead, the Enthusiast plans a better life. Some other situation, some other station in life, some other relationship to someone or something will be the solution to these feelings of being "out of it" or "lost." The Enthusiast does not sit still long enough in his despair to allow the true nature of being human to emerge in its own natural manner. He plans. He moves on. He finds something new.

These characteristics of the Enthusiast illustrate the classical deadly sin called *gluttony*. And this *gluttony* for experiences does not fill the inner void. She does not allow an obedience to The-Way-It-Moves to unfold toward true Joy, true Creativity, true Freedom in living the actual life that is given. Rather, she has become stuck in a fate of her own construction, moving in semi-desperation from one surface mode of living to another. He has become scattered rather than focused. He is doing many things, but perhaps nothing that deeply matters to him. The Enthusiast becomes gluttonous for ever new experiences that will fill the void, a void that remains unconscious as long as it is filled with ever new, ever more, ever different something or other. But sooner or later this gluttony, this scatteredness may itself become boring or downright intolerable. At such a moment, the Enthusiast is "not far from the Kingdom of God," not far from the true flow of Reality, not far from the Attuned Working that is the deep Joy of being both true Freedom and true Obedience to The-Way-It-Moves.

A Spirit-mature seven does not lose his joy and enthusiasm for living, but joins these buoyant characteristics with a depth and focus that allows a still richer and wider range of life to flow through him. She joins Reality in its always-rich profundity.

* * * * * * * * * * *

All persons fall from Spirit Freedom, but three personality types specialize in falling away from the Freedom aspect of their true nature. Type 4 specializes in falling away from a deep merger with Freedom into a bondage that defends an identification with some self-image created by the self. Type 1 specializes in falling away from the Inherent

Purity of unreservedly, spontaneously, decisively being Spirit Freedom
into bondage within the restraints of self-created standards. Type 7
specializes in falling away from the true Freedom of Attuned Working
with the flow of Reality into a bondage to self-made temporal plans.

The descriptions of these three personality types have not been exhaustive. My aim has been to show the interface between the wisdom
of the enneagram heritage and the wisdom of the Christian heritage
on fall, redemption, and Holy Spirit. For further description of these
three personality types, I recommend Chapters 5, 6, and 10 of *The
Spiritual Dimension of the Enneagram: Nine Faces of the Soul* by Sandra
Maitri. (Jeremy P. Tarcher/Putnam: 2000).

PART FOUR

*Moving Toward Full
Realization*

15.

The Penetration of Personality & the Initial Experiences of Spirit

As you read the descriptions of the nine personality types in Chapters 12, 13, and 14, you may have found that you identify with several of the nine types. This is not a sign of confusion. To some degree each of us may participate in all nine ways of escaping from our essence. All nine of the personality fixations are human potentials, and each of us may participate in every form of human perversion.

Furthermore, each of us can access all nine aspects of our common Spirit Being. Essentially and potentially, each of us is the whole of profound humanity. The whole wind of Holy Spirit may blow in each life. Each of us is all three aspects of Trust, all three aspects of Love, all three aspects of Freedom. This is our essential Being. This is the essential Being of every human being. This is who we are. This is our Spirit Home. Though I am using Christian language, the Spirit Home I am pointing to is beyond the comprehension of any language and it is pointed to by many religious languages.

According to the enneagram heritage, humanity has departed from this Home in nine characteristic ways. One of those ways of departure most characterizes the fundamental pattern of each of our lives. Even though it may seem at first that we might be several of the personality types, when we know ourselves well and understand the enneagram model well, we discover that one of these nine types is the foundational pattern in our life. Our early childhood was what it was, and we cannot change that. Our basic personality type was set in the first few years of our life. So it is important to discern which personality type is our basic fixation.

We start moving toward our Spirit Home from wherever we now are. Typically, we start our Spirit journey from some mostly unconscious identification with our particular personality, our particular default pattern for living. The enneagram is a chart of the nine major types of personality fixation. Each of us can find ourselves primarily located in one of these nine fixations. Each of us begins our journey home by dealing with our primary personality fixation.

If we are not yet clear which personality type is foundational for us, this can have two causes: (1) it may be that we do not yet understand this model of personality types clearly enough; and (2) it may be that we do not yet understand ourselves well enough to be sure how to place ourselves accurately within this array of types.

Understanding this model of personality types takes some time and deep inward attention. Also, we need to keep in mind that the enneagram is only a model, a rational model created by human minds. This model is only a lens to look through at our real life experiences. This lens (and my description of it) is not perfect. And, it may take time to get this lens adjusted so we can look through it to see the actual processes it was created to call to our attention.

More important than learning the enneagram model is seeing the real life experiences that we are looking at through this lens. We typically think we know ourselves better than we do. Our own memory provides an irrefutable bit of evidence against our claim to full self-knowledge. Do we not understand ourselves more clearly now than we once did? Like each earlier understanding of ourselves, our current understanding of ourselves will, if we live long enough, also be transcended.

Each of us began life as an infant with enormous and unique genetic endowments. These genetic endowments plus our earliest environments plus our own responses combined to produce the first layers of our personality. While each personality development is unique, it manifests one of the nine patterns described in Part Three. Upon these earliest layers of personality development, later layers were built. The building of each layer of these complex habits was (1) influenced by our genetics, (2) influenced by our environments, and (3) chosen through our specific responses.

A personality is somewhat like a very complex computer program. Its many layers of code make complex functioning possible, but this established program also limits what the computer can do as long as it operates within this set program. Our program of personality has enabled our survival and provides functionality for our current living. At the same time our personality is a program that limits us. This personality program hides and overrides our full potential, the potential that is being pointed to with such words as Spirit Being, personal essence, true nature, Holy Spirit, Trust, Love, and Freedom. Each personality type was built under the primary influence of one of the nine aspects of Spirit, but as our personality became a program it masked Spirit, hid Spirit, and became a substitute for Spirit.

As adults we each have a long history of personality development and a very complex personality pattern. We typically identify with that complex personality pattern and act it out more or less unconsciously. To the extent that this is so, we are like robots programmed to perform in predictable ways. To a large extent human life is the unconscious interaction of a vast group of such robots acting out their set patterns. This leads to the familiar tragedies that we see portrayed in ancient Greek plays, Shakespearian plays, and other great dramas.

Some connection with our Spirit Being may persist through childhood development and moderate our adult robothood, but let us assume that we have on our hands an adult who is almost entirely unconscious with regard to his or her Spirit Being. How does this person's Spirit awakenment begin?

It begins with a penetration of that person's personality habits. Many of the stories about Jesus have to do with Jesus uttering teachings aimed at particular personality patterns. In the first three New Testament gospels, the personality pattern that Jesus engages the most is the type one personality, the person who thinks he knows what is good and what is evil. The scribes and Pharisees typify this pattern. They come to Jesus complaining about what he does on the Sabbath day. Jesus penetrates their personality with sayings like, "The Sabbath was made for human beings not human beings for the Sabbath." Or they express their shock and revulsion that Jesus is eating meals with tax collectors, riffraff, and other Jewish lawbreakers. Jesus says to them, "It is the sick, not the well, who have need of a doctor."

One of the best stories about penetrating a type one personality is the story in which Jesus is having a meal and a discussion with a Pharisee who invited him for a visit and apparently has a modicum of interest in Jesus and his wisdom. While they are there at the table, a woman comes in and begins washing Jesus' feet with her tears and drying them with her hair. The Pharisee recognizes her as a woman of the streets who has probably made her living providing bodily comforts to the male population. He is repulsed that Jesus is permitting such a woman to touch him. Jesus recognizes the Pharisee's feelings and asks to speak to him. The Pharisee consents, and Jesus tells a story about two men who owe another man a debt. One of them owes a big debt and the other a small debt. The lender forgives them both. Jesus asks the Pharisee, "Which one do you suppose will love the lender the most?" The Pharisee gives the obvious answer that it is the one who owes the most. Then Jesus points out that this woman whose sins are very great is showing great love. He also points out that nothing comparable is being shown him by the Pharisee. Then Jesus makes this penetrating remark, "Her great love proves that her many sins have been forgiven; where little has been forgiven, little love is shown." (Luke 7:47) The Pharisee is left to ponder whether his harshness toward the woman and his lack of love for Jesus indicates layers in his own life that need forgiveness.

Here are some other examples of New Testament stories in which Jesus penetrates someone's personality with a challenge to that person to access their Spirit Being:

> [Jesus] said to another man, "Follow me." And he replied, "Let me go and bury my father first." But Jesus told him, "Leave the dead to bury their own dead. You must come away and preach the Kingdom of God." *(Luke 9:59-60; J. B. Phillips translation)*

Jesus sees that this man's personality includes an attachment to family obligations. For this man to enter the "Kingdom of Spirit" he must turn loose of that old pattern. Jesus' words penetrate his sense of reality, penetrate the box of personality in which he is living.

> Another man said to him, "I am going to follow you, Lord, but first let me bid farewell to my people at home." But Jesus told him, "Anyone who puts his hand to the plow and then looks behind him is useless for the kingdom of God." *(Luke 9:61-62; J. B. Phillips translation)*

In this case, the man wants to make everybody he loves feel good about his decision to be a Spirit person. This is a violation of the wholeheartedness required for living the Spirit Life. Jesus penetrates his sense of reality.

> And while he was still saying this, a woman in the crowd called out and said, "Oh what a blessing for a woman to have brought you into the world and nursed you." But Jesus replied, "Yes, but a far greater blessing to hear the word of God and obey it." *(Luke 11:27-28; J. B. Phillips translation)*

Jesus does not deny the truth of what the woman says about him, nor does he reject her enthusiasm. But he cuts through this woman's images of subservience and challenges her to be a Spirit woman herself and not simply an enabler of someone else. Her flight from Spirit is not her vision of the greatness of Jesus, but her reluctance to see herself as **the very same greatness** waiting to be enacted. If she saw for herself what Jesus was pointing to, left behind her old images, and received her welcome into the clan of Great Spirit Beings, then Spirit would be penetrating her personality cocoon. We can only guess from this short story what this woman's personality type was. But here is my guess. This woman was probably a personality type two. She sounds like a helper, an aggressive outgoing person who says what she feels to encourage others but does not appreciate fully the dynamics of her own inner being.

In such stories, the individuals in Jesus' presence are being provoked to look beyond their habituated patterns and see the hidden Kingdom, the Spirit Being, the personal essence that is our true human nature. In such initial experiences of Spirit, one is not asked to demolish personality or to be completely detached from personality or even to stop identifying with one's personality. One is asked to simply allow a bit of Spirit into one's consciousness. This is the way the Spirit journey begins for each of us. We are moving along in our mostly unconscious personality identification when another human being or some unusual life experience or some new awareness penetrates our personality pattern and enables us to breathe a whiff of fresh air from the boundless expanse of Spirit. From the viewpoint of the personality, this boundless expanse may seem like a bottomless void, a black hole into which the personality dreads to move. But this dread can unite with a fascination and a courage that forms an experience of Awe or Wonder. If we open to this Wonder, we experience a step on the Spirit journey, a fresh wind blowing through our lives.

For many years we may continue experiencing, from time to time, whiffs of Spirit interrupting our personality pattern. Perhaps one day per month we hear something that awakens a bit of Spirit. Perhaps one week in a year we attend a retreat that provides some rain for our Spirit desert. Perhaps over time our personality comes to have a number of holes punched in it. Perhaps some of these holes are big enough that we are not able to patch them or forget them. We become a personality with Spirit holes. We are still basically identified with our personality, but there are holes and the holes are getting larger and more numerous. Perhaps we wake up one day to realize that our personality is so ragged that it has more holes than cloth. On such a day we are ripe for a shift to phase two of our journey of Spirit.

16.

The Disidentification with Personality and the Recognition of Spirit Identity

At some point in our lives, it may dawn on us that our personality is not who we are. Our personality is useful along with fingernails, arms, and legs. Indeed, like head, heart, and lungs, we cannot do without our personality. Yet who among us believes that our legs are who we are? "I am the woman with beautiful legs." "I am the man with strong legs." Well, maybe I am, but is that who I am? So it is with our personality. One day we wake up to the fact that we have been identifying with our personality; we have been thinking and acting as if our personality were the "real me." It is a banner day in the journey of Spirit maturity when we notice that our personality is "not me" in the deepest sense of what "being me" means.

The teeter-totter helps me image this banner day. Picture a teeter-totter upon which one child is heavier than the other. The heavier child is in the down position. The lighter child is up in the air. If the heavier child represents our personality and the lighter child represents our Spirit, let us image what happens when the heavier child loses weight and the lighter child grows heavier. The teeter-totter tips. Spirit takes over the heavy position and personality loses control. This tip of the teeter-totter begins a new stage in the Spirit journey.

In the previous chapter I described being a personality to whom Spirit penetrations are happening. In this chapter I am describing what it is like to identify with being a Spirit Being who has a personality. After such a shift each of us still has the same personality, and each of us is still the same Spirit Being we have always been. But everything is transformed.

We sometimes speak of "being onto myself." What this phrase can mean is that we begin to see our personality for what it is – a set of habits. Whether these habits are useful or useless, functional or dysfunctional, they are just habits. They are the practiced patterns of a lifetime. In one sense it is good to have habits; a certain amount of continuity avoids the excessive pressure of having to start everything over each moment of our lives. But when we are identified with our personality, we do not see these habits as habits. We see them as "just being human" or "just being me." We do not know that these habits can be broken. We even fear breaking them because we see this as a breaking of our very self. Indeed, we think that if we break these habits, we will not know "who we are." We might think, "I am not myself anymore." And of course, that is true in a sense, for the self I have thought I was is being transcended.

This teeter-totter moment is a discovery of something about Spirit that we did not know before. Spirit is not a part of our personality. Spirit is not some inspiration for our personality. Spirit is not one of our more holy feelings. Spirit is not one of our more holy thoughts. Spirit is not something we can possess, own, or control. Spirit is wild. It is like the wind; it is sometimes a breeze, sometimes a storm. It comes from we know not where, and we cannot know where it is going. Spirit is expansive. It seems to have no borders, no edges, no confined space. Spirit cannot be put in a box. Spirit is always outside the box. Spirit is not a static state: it is a state of perpetual becoming. To arrive at identification with our Spirit Being is to transform every image we ever had about what "arriving" means. Arriving at Spirit identification does not mean some sort of safety, security, or certainty. It is not the sort of assurance we may have thought we wanted. Our Spirit Being is indeed our home, our rest, our glory, our joy, our best life scenario, but all these terms when applied to Spirit living have gone through a death and a resurrection.

When we are identified with our personality, "home" and "rest" mean settling into being our personality rather then being challenged to be something deeper. From the personality perspective, "home" tends to mean a cave into which we can escape and "let the rest of the world go by." But being at home in our Spirit Being means being ourselves as an open, constantly changing, boundlessly expanding, and continually surprising flow. And we are not letting the rest of the world go by. We are super-sensitized to the entire course of nature and history as if it were our own body, our own family, our own household. Indeed, identifying with our Spirit Being means seeing ourselves as part of the whole course of nature and history and thereby linked with that inclusive Overallness within which nature and history are nested. Our relation to this Overallness is our Spirit Being. Spirit is our relatedness to the Awesome, Wondrous Overallness. Spirit is the bubbling up of Wonder or Awe within our soul. Such Wonder is our true soul: it is our soul being its full potential. If we use the word "soul" to mean our impressionable, human mode of consciousness, then within personality identification we have a small soul, a reduced soul. When we identify with our Spirit Being, we experience our full soul – our soul as Spirit.

This post-teeter-totter phase in our Spirit journey includes the maturation of a quality we might call "chastity." According to Søren Kierkegaard, "chastity" means "willing one thing." And the "one thing" we are willing is willing to be our Spirit Being. Such willing, such intentionality, such commitment, such openness, such loyalty, such dedication is required to be our Spirit Being. The temptation to revert to being identified with our personality remains. The devil, we might say, is always at our side. When powerfully resisted, this perpetual tempter retreats for a time, but he (or she) is never entirely gone. Identification with our Spirit Being is a sort of mating or marriage to which we must choose to remain true. This covenant is plausible to us because we are experiencing the Spirit life as beloved, as true living, as the best-case scenario for our destiny. I have come to admire deeply the simple story that Jesus told about a man who discovered a treasure in a field he was plowing. He reburied that treasure, and then sold everything he had to buy that field. That is the sort of dedication required to be "chaste" in our identification with our Spirit Being. And there is a sense in which it is actually true that everything we have treasured in the past has to be sold in order to buy this new treasure. Some of the aspects of our old life are given back to us, but they come back in a new relation to the main thrust of our lives, so it is fair to say that we have lost all things in the way that we once had them.

Perhaps we know the day and the hour in our lives when the teeter-totter tipped. Perhaps we do not. Perhaps we just awoke one day and found that we were identifying with our Spirit Being. If we are indeed viewing being Spirit as the core treasure of our lives, the teeter-totter has tipped. After the teeter-totter tips, the journey still goes on. Personality, the same old personality, still characterizes a significant part of our lives. It has simply become lighter in influence. And Spirit, which is now the heavier focus, can become still heavier. Perhaps our next steps will be challenging, but we can meet them knowing that we are a Spirit Being. We need not retreat into the box of our personality. We do not need to know precisely where we are along this path of Spirit intensification; we only need to be open to taking the next step as it presents itself. The Spirit journey is endless, so we never get to a place where no further journey is possible. Each step and the next and the next is a step into Eternity. On such a journey, the last step never arrives.

17.

The Melting of Personality and the Molten Flow of Spirit

Is there a phase three in the journey of Spirit? Is there another turning point comparable to the teeter-totter tip that characterizes the turn from phase one to phase two? Based on my own experience, I believe we can describe a third major phase of Spirit journey.

As we increase our awareness of Spirit and strengthen our intentional participation in living our Spirit Being, we come into a clearer vision of the wholeness of our Spirit Being. All nine sides of the jewel of our Spirit Being are visible to us. All nine facets of this Spirit diamond are shining. All three aspects of Trust, all three aspects of Love, all three aspects of Freedom are vivid to us.

When Spirit becomes this present to us, we may notice that something is happening in our relation to our Spirit teachers. They cannot help us very much anymore. It is not that they have ceased being people who are treasured by us. And we may not have outgrown them, though we do experience outgrowing some of our teachers. But something deeper is happening than outgrowing teachers; we are moving into arenas where guides cannot help us. We must now lean almost entirely upon guidance from within our own Being. That inner guidance has always been there; but until this third stage of the Spirit journey we have not been clear enough to fully trust our inner guidance. We have needed our teachers to assist us in being clear about which inner actualities are Spirit guidance and which inner actualities are our personality reasserting itself – tempting us to another retreat from Spirit living. If our human guides have been good Spirit guides, they have always referred us to our inner guidance. Nevertheless, we needed their assistance in discovering that inner guidance.

Now, in this third phase of the Spirit journey our next steps have become so inward and so subtle and so unique to our own particular journey that we are in large measure on our own. We may even be exploring territory into which no known human companion has ever ventured. We may read about a few others who have experienced what we are experiencing, but perhaps they lived in an another era, or in another culture, or in another overall situation, or as another personality type, or as another sex. Perhaps they used another mode of expression that has to be translated to find alignment with our culture and our unique Spirit challenges. We still treasure, revere, and use our Spirit teachers. But we are more and more aware that we are on our own.

Also, we are more aware that we are Spirit teachers to others. We may have been a Spirit teacher or a Spirit guide to others for decades, but now it seems that we are some sort of Spirit guide most of the time. We may not be playing formal teaching roles, but Spirit guiding characterizes more of our ordinary relationships. Our focus has now shifted from the need to access Spirit to the need to share Spirit. Even though we have been sharing Spirit in the two earlier phases, the sharing aspect has now blossomed into a prominent flowering within our daily living and within our vocational planning.

And perhaps the most amazing characteristic of this third phase of the Spirit journey is that something remarkable is happening to our personality. It may seem to be melting. In large measure it may have already melted. Instead of being a rigid frozen cube of ice that does not move well through many of the narrow places of living, our personality is becoming integrated into the overall flow of the Spirit soul. The flow of Spirit so fully dominates the soul's experience that the habits of personality are gathered into the flow.

Or we might speak of our personality becoming transparent. Rather than being an opaque coating that dims out the light of Spirit, Spirit shines through our increasingly glassy personality pattern. It is not as if the personality has disappeared. It is not that the personality has lost its power to tempt us into reduced living. What has happened is that our consciousness has better identified the habits of our personality and distinguished them from our Spirit potentialities. Our personality's rigidities and unrealisms can be more fully marginalized in our daily living. And the more functional parts of our personality can now shine with light that the Spirit presence is providing. Our personality has been recruited and trained to be a servant of Spirit living.

However deeply we experience the qualities of this third journey, the journey of Spirit has not ended. Whatever glories we might be able to experience and describe, each of them is only a stepping stone for the next. Each experience is only a launching pad for the next flight into some still more intense Spirit realization. The Spirit journey does not become a possession we can put in our pocket. And it never becomes a plateau upon which we can forever vegetate. We may be able to discern that we have come a long way; but a still longer way stretches out before us. On this Infinite path of Spirit, the way yet to go is always longer than the distance we have come. Spirit is an Infinite relatedness, but our consciousness of Spirit and our manifestation of Spirit are a finite journey through finite temporal happenings. Though the more mature Spirit person may be further along in Spirit realization than the Spirit novice, the mature person is no closer to final realization. The Spirit journey is an endless journey. Humility deepens as we go. Any assumption that we have finally arrived is arrogance. Indeed, it is a detour away from the ongoing, ever-continuing Spirit journey.

Nevertheless, arriving in this third journey is a real experience, and one of the qualities of this arriving is that we experience with some fullness all nine aspects of Spirit depicted as the nine points of the enneagram design. That means we experience all three aspects of Spirit Trust (See Chapter 7 for a full description), all three aspects of Spirit Love (See Chapter 8), and all three aspects of Spirit Freedom (See Chapter 9). The third journey of Spirit not only renders our particular personality transparent to its associated point on the nine point circle of Spirit, but we also find ourselves accessing the other eight points of Spirit as well.

In our essential Being each of us is all nine faces of that bright diamond of Spirit essence that has been hidden beneath the opaque coatings of our personality patterns. When our Spirit journey begins we are almost entirely identified with a pattern of escape from one of these nine faces. Our escape pattern is like an opaque coating that hides that face of the diamond. As we identify with Spirit and move into the third phase of our Spirit journey, it is as if our personality (our escape pattern) turns transparent. We see through it. That face of the diamond of Spirit begins to shine through the previously opaque personality. Also, the third phase of the Spirit journey involves exposing the whole diamond, turning transparent the opaque coatings that cover all nine faces of the diamond. Our Spirit presence begins to gleam in every direction.

In our entire lifetime, this unfolding may never be complete, but the possibility of completion always stands before us. The unfolding is real, and what is being unfolded is the light that shone through Jesus who, as the Christ, became a symbol for Spirit completion. This light is the same light that shone through the Buddha, Mohammed, and others whom we have rightly designated as exemplars of Spirit. It is appropriate that we have created stories and myths and legends to memorialize these persons. Yet it does not actually matter if Siddhartha, the ancient Indian prince/monk, was or was not a perfect Buddha. The Buddha is now a symbol for the perfect life. To his followers Mohammed has also become a Symbol for more than the bare biography of this religious founder. And for we who claim a Christian heritage, we need to be clear that Jesus, the first century Jewish Nazarene carpenter/preacher, may never have fully realized all nine facets of Spirit Being. Jesus as the Christ has become a Symbol for the perfected life. The stories we tell about such exemplars are stories of possibility – the possibility of perfection for them and for ourselves, a perfection that none of us may ever reach, but a perfection that is, nevertheless, who we truly are in our essence. This perfection stands before us and calls us to the next step in our Spirit journey.

18.

The Beatitudes and the Three Journeys of Spirit

Verses 3 through 10 of the fifth chapter of Matthew are often called the Beatitudes. They are eight cryptic sayings each beginning with the word "Blessed" – which is sometimes translated "Happy." These "sayings of Jesus" were probably augmented somewhat by his followers, but I am going to assume that these followers continued to express the same Spirit that Jesus embodied.

Over fifty years ago, I wrote my first theological paper on these eight verses. Much water has passed under the bridge since that first encounter with the profound inwardness of Jesus' teachings. My understanding of Spirit and capacity for living Spirit has deepened. I am now able to see more in these verses.

In the last three chapters, I shared how I have come to discern three distinguishable stages in the journey of Spirit, three types of journey in the one journey of our lives. Recently, I noticed that the eight Beatitudes also express this threefold journey of Spirit. The following prose poem shares how this came together for me. In this poem I am translating the classical words of the Beatitudes into contemporary language that I believe clarifies the Spirit depth of these sayings.

Journey I: The journey **to** Spirit presence
— the appearance of Awe or Spirit from beyond personality

B1. Blessed are those who experience their profound need, for they shall find the Commonwealth of Spirit.

B2. Blessed are those who experience sorrow, for they shall find unassailable comfort.

Journey II: The journey **with** Spirit presence
— the identification with Spirit rather than personality

B3. Blessed are those who are detached from celebrity, status, ownership, and acclaim, for they have the entire natural realm as their inheritance.

B4. Blessed are those who hunger and thirst for Spirit realization, for they will be fully fed.

B5. Blessed are those who forgive everyone, for they shall be forgiven everything.

B6. Blessed are those who inquire with pristine honesty into the depths of Spirit, for they shall experience the Absolute Wholeness of Being.

Journey III: The journey **in** Spirit presence
— the integration of Absolute Spirit with all aspects of living

B7. Blessed are those who integrate all the conflicting aspects of living into the unitary life of Absolute Peace, for they are the vanguard of human history.

B8. Blessed are those who suffer human opposition to their manifestation of Spirit, for the Commonwealth of Spirit is their Eternal Home.

I will comment further on each of these three journeys and each of these eight blessings.

Journey I

If "soul" is a term for our ongoing consciousness of consciousness, then we begin our journey as a restricted soul. We are a soul confined in the box of our own personality. We think that this box of habits is who we are. The box may provide room for many pleasures and exciting activities, but sooner or later we become aware that we live in a box, that there is much more to living than what goes on in our box. The blessings of the initial journey of Spirit are about Spirit penetrating our box of personality habits.

Blessing 1:

Blessed are the poor in spirit, for theirs is the kingdom of heaven.[11]

Blessed are those who experience their profound need,
for they shall find the Commonwealth of Spirit.

Living exclusively in the box of personality sooner or later becomes a desert, lacking moisture, water, juice. Repeating old dry habits over and over ceases to be an alive and vital participation in life. Also, we begin to be more aware of the devilish quality of our own personality. Its addictions, defensiveness, reactive behaviors, violence, meanness, bitterness, and despairs become a never absent pain that haunts our box. Soon life in this box becomes a meaningless life, a thing of dust, useless worthless dust, like some old discarded something found in an attic, so useless that we might as well be a corpse rotting in the grave. These are examples of that sense of profound need that the first Beatitude calls "blessed."

---

[11] Matthew 5:3; Revised Standard Version

Such experiences are blessed because they indicate that the Commonwealth of Spirit is near, that the Kingdom of Full Reality is close by. The box of personality is being penetrated by a larger sense of Reality. This moment is blessed because the Reality that is seeping into our box is a moisture, a refreshment, an innocence, a vitality that we are missing and very much need. We can call this seepage Awe or Spirit, but whatever we call it, it is something more than living in our box. It is something from outside the box of personality. It is getting in touch with the Mystery and Fullness of death and life and change and transformation and surprise and newness. It is a new world, a Spirit Commonwealth, a Kingdom of Divine Reality.

An autobiographical note: While still in college I attended a lecture by an African American preacher who had written a novel about the life of Jesus. He made it plain that the power and courage of Jesus were possibilities for all human beings. He also made it plain that accepting this simple truth would be costly in terms of one's acceptability to others. In a private conversation, he chided me that I might not want to pay this price. For some reason, perhaps my own stubbornness, this chiding prompted me to push into the matter even more vigorously. I began to look beyond the box of being a mathematics scholar and teacher acceptable to my parents and expected by my friends. I began to become poor in spirit in the sense that I began to sacrifice my riches of approval by friends and family in order to open to some radical qualities of awareness that most others found foolish and dangerous. But I experienced this openness as a blessing, a road to happiness.

Blessing 2:

Blessed are those who mourn, for they shall be comforted.[12]

Blessed are those who experience sorrow, for
they shall find unassailable comfort.

There is sorrow involved in saying goodbye to the particular person that we have been. To see an old box, an old self, die away is a sad

---

[12]   Matthew 5:4 ; R.S.V.

experience, however crummy that old self may be. "I don't know who I am anymore," is an expression of this sadness. In fact, the true depth of all sorrow is losing an old self. When someone we love dies or leaves us, the loss for us is losing the self we were with that person in our lives. If we lose our dog, we lose a self-with-dog, with one particular dog. We might find a new dog, but it won't be Skippy. Sorrow is always the sorrow of saying goodbye to something we have been and can no longer be. Every fragment of who we think we are is treasured by us, even if we also hate that same treasured aspect. We have identified with the fragments that we are losing. We may feel insecure and frightened about no longer being the person who we thought we were.

To call such sorrow blessed is a transformation in our perspective. As a first impression, the challenge to be something more and different may seem frightening rather than encouraging. We might say, "Is endless and hopeless sorrow to be my lot?" Reality seems to smile back at this question with a firm, "Of course not." What awaits us beyond all our sorrowing is an unassailable comfort that can never be taken away from us and, therefore, about which no sorrow is possible. Life beyond the box of who we thought we were is more, not less. An enduring Great Self awaits us, and it can gather all our sorrow into itself as one of its lovely children.

An autobiographical note: My first quarter at a Christian seminary was in many ways a sorrowful experience. After viewing myself as the top student of my university in mathematics and physics, I now found myself taking a remedial philosophy course and making a "C" in my favorite theology course because my spelling and typing were so poor. I was sorrowful over no longer being the smartest one in the room. I had never worked so hard for so little acclaim. This seems very minor to me now, but it was not minor at the time. Also, when I was a young pastor of a local church, a young man in my congregation shot and killed his buddy in a hunting accident. I discovered that I did not know how to talk with the friends and family who were there facing that sorrow. I was in sorrow for my own self as a frightened and immature person. And this was only the beginning of humiliations and sorrows that have happened to me over the last half-century.

Some sorrows are hard to tell briefly, such as the repeated discovery of a pattern of being lost in mental worlds of my own making and thus out of touch with my own feelings and the feelings of those around me. I lived through many such experiences before I heard this saying attributed to some Buddhist teacher: "Humiliation is the road to enlightenment." This saying illuminated a great deal of my life. Enlightenment is the comfort promised to the sorrowing. But enlightenment, Spirit Reality itself, is not a sorrow; it is a type of happiness, a joy and a courage that can endure no matter how great the sorrows of losing my old sense of who I thought I was.

Journey II

The first journey of Spirit can continue for many decades, perhaps a whole lifetime. What characterizes those first years of our journey is that our Great Self, our Spirit Self, our Awed consciousness of consciousness happens to us as if from the outside. We view our Great Self as a kind of "not me" because we still identify with our basic personality that we spent our entire life designing and defending. We sometimes speak of the experience of our Great Self as being "beside ourselves." What a wonderful metaphor! Spirit, in the first journey of Spirit, means becoming "beside ourselves," outside our ordinary selves, a trip to a land of Mystery, an experience of ecstasy or Awe that seems, at first, quite alien to our ordinary lives.

The second phase of our Spirit journey begins as we shift our identification from our personality to our Spirit Being. No longer am I a personality having Spirit experiences. I am a Spirit Being who has a particular set of personality habits. This shift in identity is the beginning of a different quality of Spirit journey. This second journey includes moving deeper and deeper into understanding the specific patterns of our personality and how it restrains Spirit living. It includes moving deeper and deeper toward realizing what Spirit is like. The next four Beatitudes depict elements of this second journey.

Blessing 3:

Blessed are the meek, for they shall inherit the Earth.[13]

Blessed are those who are detached from celebrity,
status, ownership, and acclaim,
for they have the entire natural realm as their inheritance.

In our customary flow of life we fill up the box of our personality with celebrity, status, possessions, and acclaim. Filling our box is the opposite of this Beatitude's challenge to be "meek." "Meek" does not mean being a Mr. Milquetoast who knuckles under to all challenges and opposition. "Meek" here means a bold surrender to living life the way life actually is.

Instead of being meek, we are typically boastful. We promote ourselves, our finite selves, our personality, our habituated person. We surround our personality with defenses of all sorts. We assume that we need more wealth, more popularity, more friends, more things to do, more skills, more fun, more excitement, more, more, more. "More" is the opposite of being meek.

"Blessed are the meek for they shall inherit the Earth." What a strange saying! To understand it we must look beyond the beliefs of our personality to the actual experiences of our Spirit Being. When we are meekly willing to be the Spirit Being that we are, we do not need to pull in more and more support. As a Spirit Being we already possess it all. The entire Earth is ours. The entire cosmos is ours. All of nature is our family, our mother, our father, our brothers, our sisters. We do not need to own nature; we do not need to have a deed to pieces of the planet. All of nature is already ours as a gift. We cannot own the air, but we have it as a gift to breath. We cannot own the water cycles of the planet, but we have water as a gift to drink. We cannot own and control the biological systems of the planet, but we have food to eat. Jesus chided his disciples, "Why are you anxious? Look at the birds. The Final Papa feeds them; are you not more valuable than they?" Indeed, everything, entirely everything belongs to the meek. There is no need to fill our narrow little box. When we are living outside the

---

[13] Matthew 5:5 ; R.S.V.

box, everything belongs us. That is, everything is on loan to us for the time we need it. We are given the Earth as we need it. It is also true that everything will be taken away from us, for it is only on loan. But even our losses belong to us. Everything belongs to us. We need nothing whatsoever. As personalities we think we need everything. As Spirit beings we need nothing. "The Lord is my shepherd; I shall not want." "Blessed are the meek."

An autobiographical note: I have lived in times in which I had almost nothing of worldly goods and I have lived in times when I had more than I needed. During the fourteen years I lived in a religious order of families, I had little. My parents shamed me for being so poor. They also worried about me. Being meek in those years meant not giving in to those feelings of shame and anxiety. Being meek meant willingly, even joyously, keeping on with my heart-felt tasks – often with little or no appreciation from others and with almost no clarity about my economic future. Those years required disciplined attention to my meager resources and doing without many things; nevertheless, I was continually surprised at how abundant the cosmos continued to be in every way that was absolutely necessary to my vocation. In some measure, I accessed a sense of what it means to be meek, and to find that a blessing.

In more recent times, I have had more than I needed. In this period meekness has meant something different. I discovered that the anxiety over losing something can be as great as the anxiety over not having it. Having a house, I have worried about tornadoes taking my house. I have had to learn to enjoy my abundance with detachment. I have also had to learn to become detached from my miserly styles that were appropriate during my times of scarcity. I have had to learn the blessing of fearlessly spending a chunk of money for some important cause or training or benevolence.

In both of these periods, I also noticed the blessing of being detached from acclaim. My meekness with regard to having to be somebody has enabled me to do some unpopular things, abandon some old friends, find some new ones. It is clear to me now that when I calmly, simply surrender to the meekness of such inner detachment, there is no doubt about the liveliness of the accompanying blessing. The lack of anxiety that characterizes the life of the meek is indeed a great happiness.

Blessing 4:

Blessed are those who hunger and thirst for righteousness, for they shall be satisfied.[14]

Blessed are those who hunger and thirst for Spirit realization, for they will be fully fed.

Blessed are those who hunger and thirst for being a full manifestation of their Spirit beings. Most of us hunger and thirst for everything else. We know what hunger and thirst means. In these two strong words, we feel the power of our aggressive being. Blessed are those who are aggressive in their quest for Spirit realization. This hunger and this thirst will be satisfied. Spirit is there for us in absolute abundance. Going for it succeeds. This is part of the blessing. One might hunger and thirst for food and water and not get them. But those who hunger and thirst for Spirit shall be fed. Those who hunger and thirst to "be somebody" in the eyes of others may experience starvation. But those who hunger and thirst for Spirit shall be fed. I could go on with this, but this point is so simple it only needs to be tried to prove its validity.

An autobiographical note: My hunger and thirst to be a widely read author may never be satisfied. Even if this were to come to pass, I am quite sure this would not actually feed my Spirit. But the investments I have made in going to Spirit-quality classes, workshops, retreats, and conferences have certainly paid off in deep satisfaction. This is also true of the many hours I have spent reading Spirit books, meditating, writing in journals, doing reflective writing, and holding deep conversations with Spirit friends. It now seems to me that every movie, every TV news program, every bit of music or art or drama can be a time when this hunger and thirst for Spirit realization can come into play and can be satisfied.

---

[14]   Matthew 5:6 ; R.S.V.

Blessing 5:

Blessed are the merciful, for they shall obtain mercy.[15]

*Blessed are those who forgive everyone, for
they shall be forgiven everything.*

Receiving mercy means being forgiven. Everyone has need of being forgiven. We often expect mercy for ourselves. But the mercy of
the Final Papa/Mama is indiscriminate. It does not forgive some and
not others. It does not forgive me but not those who have hurt me and
rejected me and opposed me. Everyone is forgiven. If we do not grasp
the universality of forgiveness, we do not grasp that we are forgiven,
eternally forgiven. Most human beings will never forgive us, but we are
eternally forgiven. The cost of accepting that forgiveness is accepting
it for everyone. So if we are not merciful toward others, we are rejecting the mercy of God toward ourselves. And if we are willing to be
merciful toward others, we have already accepted mercy for ourselves,
a mercy that knows no limits and no end.

We need to reflect on how important this mercy is. For the second
journey of Spirit, the need for mercy is especially deep. As we proceed
on this journey, more and more awareness of our own personality comes
into view. In the early stages of our Spirit journey we do not know how
addicted we are, how selfish we are, how weak we are, how mean we
are, how guilty we have felt, how numb we have become, how lame,
how blind, how deaf, how dead to true living our life has been. As we
partake of the second Spirit journey, we see, as we have not seen before,
how much our personality habits have constrained us. We know more
fully our need for mercy. We not only know more clearly what we
need to be forgiven for, we also know that there are still vast currently
unknown estrangements for which forgiveness will be needed. "Lord
have mercy!" This is perhaps the key prayer for taking the second Spirit
journey. And it is a wonderful prayer, for it is immediately answered.
No matter what horrors of guilt come to the surface, we can say, "Lord
have mercy!" and the Final Absolute Overallness answers back immediately, "OK."

---

[15]   Matthew 5:7 ; R.S.V.

An autobiographical note: I was lying on a divan listening to a tape while I was waiting for a heart operation. My heart was having a flutter problem, racing up to 120 beats a minute, and those beats were weak. If I exerted myself blood would not reach my head and I would get dizzy. So I had to take it easy in order not to have a heart attack before the operation could be done. Earlier during this period, I had had a very bad night after watching an NBA playoff game. That second over-time had been too exciting for me. So I was taking it real easy. On the tape I was listening to, the presenter was talking about the heart chakra as one of the seven Spirit energy places on the human body. She was saying how these energies either flow or get blocked, and how blocked energies could even affect the operation of the physical heart. That got my attention. She went on to explain how we block the energies of the heart chakra by not forgiving other people – that not forgiving other people is a strain, indeed a waste of energy. For the energies of the heart chakra to flow, a person has to give up grudges against other people. So I began to reflect on who I had grudges against, and two particular persons came to mind. Several decades ago these two close friends with whom I had worked for years let me down. When I decided to divorce my first wife and marry my current wife, they had abandoned me. I recalled a particular event in which the two of them had taken me aside and asked me to leave a meeting claiming that I was a bad influence. Lying on my couch recalling this event, I realized that I still held a grudge against these two. I could see that it was true that this grudge was wasting energy, energy I needed. As I now faced the prospect of my own death, what did it matter that these two men had betrayed me decades ago? I might as well forgive them. Perhaps that would indeed take away some strain, loosen the flow of my heart chakra, perhaps even aid me in making it to my heart operation. So I did. I simply gave up any right or need to hold grudges against these men any longer. And I did experience a profound relaxation. I felt warmer and more compassionate toward myself and all the persons who had given me a hard time. I don't know whether this helped me make it to my heart operation or to get through the trauma of it. But it certainly helped me feel differently toward myself and toward all the persons who had ever misunderstood me, betrayed me, abandoned me, hurt me. I could see that mercy did indeed flow through my life when I turned loose of my grudges. By being merciful, I received mercy. I received forgiveness for my grudges as well as for those against whom these grudges were held.

Blessing 6:

Blessed are the pure in heart, for they shall see God.[16]

Blessed are those who inquire with pristine
honesty into the depths of Spirit,
for they shall experience the Absolute Wholeness of Being.

Purity of heart does not mean something pious and sentimental. In the context of the Beatitudes purity of heart means an open, dedicated, honest inquiry into the depths our Spirit Being, yes, into the depths of Overwhelming Awesome Reality.

Søren Kierkegaard wrote an entire book on purity of heart in which he suggested that the pure in heart are those who "will one thing." Most of us most of the time are devoted to many objects of devotion. We are conflicted by the many meaning givers that we have chosen to give meaning to our lives. We are not willing one thing but many things. Those who have one meaning giver are those (and only those) who have chosen that One, Final, Absolute Mysteriousness as their one all-consuming focus of loyalty and meaning. The pure in heart see God, but what do they see? They see the Final Absolute Mysteriousness as trustworthy. They trust that the meaning and purpose of their lives is found in trusting this Finality.

Seeing God is a paradoxical seeing. The Gospel of John says bluntly (John 1:18) "No one has seen God." I assume that this includes Jesus and Moses and everyone. In the same verse that says, "No one has seen God," the gospel of John goes on to say that Jesus, the offspring of God, has made God known. But the word "known" in this statement should not be interpreted to mean "imaged" or "understood" or "made part of a worldview." God, even when known in the sense that

---

[16] Matthew 5:8 ; R.S.V.

Jesus knew God, remains unknown – the Unknown Unknown, the unknowable absolute Mystery.

When the Gospel of John says that Jesus made God known, he did not mean that God was no longer the Unknown Mysteriousness. He meant that Jesus had made God known as Love for us, as forgiveness for us. Indeed, this is the meaning of trust in God: that this Final Mysterious Power fosters our happiness by leading us to our Spirit greatness. This is what Jesus had "made known." In virtually every one of his teachings, Jesus was making it known that the Final Papa is benevolent, forgiving, and loving. This God is the provider of profound aliveness, the treasure worth selling everything to possess, the only aliveness that cannot be taken away from us, the true home to which every prodigal needs to return.

Seeing God does not mean understanding this Mystery of All Being with our minds. It means a direct experience of this transrational, transconceptual fullness of that Final Mystery that we can never understand with our minds. If we are intent on putting the right doctrines or right theories in our hip pocket and using them to control our lives, seeing God may seem like an irrelevant blessing. But in the context of the Beatitudes, seeing God includes experiencing in full measure the Spirit being that we essentially are. And it also means experiencing in full measure the essential nature of Reality.

So what is it like to experience the fullness of Reality? This question can only be answered in poetry, and the poetry can only be understood by those have also arrived at an actual experience of purity of heart – that is, a place of wholehearted dedication and honest inquiry into what is so and what is not so. Only those who share in this direct vision of God can recognize the descriptions made by other visitors to this "PLACE of VISION." When we have been "THERE," then we can hear others speak about THERE. This PLACE of VISION is the end of the second journey, the end toward which the second Spirit journey moves.

An autobiographical note: So, have I been THERE? Have I seen God? When have I been pure in heart? Most of what I learned from reading Søren Kierkegaard's book *Purity of Heart* was how I was not willing one thing, but was instead a scattered person willing many things. Nevertheless, I have some resonance with the image of willing one thing. I know that the Spirit life is indeed singular, that the fullness of Spirit life realizes a Truth that unites all the little truths that life presents.

The experience of such unity and "purity of heart" I associate with moments of immediate awareness of the Vastness of Reality. When have I experienced this Vastness? At times, the vastness of the cosmos has become more than an idea in my scientific mind; it has become an experience in my soul. Reality is BIG. An experience of this vastness has also happened to me in quite mundane circumstances, reading a book, meditating, looking out the window at the trees. Vastness is always there, behind and within each event. It is I who am not always present to the Vastness.

Seeing God can also be likened to an experience of Infinite Blackness. A. H. Almaas calls it "Shining Blackness." The mind cannot penetrate it, but the Blackness shines in the soul as a sober and trustworthy truth. The human consciousness of consciousness reaches a boundary where consciousness becomes absorbed into a boundless Blackness from which all consciousness comes and into which all consciousness returns. It is this brilliantly Shining Blackness that is the object of worship recommended in the biblical literature. As Christians, this Shining Blackness is our God. And while elements of my life may experience a deep dread of this Blackness, the True Me experiences this Blackness as Peace, as a place of Rest in the hectic march of time. Indeed, the Blackness is Light that illuminates my life.

Journey III

Seeing God is not the end of the Spirit journey, but the beginning of another journey. Traveling beyond our thoughts and specific sensations to an awareness of the transrational Vastness, the Shining Blackness, the Eternal Peace of seeing God is an important Spirit awareness, but we must return from such moments to our everyday living. In fact, we never leave everyday living, we only expand the context in which it proceeds. Journey III is the journey of the Spirit person who shared this direct vision of God and now returns to the ordinary aspects of living, finding it needful to integrate these ordinary experiences with remaining THERE with God. Most of us have probably hoped that being THERE with God would mean that our journey was over. Indeed, being THERE is full of wonder, full of peace, full of satisfaction, full of joy, full of the unassailable power of Being. Nevertheless, the journey continues. Life goes on. And this continuing life goes on in the same body, with the same parents, having the same personality, having the same flaws, living in the same culture, living with the same people, facing the same challenges that existed before the Journey to THERE with God took place. And this third journey is not an easy journey. Yet, however surprising, disagreeable, or disappointing it may seem to continue the Spirit journey, taking this third Spirit journey is also characterized by blessings. And here are two of them:

Blessing 7:

Blessed are the peacemakers, for they shall be called sons of God.[17]

Blessed are those who integrate into the life of Absolute
Peace all the conflicting aspects of living,
for they are the vanguard of human history.

Finite living is characterized by conflicts not peace. So what is this Peace and who are these Peacemakers. In our ordinary finite living there is a conflict between our inner life and our outer life. There is a conflict between our left-brain and our right brain. There is a conflict between our feminine aspects and our masculine aspects. There is a conflict between our social being and our natural being. There is a conflict between our society and the natural planet. There is a conflict between our society and every other society. There is a conflict between our social class or group and every other class or group. And this is only the beginning of the innumerable conflicts that comprise our living.

Let us picture the person who is living the third phase of the Spirit journey as one who is returning from the place of PEACE with the Infinite THERENESS. Such a returnee is a bringer of Peace to all the conflicts of finite living. The blessing promised to these peacemakers is that they shall be the vanguard of history (the sons and daughters of

---

[17]   Matthew 5:9; R.S.V.

God), the ones who set the course of the future in potentially positive directions, the ones who provide a Presence that can endure the conflicts and resolve them for this generation of humanity. This capacity for service is the blessing.

The peacemaker has already received the blessing of Peace. Seeing God means finding Peace, the peace that passes all understanding. Now the Peaceful One returns as peacemaker to all the conflicts of the ordinary realm of living. The Peaceful One makes peace between men and women, between society and nature, between upper classes and lower classes, between East and West, between humanity and all the other life forms of the planet, between minds and emotions, between finite sensitivities and Spirit awareness.

Some of these conflicts can be ended. Any conflict that is based on lies can simply end when those lies are no longer told. Other conflicts are based on life polarities that never end – such as masculine and feminine, nature and society. In such cases, the peace made by the peacemaker does not end all tension between these ongoing poles of living. Rather, these basic polarities of life are blessed with the capacity of having respect for one another. The peacemaker reconciles and integrates masculine and feminine, nature and society back into the whole to which these polar parts belong. The Final Whole contains all such parts in a mutually enhancing harmony. How this reconciliation is to be accomplished in each generation is for the peacemaker to work out. He or she is capable of doing this because the vision of God has revealed how all the parts are at Peace in One Reality. This vision of Peace is the peacemakers authority and qualification for peacemaking. The peacemaker sees the Whole and is thus made capable of choosing new directions within the manyness of ordinary life. The peacemaker also has the power to assist new directions to take on actuality. This is the blessing offered to the peacemaker: to be a bringer of peace to whatever causes the peacemaker chooses to bless. This is the blessing to the peacemaker: to be able to bring peace to the conflicts.

Every instance of such peacemaking is complex and difficult even to talk about, but peace can be made when we assist members of any truth-seeking group to begin with the experience of THERE, the experience of the Wholeness in which all parts cohere. Those who make such peace are the sons and daughters of God. Why? Because they are experiencing the Eternal Peace that can make peace on Earth among the fragments of reality that destructively conflict with each other.

An autobiographical note: I began my life as a mathematician, an abstract artist of the possibilities of the human mind. The human body and its emotional intelligence were relegated to secondary status. I was, as one therapist said to me, an expert at "feelingless verbosity." I could talk about or around some of my feelings, but I was unable to express them plainly and openly and simply. I will not attempt to itemize all the therapies, workshops, humiliations, and illuminations it took to make peace between my emotional intelligence and my mental intelligence. I will simply report this: I have found peace within myself by becoming aware that the same God who made the mind also made the body with all its emotional wonders. Indeed, I came to see that every emotion is good, including anger, fear, terror, shame, and guilt as well as the more sweet, restful, exciting, satisfying feelings. All feelings are a gift from God; they are integral parts of the situation that God is giving to me. Some emotions may be showing me that my relationship with life is delusory, but that is a gift. Some emotions may be practical guidance, telling me something specific about my real self and my real situation. That is also a gift.

I have learned to see that each of us is supplied with an emotional intelligence that can enable us to sort out the meanings of our various emotions, and thus affirm them all. This intelligence is very different from the intelligence used by the mathematician or scientist. Scientific truth seekers have had to learn how to keep emotions out of their scientific work. The pure scientist is dedicated to objective mental work. The body and all its functions can be an object of our scientific investigation, but we do not count on the body's emotions to assist us with our objective work. It is as if a war is going on within me and within my society, between science and the more artistic and religious feeling-laden aspects of humanness. Nevertheless, I have made some sort of peace between my scientific mind and the emotional intelligence of my body. And this peace enables me to be a peacemaker in my associations with other people. Perhaps I first recognized the power of this peacemaking potential while working though issues with my wife and forging new relations with my adult children. And this peacemaking has also enriched my work as a teacher and writer within this conflicted culture.

Blessing 8:

*Blessed are those who are persecuted for righteousness' sake,
for theirs is the kingdom of heaven.*[18]

*Blessed are those who suffer human opposition
to their manifestation of Spirit,
for the Commonwealth of Spirit is their Eternal Home.*

Estranged persons and estranged societies of persons will inevitably find ways to oppose the sons and daughters of God, the vanguard, the peacemakers, the visionaries who see the truth about life and witness to it, the activists who see what needs to be altered and choose to show how to do it. The eighth and last Beatitude says that these sons and daughters are blessed, even though they are opposed by many and frequently suffer bitter persecution.

So what is the blessing? It is not that those who are persecuted today will be rewarded later with a heavenly blessing that compensates them for their hard times. No, like all the other blessings, this last blessing is operative right now, right here in current living.

Further, this blessing is not the assurance that we are on the right track because we are being rejected and persecuted. Those who are returning from having seen the vision of God need no assurance that they are on the right track. Having been THERE is all the assurance needed. Seeing the Infinite Shining Blackness, experiencing that Peace, and integrating such Peace with all the ordinary challenges of daily living is the right track. It remains the right track whether we are persecuted or not.

Furthermore, opposition from one's social peers can mean different things. It can mean that we are being an obstinate, tyrannical, self-centered bully. It can mean that we are being an unconscious nerd.

---

[18]   Matthew 5:10; R.S.V

Whatever the case, no assurance that we are on the right path comes from being opposed or persecuted.

So what is the blessing associated with being rejected and persecuted? It is the same blessing that attracted us at the beginning of our Spirit journey. It is the same blessing offered those who are in deep Spirit need. The blessing is participation in the Kingdom of God, the Reign of Reality, the Commonwealth of Spirit, the Communion of Spirit Realization. The blessing is a living communion with those who live, have lived, and will live from this Spirit place. Whether we are experiencing our Spiritual poverty or are being persecuted for our Spirit maturity, the blessing is participation in the Commonwealth of Spirit, the Communion of Saints. This is our eternal home, our rest, our life. And this blessing is not lessened by being opposed or persecuted for our work in manifesting this Spirit aliveness. Indeed, any opposition only intensifies the blessing.

Why is the blessing intensified by opposition? A deep paradox is revealed here. The opposition that the defenders of fallen living make toward the Spirit vanguard reveals or can reveal to these defensive persons what they need to know in order to be healed. Their irrational, compulsive opposition toward the true sons and daughters of God is itself God's judgment on their patterns of living, the patterns that are preventing their own blessedness. Experiencing such judgment is the first step in the process of Spirit healing, for it means realizing the unconscious layers of hatred toward Reality, toward authenticity, toward God, and thus toward God's servants.

The second step in Spirit healing is experiencing one's welcome home to Reality. This also is communicated to them by the Spirit vanguard. The Spirit vanguard manifests a witness to forgiveness for their own selves and all others. They are the ones who know, live, and thus communicate the truth that Reality is merciful, forgiving, accepting, welcoming to all prodigals.

The third step in Spirit healing is accepting one's acceptance, choosing to be home. The Spirit vanguard by their very being, their words, their deeds beckon people to accept their acceptance. The Spirit vanguard is the walking breathing presence of the Kingdom of God. They are the "Home," the "Rest," the "Commonwealth" toward which all are called. Therefore, those who persecute this "Home" may discover that it is their own Home they are persecuting. They may turn homeward and be healed.

The eighth blessing is simply that beloved Kingdom, of which the persecuted ones are already members. That Kingdom is being expanded or spread by their persecution. The more vigorously they are opposed, the more quickly the opposers are absorbed into the beloved Kingdom. Do not ask why this must be so, simply notice that this is the case, and that this is a blessing! Like seed that falls into the Earth, the persecuted create a harvest of Spirit living and thus many more seeds for still other harvests.

The sons and daughters of God are the peacemakers, the visionaries, the vanguard of Reality, the servants of the Whole. Being opposed and persecuted is part of their service, part of what it means to take the third journey of Spirit and be blessed in doing so. The gospel writer of Matthew expands on this last Beatitude in the verses that follow it:

> How blessed you are when you suffer insults and persecution and every calumny for my sake. Accept it with gladness and exultation, for you have a rich reward in heaven. In the same way they persecuted the prophets before you.
>
> You are the salt of the world, and if salt becomes tasteless, how is its saltiness to be restored? It is now good for nothing but to be thrown away and trodden underfoot. (Matthew 5:11-13 New English Bible)

The "heaven" spoken of here can best be understood in modern metaphor as "the living NOW of holy Reality." The salt spoken of here was probably salt-laced rock. The saltiness of such rock is being used as a metaphor for manifesting the sting or taste of Spirit. By actively being who they are, the sons and daughters of God are this saltiness. This is the character of the third Spirit journey, having moved away from the box of our habituated personality and social conditioning to the Final Source of all Spirit saltiness, we now return to the entire round of human experience within this estranged world to be the ongoing sting of saltiness.

An autobiographical note: Only recently have I understood how profound this Beatitude is. Early in my life, I met rejection from my parents when I chose a religious vocation. I met rejection from my first congregation to whom I attempted to preach honestly. Later, I met rejection from dear friends who could not understand my need to reconstruct my marital life. Indeed, I have been and am still being rejected by both friends and enemies in almost every organization to which I belong. I have had many opportunities to learn all over again that the best way to live is to charge ahead with my best grasp of my own integrity and my own grasp of truth and simply let the chips fall where they may. But not until recently have I seen how important it is to intentionally provoke others into their rejection of the truth. Strange as it may seem, rejecting me can be a way other people discover their own issues. It is almost impossible for people to know what their own issues are until they see themselves rejecting what is clearly true.

So I am now learning that the blessing of this last Beatitude has nothing whatsoever to do with my need for acceptance or my wish to avoid rejection. I am learning to see the blessing from the perspective of awakening Spirit in the world rather then from the perspective of my comfort. My task is presenting truth to other persons, not in order that I can be proud about my correct behavior as a truth presenter, but so these other persons can hear the truth. And their rejection of truth or their acceptance of truth is interesting only as it pertains to them. Are the persons who are rejecting truth learning something thereby about themselves? Are the persons who are accepting truth learning something thereby about themselves? The blessing I am experiencing is the blessing of seeing other people move into better alignment with their own happiness, their own Spirit being, their own meaningful vocation, their own fellowship with other aware members of the Spirit Commonwealth. The more deeply and the more courageously I present truth, stand by truth, be truth in my every movement, the more rejection I am going to encounter. This is absolutely necessary. Truth must always fight its way through the defenses of those who do not wish to embrace it. In most situations my challenge is to work harder at being rejected. I am not conducting a political campaign or a popularity contest. As a returnee from the THERE of seeing God, my task is to tell humanity what I have seen and to be rejected for making this witness. This is what makes me the salt of the Earth. If people are learning who they are through rejecting me, Spirit is winning. I am being that salt without which Christianity or any other religion is good for nothing but to be trodden underfoot. This is the blessing.

* * * * * * * *

All eight of these blessings and all three of these journeys of Spirit continue indefinitely. We never complete any of them. There is a progression from Blessing 1 to Blessing 8, and from Journey 1 to Journey 2 to Journey 3. Nevertheless, each of these blessings continues to take place in our lives. The progression in our Spirit journey might best be understood as how the focus of our Spirit journey changes over the years. But it does not matter where our focus happens to be at this time. Our current focus is given to us by God, and we are called to focus on that focus. Later, our focus will be different. Spirit is a journey, influenced by what we do, but fundamentally determined by God, a Power beyond our control.

And it is foolish and despair producing to compare our journey with anyone else's journey. Each of us is uniquely placed to journey the journey we are journeying. Blessed are the meek: blessed are those who surrender to journeying the journey that they are required to journey.

19.

Nine Ways Home

In the last four chapters I described three stages of Spirit journey: (1) our initial experiences of having our personality penetrated by Spirit, (2) our surrender to being a Spirit Being rather than identifying with our personality, and (3) the melting of our personality fixations and the shining forth of the entire diamond of our Spirit Being.

In this chapter I will take another look at the enneagram overview. I will emphasize that we begin our journey where we are, namely deeply identified with our unique personality, a personality that can be seen to be one of the nine types of personality depicted in the enneagram analysis. The enneagram heritage can be used to assist us to focus on our personalities, and to do so in a manner that can also be a focus on our Spirit realization – on Trust, Love, and Freedom. While our journey of Spirit begins as a challenge to our identification with our personality, it moves toward a realization of all aspects of Trust, Love, and Freedom.

A profound knowing of our personality pattern includes knowing the Spirit aspect from which our personality is a falling away. Seeing the falling away aspects of our personality fixation can be valuable to us in taking our journey home to Spirit. The falling away aspects of our personality can be viewed as a map back to our essence. Consider this analogy: if we notice that we are walking north away from our home, this noticing can be a guide for us. If north is away from home, then walking south is heading home.

Further, noticing our personality pattern includes noticing our despair over being stuck in the box of personality. Noticing this despair is a doorway to Spirit realization. The departure from personality identification into the wide-open spaces of Spirit realization means passing through the doorway of despair.

THE DOORWAY OF DESPAIR

If our primary identification is with our personality, we are living in a despairing state of life. We may not be currently experiencing that despair; nevertheless, it is despair because our personality is not who we are. As who we truly are becomes more conscious, our despair over our personality identification also becomes more conscious. Until this consciousness of our despair dawns upon us, we are not in the process of leaving our personality fixation; we are content with it. This is why despair is a blessing. As Paul Tillich pointed out, experiencing our despair is step one in the happening that Christian heritage points to with the term "grace."

The journey home to our Spirit essence entails experiencing our despair as a doorway, not a catastrophe. How strange this seems to our typical approach to living! The way forward on our Spirit journey includes the pain of losing our personality as our basic identification, losing who we think we are in order to become who we really are. Even though becoming who we truly are is a blessing, we nevertheless experience despair over losing our self-constructed facsimile of our self. Even though this "losing" leads to abundant life, we still feel the losing. Most of us flee from our feelings of gloom, hopelessness, dark night, horror, dread, grief, anxiety, and other such feelings that attend our states of despair; nevertheless, feeling our despair is our doorway home. Despair over our false self is the path toward being our true Self. Despairing feelings merely mark the doorway through which we must pass. These feelings are aspects of those dark nights spoken of by the mystics. The dark nights of the Spirit journey can seem horrific, but each dark night is our friend. It is an opportunity for deep change, our sign that we are leaving our personality identification and finding our way home to our true essence – to our Spirit Being of Trust, Love, and Freedom.

Each personality type experiences a characteristic type of despair, a commonly met doorway through which this personality type must pass in order to return to Spirit essence. Every person may pass through many despair doorways, but each personality tends to begin with its own most characteristic doorway. We could write an entire novel about Johnny Five or Suzy Three or any other personality type. Indeed, these novels already exist. In every novel that accurately portrays realistic characters, I find it possible to identify the personality types of the main characters.

If I were to write a novel based on my own experience of my number five personality, here are some of the dynamics that might appear in that story. I tend to hide in my self-built world of mental constructs. I feel free to work with these constructs. Indeed, I am free to learn new ways to think. I am free to take in new data. I am free to change the ways I think. But as long as I limit my living to the world of thinking, I am not truly Free in the Spirit sense; I am bound to that inner world of my own thoughts. And the wholeness of real life does not go on within the life of my mind. Reality breaks into the mental world. I only come to know Reality when I come to know mental ignorance. Indeed, no matter how much I know, it is trivial in relation to what is still unknown. I actually live in a strange land of Mystery, the Unknown Unknown. Only in this land are there Spirit Trust, Spirit Love, and Spirit Freedom. So if I wrote a novel about Johnny Five becoming his Spirit Being, I would need to describe how Johnny discovered Mystery and learned to Trust that Mystery, Love that Mystery, and be the Freedom bestowed by Mystery.

As a five, I tend to trust only what my mind can categorize, make orderly, and render consistent with what I already know or think I know. I don't trust my feelings. They are too disorderly. I don't know what they mean, and I am not inclined to simply feel them and wait to understand what they might mean. I want to know now, so I am paranoid about my own feelings rather than trusting them to mean something. I am intolerant of ignorance, especially of my own ignorance, which I tend to deny. I am especially defensive with respect to feelings of despair related to my not knowing. I hate for people to correct what I say or even interrupt me before I finish saying it. I hate for people to oppose or correct my writing in any substantial way. My Spirit journey can only proceed when I am able to trust that these experiences of despair are doorways to my glorious being of Trust, Love, and Freedom.

Every personality experiences doorways of despair. Why is this so? It is so because our Spirit essence means experiencing Reality beyond the boundary of our self-constructed personality. The experience of despair is the experience of that boundary. It is our identification with our personality that is doing the despairing. Our Spirit Being does not despair. But when we are identified with our personality, we do not yet know the glory of our Spirit Being. As personalities we are tempted, whenever we are experiencing despair, to turn back from this boundary of the personality into the personality itself, rather than going forward through that boundary of despair into the open country of Freedom, Trust, and Love.

SORTING OUT PERSONALITY FROM SPIRIT

Returning home to our Spirit essence means clarifying what part of our experience is the operation of our personality and what part of our experience is a manifestation of our Spirit essence. This sorting out includes seeing the ways that our personality is a block to experiencing and living our Spirit essence.

Seeing our personality identification as a block to Spirit realization does not mean any sort of animosity toward our personality, or any sort of demeaning of the importance of our personality. Our personality is necessary for our survival and functionality. Each personality is a partial hold on reality. But because it is partial it is a perversion – a facsimile of our true nature – a falling away from our true nature. The personality is thus a box that protects us from our true nature. If our personality had contained nothing of our real lives, we could not have survived. When a personality incorporates very little reality, we commonly call this a "dysfunctional personality." Yet even the most dysfunctional personality contains a trace of our essential nature, and even the most functional personality operates as a block to returning home to the fullness of our Spirit essence.

So it is key to our Spirit journey to become aware of what part of our experience is our Spirit essence and what part of our experience is the behavior of our personality. Typically, we do not notice this distinction. And even when we do notice this distinction, we typically minimize the difference between personality and Spirit. But that difference is very great. Indeed, it is infinitely great.

Personality is a human-made design, a past-oriented construction, a default pattern for living. Spirit is not human-made; and it is not past-oriented. Spirit is present reality, and it is not a pattern of any sort. When we talk about our Spirit essence, we construct rational patterns with which to talk about it. For example, the categories "Trust," "Love," and "Freedom" form such a rational pattern. But the terms "Trust," "Love," and "Freedom" do not point to patterns; the realities meant by these words are the very opposite of patterns. Trust, Love and Freedom are wild energies of upwelling response. They are like wind. "The wind blows where it wills; you hear the sound of it, but you do not know where it comes from, or where it is going. So with everyone who is born of Spirit." (John 3:8) I will expand upon this:

Freedom is not a pattern; it is that which creates all patterns. There is no pattern called "Freedom." And any understanding of "Freedom" that construes Freedom as a pattern created by human beings is a misunderstanding of that primal Freedom that is our human essence. Freedom is a non-patterned Void out of which all pattern comes. We are such Freedom. We are not primarily rational beings. We are transrational Freedom. We use our reason to talk about our Freedom and to enact our Freedom, but Freedom itself is transrational. When we speak of knowing our Freedom, we do not mean getting our mind around it. We mean noticing that there is a creativity in the depths of our being that our mind cannot comprehend. Personality is a construction of Freedom, but personality is not Freedom itself. Personality contains no essential Freedom. It is a building built by Freedom; Freedom is the ongoing building process. Our personality might seem to contain an element of Freedom, but that element is better understood as "free will" operating within the limitations of the personality design. Since this "free will" is limited by the personality, it is also a bondage in relation to the fullness of Freedom. Though we might say that Freedom is reflected in this "free will," Spirit Freedom is infinitely deeper and boundlessly more than "free will."

Similarly, **Trust** is not a pattern, not a set of beliefs. Trust is beyond belief. Trust may be expressed through statements of belief, but Trust itself is infinitely different from those beliefs through which Trust may be stated. Trust is a movement of our being on the transrational level. It precedes thinking about it. It functions as a core passion, loyalty, devotion, dedication out of which all our philosophical, theological, and ethical thinking emerge. And Trust is not created by human effort; it comes with our true nature. All beliefs and all other elements of our personality have been and are being created by human effort. Trust includes Freedom in the sense that Freedom freely chooses to Trust. This does not mean, however, that Freedom creates Trust. Rather, Freedom and Trust exist together as inseparable aspects of our true being.

Spirit Love is also part of our true being. Love lives in an inseparable meld with Freedom and Trust. Spirit Love is infinitely different from the emotional sentiments that are aspects of our personality. Spirit Love may be attended by tender feelings, sadness, joy, states of delight, sweetness, outrage, fury, and many other feelings, but Spirit Love itself is not a feeling. It is an infinitely deeper experience than feelings. All our feelings are operations of our biological/psychological person. Spirit Love is a complete detachment from all feelings as well as a complete engagement in our feelings and an affirmation of all our feelings. And, Spirit Love is an affirmation of all those realities about which we have feelings. Spirit Love is an enchantment with Being, and this includes our own being and the being of every other person and thing.

The journey from living within the limits of our personality into living from our Spirit Being is a departure from patterned living into a wildness, a spontaneity, an unpredictability that tends to make all personality-identified persons shudder.

NINE WAYS HOME

With the above fundamental dynamics fresh in our minds, let us review the nine personality types. In this review I will emphasize the characteristic journey home of each type. Three personality types (8, 9, & 1) can be said to be power-based or anger-based. Three others (5, 6,

& 7) can be said to be escape-based or fear-based. The remaining three (2, 3, & 4) can be said to be self-image based or humiliation-based. All of us experience feelings of anger, fear, and humiliation, but each of these three sets of personalities specialize in one of these three basic relationships toward Reality. In each case the healing journey includes accessing our Spirit life beyond the anger or fear or humiliation. We do not have to flee from our anger, fear, or humiliation. We only have to experience what is real, including our anger, fear, and humiliation. When we do, we are also in position to experience the still deeper realities – Trust, Love, and Freedom.

The Anger-Based Personality Types

The limiting fixations of the 8, 9, and 1 personality types have to do with personal relations and with anger. These three anger-based personality types are preoccupied with power and integrity in their relations with others. The 8-fixation might be described as a form of rationalism that justifies bullying people with an assumed "truth." The 9-fixation might be described as a form of sentimental peacemaking that suppresses anger. The mild-mannered nine is a cover for some deep rage against the intensity of actual living. The 1-fixation might be described as a form of moralism that supports being right and making others wrong. Their anger is a righteous resentment against violations of their principles. Handling anger clearly and cleanly will bring healing to all three of these anger-based fixations.

All of us (not just eights, nines, and ones) experience anger. And in order to access our Spirit Being all of us need to work through our anger. But for eights, nines, and ones, working through their anger is a first order of business.

Here is a description of the positive journey for those of us with a **personality-type-8 fixation**. In order to move through an angry mistrust of Being to accessing our essential Trust of Being, we have to experience our anger and detach from the rationalism that sustains our ongoing warfare with Reality. Experiencing our anger fully and going public with our anger in a vulnerable fashion can enable us to move beyond our bullying of others, of ourselves, and of Reality. Experienced anger can then flow rather than fixate as personality patterns of frustration and hostility. The anger can become a component in our overall

energy for living rather than a malice toward Reality. Anger can be part
of our basic Trust of Reality. This Trust has been eclipsed by our attempts to bully Reality. In the context of Trust, our anger can become
part of a program for justice and honesty rather than a defense of ego
or personality. When this happens, we are experiencing the positive
journey of the person with a type-8 fixation

Here is a description of the positive journey for those of us with
personality-type-9 fixation. For nines the issue is to move beyond a
deep suppression of anger. As nines, our Spirit journey includes letting
our consciousness view the rage that is hidden below the surface of
our peace-making patterns. Such awareness can open us up to a fuller
expression of our essential Love of Being, but this entails fully facing
the anger that has become a deep rage because of its suppression. In
order to access this anger we need to become detached from our sentimental peacefulness that is suppressing the raging malicious anger that
we cannot abide and so suppress. The positive journey of the person
with a personality-type-9 fixation is to move beyond this sentimental
peaceable suppression of rage into a full experience of the rage that can
then lead us toward experiencing that intense, wildly energetic Love of
Reality that the rage is eclipsing. When this happens, we are experiencing the positive journey of the person with a type-9 fixation.

Here is a description of the positive journey for those of us with a
personality-type-1 fixation. For those of us with this personality the
issue is moralism, a bondage to principles – to some system of rights
and wrongs. This moralism is anger based. Such anger flares into
action as powerful resentments toward those who violate our beloved
principles. In order to move beyond this trap, we need to experience
this underlying anger, see how it is held in place by our devotion to
principles. Thereby we allow such anger to pass, opening up our consciousness to an experience of the purity of our essential Freedom, a
Freedom that sees through the relativity of our principles and guidelines and relaxes in our ambiguous decision-making situations. When
this happens, we are experiencing the positive journey of the person
with a type-1 fixation

All of us may take all three of these journeys, but personality types
8, 9, and 1 are especially focused on an anger journey. These are the
anger-based personalities.

The Fear -Based Personality Types

Personality types 5, 6, and 7 are fear-based personalities. These three fixations tend to be paranoid about fully real experiences. All three fixations manifest a deep dread of Reality. The 5-fixation might be described as a form of rationalism that dreads challenges to current beliefs. And the 6-fixation might be described as a form of sentimentality that dreads personal power. The 7-fixation might be described as a form of moralism that dreads being bored or left out. Handling fear clearly and cleanly will bring healing to all three of these fear-based fixations.

All of us (not just fives, sixes, and sevens) experience fear. And in order to access our Spirit Being all of us need to work through our fear. But for fives, sixes, and sevens, working through their fear is a first order of business.

Here is a description of the positive journey for those of us with a **personality-type-5 fixation**. As fives we live in our minds in order to avoid our dread of the fullness of Mysterious Reality. This deep dread is a product of the five's insistence that life make sense. In order to realize our Spirit essence those of us with a personality-type-5 fixation need to fully experience our dread of not knowing. Sitting with this dread tends to make it laughable, for as we face this dread we learn that our dread of ignorance is a silly avoidance of the full Mysteriousness of life and of the unavoidable dumbness of the human psyche. When such insight works its way through the hell of our resistance to being stupid, our dread does not go away; it mutates into something larger. Dread of mystery and ignorance is gathered up into a fascination and courage to be curious and open toward the yet to be known. Such openness is still scary, but it is now an excited sort of fear that is nested in a vast sea of equanimity. When this happens, we are experiencing the positive journey of the person with a type-5 fixation.

Here is a description of the positive journey for those of us with a **personality-type-6 fixation**. Sixes are also paranoid about fully real experiences. Those of us with this fixation revert to a type of sentimentalism, living in shallow states of loyalty or daring. The six's dread is a dread of personal strength, of the full power and autonomy of being oneself. Those of us with a six fixation need to pay attention to and fully experience our dread of being powerful and autonomous. Sitting with this dread tends to be sobering but also refreshing, and perhaps amusing, leading to a willingness to poke fun at ourselves. When the full wildness and raw power of human selfhood works its way through the hell of clinging to our fabricated weakness, it seems ironic that we have tried so hard to be strong some other way. When led to such insight, the dread of personal power does not go away; it mutates into something larger. The dread of personal power is gathered up into a fascination and courage toward the risk of being our full selves. Being powerful is still scary, but this fear becomes part of an excitement about challenging our own and other people's shallowness. When this happens, we are experiencing the positive journey of the person with a type-6 fixation

Here is a description of the positive journey for those of us with a **personality-type-7 fixation**. Like fives and sixes, sevens are paranoid about fully real experiences. We who have this fixation revert to a type of moralism that insists that one should always be excited and never bored. Sevens flee from their dread of realism by jazzing up one experience after another. This tends to manifest as a shallow mode of living, moving from one thing to another without ever pushing anything all the way to its horrific and glorious depths. Beneath this restlessness is a dread of boredom. Those of us with a 7-fixation need to experience fully our basic boredom. Sitting with this boredom and this dread of boredom feels like hell at first, but in the end becomes profoundly relaxing. It releases us from our restless panic about missing out on some exciting adventure or state of being. When we simply surrender to real life with all its boring lows and outlandish highs, our restless panic relaxes. Our dread of a boring life is gathered up into the fascination and courage to simply let our lives unfold naturally. This may still be scary, but this fear becomes part of a relaxed excitement, an anticipation of surprise and fresh depth. When this happens, we are experiencing the positive journey of the person with a type-7 fixation.

All of us may take all three of these journeys, but personality types 5, 6, and 7 are especially focused on a fear journey. These are the fear-based personalities.

The Humiliation-Based Personality Types

Personalities 2, 3, and 4 are preoccupied with self-image, with a defense of self-image from experiences of humiliation. All of us defend our self-image, but these personalities are especially fixated in this arena. Personality types 2, 3, and 4 are fixations that focus on protecting the existing self-image. These personality types often become what we sometimes call "hysterical" with restimulated thoughts and behaviors over threats to the qualities of their "person" (that is, their ego). Healing involves interrupting these intense feelings and thoughts, reinterpreting them, and revealing something beyond them – revealing the presence of our quiet, silent, invincible Spirit Being. Buddhists often call this a discovery of our "no self" – a state of being that knows no humiliation. The "self" that can know humiliation is our ego or our personality. Like all temporal constructions, self-images and personality formations do not encompass the fullness of Reality. So Reality continually humiliates our self-image.

The 2-fixation might be described as a form of moralism that knows how others need to be helped. The 3-fixation might be described as a form of sentimental achievements of outward shells of living that are not rooted in our true and vulnerable being. And the 4-fixation might be described as a form of rationalism that counts deep feeling as special and insensitivity as crass. Handling the humiliations that come to these fixations clearly and cleanly will bring healing to all three of these humiliation-based fixations.

All of us (not just twos, threes, and fours) experience humiliation. And in order to access our Spirit Being all of us need to work through our humiliations. But for twos, threes, and fours, working through their humiliation is a first order of business.

Here is a description of the positive journey for those of us with a **personality-type-2 fixation.** The humiliations that come to those of us with this fixation derive from a commitment to being a helpful person and a desire to be appreciated and reciprocated for being help-ful. Those of us with a type-2 fixation are typically gushy, outgoing, positive people. And we are proud of that quality and active in being that quality. We are therefore vulnerable to the humiliations that come to all helpers. For who is ever fully helpful to another person? Humans can assist each other, but in the deeper matters every person must help himself or herself. Thus people tend to be resentful or even contemptuous of persons who get their juice from being helpful to them. So we type-2 personalities cannot avoid the hell that goes with being helpful. To find our true rest of Spirit and our true ability to assist others, we twos benefit from opening to a deeper consciousness, especially a consciousness about the futility of all helpfulness. Experiencing this helplessness of our help will be humiliating, but we can find thereby our true and Trusting being, which cannot be humiliated. When this happens, we are experiencing the positive journey of the person with a type-2 fixation.

Here is a description of the positive journey for those of us with a **personality-type-3 fixation.** The humiliations that come to the person with this fixation derive from the three's commitment to being a successful or beautiful person and to being acknowledged by others for this accomplishment or capacity. Those of us with a type-3 fixation are typically workaholics and are keenly focused on outward results and outward qualities of personhood. We expect affirmation for these qualities; therefore, we are vulnerable to the humiliations that come to all those who are attached to the passing things of their external lives. We type-3-personalities cannot avoid the hell that goes with failing or with becoming ugly. To find a true rest of Spirit and the ability to truly glow with effective living, we threes can benefit from a deeper consciousness, especially a consciousness about the futility of all success and beauty. Acknowledging our shells of pretence will be humiliating, but we can find thereby our true and Loving being, which cannot be humiliated. When this happens, we are experiencing the positive journey of the person with a type-3 fixation.

Here is a description of the positive journey for those of us with a **personality-type-4 fixation.** The humiliations that come to a person with this fixation derive from the four's commitment to being a deep, insightful, creative person and to being appreciated for these qualities. Those of us with a type-4 fixation are typically emotionally sensitive and creative people. We are proud of these secret depths and we expect to be noticed as special people; therefore, we are vulnerable to the humiliations that come to all self-adulating persons. Others almost never notice us fully, at least not fully enough to suit us. And those who do notice us may also notice that we fours, like everyone else, are less than fully deep or insightful or creative. All humans are flawed, shallow, stupid, and ordinary. We four-personalities cannot avoid the hell that goes with demanding more of ourselves than what is ordinary and common to all of us. To find a true rest of Spirit and the ability to be truly deep and creative, we fours can benefit from a deeper consciousness, especially a consciousness about the futility of all specialness. Grasping that we are no more than ordinary will be humiliating, but we can find thereby our true Free, creative being, which cannot be humiliated. When this happens, we are experiencing the positive journey of the person with a type-4 fixation.

All of us may take all three of these journeys, but personality types 2, 3, and 4 are especially focused on a humiliation journey. These are the humiliation-based personalities.

COMPLETE SPIRIT UNFOLDMENT

All nine of these journeys home can take place in every life, but each of us must begin where we are. Since I am a five, I must begin with experiencing my paranoia, my fear, and my despair over the fragile nature of all knowing. As I access the Trust of Reality that is my essential being, I move toward aggressively being that Trust. This is a move toward the essential quality that is associated with the type-eight personality.

As a five my next movement toward full Spirit maturity tends to be toward the Spirit strengths located at point eight on the enneagram chart. This order of unfoldment is said to be related to how my five pattern arose, namely through a denial of the aggressive being of Trust that characterizes the Spirit quality at point eight. As a small child I was, in childlike ways, a little eight. The development of my type-5 personality took place in a family in which eightishness was discouraged. In order to survive or be approved, I suppressed my point eight qualities. So when I begin expanding my experience of life beyond my type-5 box, accessing the Spirit qualities associated with point-8 on the enneagram chart arises as a first order of business.

Each personality type has such a next place on the enneagram diagram toward which Spirit realization tends to move. The following diagram depicts these next movements for each personality type. The arrowheads mark the point on the enneagram chart toward which each personality type moves next. Then each personality type may keep moving on its realization journey around the entire chart of enneagram qualities. This is the theory. This theory needs to be tested in each individual life. Since each life is complex, this theory is not easy to test. Whether the theory proves entirely true or not, it states something important: being a particular personality type does not mean that a person's Spirit realization is restricted to one and only one point on the spectrum of Spirit qualities. All of the Spirit qualities on the enneagram chart are aspects of the essential Spirit Being of every person.

The five, after moving toward point eight, wrestles with the personality fixation at point eight and moves toward point two, then four, then one, then seven, and then back to five. Each personality type in this sequence takes a similar journey. This is the theory. Here is a chart of these orders of unfoldment.

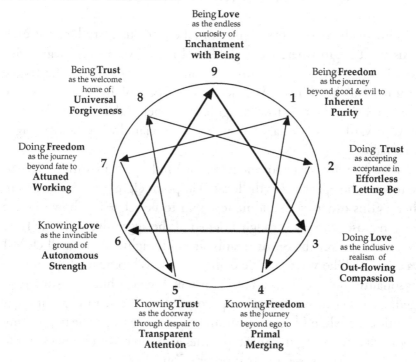

So how does a type-5 personality access Love, the Spirit aspects at points 6, 9, and 3? Here is my guess. Each personality type has two wings, one on each side. The five has a six wing. That wing takes a journey from six to nine to three and then back to six. The five also has a four wing. That wing takes its journey from four to one to seven and then back to five. Our wings enable us to complete the journey to all the Spirit qualities. This is my theory. Again, each of us will need to check out this theory for ourselves. Below is a listing of the next enneagram points on the journey of each personality type and its two wings.

The Next Realizations for each Personality Type

Primary for the 1 is recovering being Freedom by moving toward doing Freedom (7), also as a 9 wing recovering being Love by moving toward doing Love (3), and as a 2 wing recovering doing Trust by moving toward knowing Freedom (4).

Primary for the 2 is recovering doing Trust by moving toward knowing Freedom (4), also as a 1 wing recovering being Freedom by moving toward doing Freedom (7), and as a 3 wing recovering doing Love by moving toward knowing Love (6).

Primary for the 3 is recovering doing Love by moving toward knowing Love (6), also as a 2 wing recovering doing Trust by moving toward knowing Freedom (4), and as a 4 wing recovering knowing Freedom by moving toward being Freedom (1).

Primary for the 4 is recovering knowing Freedom by moving toward being Freedom (1), also as a 3 wing recovering doing Love by moving toward knowing Love (6), and as a 5 wing recovering knowing Trust by moving toward being Trust (8).

Primary for the 5 is recovering knowing Trust by moving toward being Trust (8), also as a 4 wing recovering knowing Freedom by moving toward being Freedom (1), and as a 6 wing recovering knowing Love by moving toward being Love (9).

Primary for the 6 is recovering knowing Love by moving toward being Love (9), also as a 5 wing recovering knowing Trust by moving toward being Trust (8), and as a 7 wing recovering doing Freedom by moving toward knowing Trust (5).

Primary for the 7 is recovering doing Freedom by moving toward knowing Trust (5), also as a 6 wing recovering knowing Love by moving toward being Love (9), and as a 8 wing recovering being Trust by moving toward doing Trust (2).

Primary for the 8 is recovering being Trust by moving toward doing Trust (2), also as a 7 wing recovering doing Freedom by moving toward knowing Trust (5), and as a 9 wing recovering being Love by moving toward doing Love (3).

Primary for the 9 is recovering being Love by moving toward doing Love (3), also as an 8 wing recovering being Trust by moving toward doing Trust (2), and as a 1 wing recovering being Freedom by moving toward doing Freedom (7).

Whether all of this is entirely true, I do not know. It seems plausible to me. It seems plausible to me that every personality type and its two wings unfold all nine aspects of Spirit. Perhaps the main point here is not the precise order of unfoldment, but the glorious truth that each of us has the possibility of accessing all nine facets of Spirit.

In Chapter 6, I described how Spirit unfolds in a knowing-being-doing direction and how retreat from Spirit develops in a doing-being-knowing direction. This order of unfoldment is also manifest in the enneagram directions of unfoldment diagramed in the chart above. But I am not asking the reader to simply trust the enneagram heritage on these matters. The final test is seeing for ourselves how the journey of unfoldment takes place in our own lives.

I can bear witness to the validity of at least part of this prediction of a five's unfoldment. As I have become more liberated from being withdrawn into my personality-type-5 paranoid mind-world, I have been able to access the more aggressive, lustful, outgoing, pushy qualities at point 8 on the enneagram chart. I have increasingly experienced the Spirit power of confidence in the Absolute Truth of Universal Forgiveness. I can see that my journey of unfoldment has moved from point 5 (knowing Trust) to point 8 (being Trust).

Next, according to the enneagram tradition, I move to point 2 (doing Trust). This also seems to be an experience to which I can testify. As I have persisted on the Spirit journey, I have indeed felt more identity with the emotional powers of the two and the Spirit gift of Rest in Effortless Letting Be.

From point 2, according to the enneagram tradition, I move to point 4 and then to point 1 and then point 7 and then back to point 5. I am less clear whether or not my life has unfolded or is unfolding in this way, but I seem to have increasing familiarity with all of these points of Spirit.

I also have some familiarity with points 6, 9, and 3, the knowing, being, and doing dimensions of Spirit Love. I am quite confident that all of us have the capacity to access all the aspects of Holy Spirit. Our journey may never be complete, but the COMPLETE is here for each of us. Also, my or your journey may have unique regressions, twists, and turns. But however that may be, I feel confident in pointing to this key awareness: each of us is capable of growing up into the full stature of Christ Jesus, as Paul put it. (Or if you like, each of us is capable of accessing full Buddhahood – or some other image of complete Spirit realization.) This COMPLETENESS is not a Christian matter, but a human matter. "Holy Spirit" is just a term used by Christians to point to the True Nature of every human being.

Finally, we need to be patient with whatever incompleteness in Spirit realization we find in our lives. Our first imperative is to face our flight from and fight with Reality; our anger, fear, and humiliation; our despair, malice, and bondage; our lack of Spirit. Facing this lack (this sin) is part of our Spirit realization. Spirit flows into our lives when we are consciously aware of our lack of Spirit. It takes no effort or struggle to become our Spirit essence. Struggle is the struggle of our personality to retain its claim on our lives. Our Spirit nature already owns us eternally. My Spirit essence is the real "me." Your Spirit essence is the real "you." We have only to surrender to that essence and allow it to flow in its own mysterious and unpredictable fashion.

PART FIVE

*Spirit Guidance and the
Need for Community*

20.

Spirit Essence is the Only True Guide

This will be a short chapter, but I want to indicate that this point is of chapter-level importance. **THE ONLY TRUE GUIDE FOR OUR SPIRIT JOURNEY IS OUR OWN SPIRIT ESSENCE.**

No other human being can tell us whether we are or are not living out of our Spirit Essence. Only our own Spirit Essence can tell us. If the teachings of Jesus, the teachings of the Buddha, or any other person (living or dead) seems to tell us something about our Spirit Essence, it is only because our own Spirit Essence resonates with what they say.

If this were not so, then we would not be an autonomous Spirit Being, but a slave dependent upon some other person, guru, pastor, teacher, pope, saint, leader, mentor, adept, monk, rabbi, priest, avatar, shaman, etc. In the final analysis we are on our own. We must follow our own lights, our own angels, our own Spirit Essence.

We know that other people have been useful to us in our Spirit awakenment. When we have been in illusion, others have seen what we could not see about ourselves. And we have needed others to call our attention to our own Spirit Being. Others have inspired us by their presence, their words, and their deeds. We know that we have profited from following them.

But we need to also know that we are on our own. We have always been on our own. We only knew whom to follow because of some connection with our own Spirit Essence. We only chose to follow because we sought further connection with our own Spirit Essence.

We may also have chosen to follow or continue following in order to get out of being on our own, in order to shift the responsibility for being our Spirit Being onto someone else. If we did, we were disappointed, or we will be disappointed. For no human guide is a perfect guide; at some point any guide may mislead us. And here is an even deeper truth: we were never actually guided by another person; we were always guided by our own Spirit Essence which others assisted us to access.

EACH OF US IS ON OUR OWN. WE HAVE ALWAYS BEEN ON OUR OWN. WE WILL ALWAYS BE ON OUR OWN.

The Spirit journey is an infinitely solitary journey. As a Spirit Being, we are an Awed One who is being Awed by the Awesome and filled with Awe. This is our very own experience of the Holy Spirit.

In the Fourth Gospel, the anonymous author of this wild drama has Jesus make a long farewell speech before his crucifixion. Here is a fragment of that speech:

> I will ask the Father and he will give you another to be your Advocate, who will be with you forever – the Spirit of truth. The world cannot receive him, because the world neither sees nor knows him; but you know him, because he dwells with you and is in you. (John 14:16,17; The New English Bible)

21.

The Need for a Human Guide

Though we are on our own with our own direct experience of the Awesome Mystery and with our own participation in the Awe of Holy Spirit, we also need Spirit guidance from other human beings. Sometimes a whole community of people guides us by their presence, words, and examples. Sometimes we need to study with, consult with, or work with one or two talented Spirit companions who provide the guidance we need during a particular period of time.

When I reflect back over my own life, I can see that I have been very fortunate to have had great guides of many types in each period of my life. I recall an eighth grade English teacher, a student pastor in college, three seminary professors, a mentor I lived with for decades, a whole group of people in a family order, several therapists, several Buddhist meditation teachers, some Diamond Approach teachers and therapists, some Radical Honesty therapists, two Hindu satsang leaders, my wife Joyce, my weekly-meeting Christian Circle, scores of book authors, numerous working colleagues, and more.

Why are these human guides needed? Each culture of humanity and each human person is entangled in patterns of habitual living about which we are largely unconscious. If another human being is more conscious than we of the patterns that limit us, that person can be our guide. This is especially true with regard to core patterns in our lives. We are often almost completely unconscious of our most serious patterns of escape from Spirit living. Even if we are somewhat conscious of them, we are often so consumed by them that we forget them and thus fall into states of unconsciously living in these chronic patterns.

The job of the Spirit guide is to assist us to notice or to remember what we already know; namely, that specific patterns restrain us and that specific excuses are used by us to avoid our experiences of Spirit. The Spirit guide may also lead us on "trips" that enable us to experience specific aspects of Spirit that we have been overlooking. We take such direction from others because we trust these persons to lead us toward real experiences of our own Spirit essence.

We often tolerate tough Spirit guides because we know that our escape routes are toughly defended and that our aversion and resistance is often strong toward important next steps on our Spirit journey. I think of a Zen teacher who typically strikes slouching meditators with a bamboo stick. Amos, Jeremiah, John the Baptist, Jesus were all tough teachers. It is compassion to be tough when strong patterns persist. Most of us can remember with gratitude many sharp words or actions that have rocked us to attention.

We tend to choose as our Spirit guides, persons who are onto us, persons who see beyond what we see, persons who are skilled in visioning for us the next steps on our road ahead. Many of us have spent considerable money and traveled many miles to sit with workshop leaders and retreat masters whom we anticipated were capable of seeing further than we could into our own lives.

Sometimes we find that whole communities of people are serving as our Spirit guides. When we are in group meetings with alive Spirit people, we do not know which person will be our guide on each occasion. We may not even know at the time that guidance was happening to us. Perhaps later we notice that we are operating differently, that Spirit is flowing, and that our chronic patterns are sitting in some corner with dunce caps upon their heads.

When we rerun our Spirit journey in slow motion and look at it carefully, we may see some of what our Spirit guides have done for us. We may become more clear about the healing process and thus appropriate our next steps more readily. Here, in slow motion, is a view of what a Spirit guide does for us:

(1) The Spirit guide assists us to be aware of some specific pattern of un-Spirit. In the end we may be grateful for this, but in the first instance this can be extremely embarrassing. We almost never want to see what a dunce at Spirit living we have been. We are often defensive, but the defending one is our ego, not our Spirit Being. Our habitual patterns with which we have identified ourselves typically rise to defend themselves from exposure as the patterns of destruction and silliness that they are. An expert Spirit guide assists us to see these defenses and to see them for what they are – silly attempts to hang on to delusions we have felt comfortable harboring. A guide does not have to be harsh with us to be effective, but sometimes our stubbornness needs a certain amount of firmness, even harshness, to break its hold. Usually, a skillful Spirit guide, in addition to challenging us, also maintains contact with us and exudes good will toward us. A skillful guide may communicate a patient understanding, reassuring us that breaking old habits of living may require time and persistence. Yet our slowness to change may also prompt a guide to reject being our guide any longer. This may be the action needed to communicate to us the extent of our obstinacy. The guide is free to use any methods that seem appropriate to that guide. We must not tell our guides how to guide us. When we choose our guides, we should look for guides who have the wild freedom to be as outrageous as they need to be. At the same time, those who are guided need to be willing to investigate for themselves the truth and the error in the guide's guidance.

(2) In addition to assisting us to see our patterns of un-Spirit, the Spirit guide assists us to see the welcome home that Spirit-rich Reality has for us. The guide may do this by simply being happily present in her own Spirit-rich living. Or it may take spoken words for us to hear the promise and glory of returning to our Spirit Essence. We may need a big push to overcome our fears of doing so. We may need direction for accessing our courage to hang in there with some purgatory process that brings us from spirit death to Spirit life. The Spirit guide may need to articulate over and over again the truth that we are indeed welcome home to our True Nature, to our Spirit selves. Perhaps this is done with the guide's own celebration of our progress. But the guide

may not know what our actual progress has been. We need to share our perceptions of Spirit progress with our guide and listen to our guide's responses. And then we need to decide for ourselves what is guidance and what is not, what is progress in being ourselves and what is more illusion that we need to move beyond.

The guide can help us see when we are not home, when we are home, what home is like, what next steps toward home might be appropriate for us. The guide can guide because the guide has experienced home and the process of arriving home in his own life. But the guide may not know how to apply that wisdom to another person. And the guide can never take the place of the solitary autonomy of each Spirit journeyer.

(3) Finally, the Spirit guide assists us to see that it is you alone (me alone) who must decide to be on this Spirit journey. Each of us alone has to accept our welcome home. Each of us alone has to be home. Each of us alone has to choose to stay at home. The guide cannot make these choices for us. The guide might yell at us for not making choices. The guide might beckon us to step out. But however forceful or gentle the guide may be, the good guide will understand that in the end she must remove herself and not be in the way of each of us making the choices that we and we alone must make.

Each of us will need to find our own balance in these paradoxical situations. We need human guides, but they cannot take our journey for us. We need to be on our own, and yet we may not know where we are or where to head next without our human guides. We may not even notice the number of human guides we have. We may have thousands of voices in our inner council of human relations that are in some measure Spirit guides to us. But we have to choose which of these voices to listen to now. We need to seat these voices near or far in relation to our present journey of living. We need to discern truth and untruth in each of our inner guiding voices. We are on our own, and yet we have centuries of human adventurers who stand ready to assist us. And most important of all, there are still living in the world today many Spirit persons who may be willing to be present with us and to be our guide in a personal fashion, in a fashion we need at this time in our lives.

22.

The Need for Spirit Community

The human species is an intensely communal species. A human child raised by animals may be denied ever realizing her potential for the human quality of consciousness, for language, for art, and for religion. Similarly, only in Spirit communities do Spirit persons come into being. It may seem at times that some great soul, some great Spirit teacher, has arrived from nowhere. But this is not so. Communion with many others has been the actual history of each profoundly realized Spirit person. Then these persons enrich the Spirit communities in which they participate. Spirit communities come into being through the lived lives of Spirit persons. And Spirit persons come into being through the efficacy of Spirit communities.

Each journeyer into Spirit realization needs community to nurture that journey. And each of us needs a community with whom to share our realizations. These needs are profound.

SPIRIT COMMUNITY AND
RELIGIOUS PRACTICE

A Spirit community is something more than a group of Spirit individuals. A Spirit community includes cultural fabrics as well as political and economic structures. A Spirit community is a religion. Almost all of us have been burned by sick religion; we may have been burned to the extent that we have aversion to the very word "religion," and to any practice that looks like religion. Such aversion is understandable, but it blocks our understanding of this topic. Religion is as much a part of every human society as economics or education. We don't reject economics as a whole because we experience bad economics. Similarly, we err to reject religion as a whole because we experience so much bad religion. Like economics, religion is an essential part of social life.

To say that religion is an essential part of human society is to say that religion is a very down-to-Earth sort of thing, right alongside language, art, food, housing, and sewage disposal. Religion is not Spirit. Religion is not holy. Religion is a finite, temporal, sociological fabric capable of vast perversions, just like economics or politics. There is no true religion, final religion, or absolute religion. There is just good religion and bad religion, healthy religion and sick religion.

Healthy religion fulfills a function needed in every human society – the function of expressing Spirit and nurturing singular humans in their Spirit journey. Healthy religion also infuses Spirit into the arts and languages of the whole society as well as into the modes of education, life styles, economics, and political ordering. Religion, both healthy and sick, is always going on in each society. Sick religion cannot be properly called "Spirit community," for what makes sick religion sick is its suppression of Spirit. Healthy religion is healthy when it is an outgrowth of Spirit community. And Spirit community never exists in the heavenly clouds, purified of all Earth-bound religious structure. Spirit community is always embodied as some form of relatively healthy religion. Spirit community always appears in some sort of religious container.

CHRISTIAN RELIGIOUS PRACTICE

We must again remember that Spirit community is not limited to a Christian religious practice. There are many forms of non-Christian religion that have been outgrowths of genuine Spirit community. Furthermore, religions are not separated from one another; they influence one another deeply. In their creative stages, all religions learn from other religions extensively. Recent scholars of the New

Testament formation have made clear how much the New Testament writers incorporated from the religious ferment around them. In North America today, creative Christians are learning from Buddhists and creative Buddhists are learning from Christians in an extensive exchange of insights and practices. This exchange is possible because all healthy religions are attempts to express and explore the very same Spirit nature of humanity. Our religious languages, methods, and practices may differ widely, but Spirit is Spirit wherever and however it appears.

Every healthy religion is in a constant process of creating itself anew. I emphasize the Christian dialogue with Buddhism because Buddhism has been recovering and teaching contemplative methods that are deeply needed in contemporary U.S. culture. North American Christianity is also learning from many other heritages: Taoism, Hinduism, existential Judaism, mystical Islam, Earth-affirming tribal and pagan heritages, and so on. Healthy religion is not a tight box, but a process of creative formation that reaches anywhere and everywhere for whatever it needs to accomplish its task of Spirit expression and nurture.

Healthy religion is needed by each individual Spirit journeyer. And the fruits of healthy religion are needed by every human society. Healthy religion is a liveliness that is essential to the optimal liveliness of the planet as a whole.

In this book I have been focusing on Christian heritage and Christian language, and in the remaining chapters I will be focusing on Christian religious community. One of the most confusing topics in Christian heritage is the recurring insistence that there is no Spirit realization outside of Christian community, outside of being grafted onto the Body of Christ. In order to understand this claim properly, we have to understand that the term "Christ" points beyond Jesus and his followers to a universal dynamic of the cosmos. Anyone, anywhere, practicing whatever religion, is part of the body of Christ if they are living in genuine Spirit community. Only in that sense is it true that there is no Spirit realization outside of Christ. In a competent Christian theology, the Body of Christ means everyone who is manifesting the Spirit Essence of being human.

This universal understanding of the essential nature of Christian community does not mean, however, that the Christian religion and practicing a Christian religion is unimportant. Choosing a religious practice is like choosing a place to live. We cannot live every place; we have to cook our food and sleep our body somewhere. So it is with our religious practice. We cannot practice every religion. We might study many religious heritages, but each long-standing religious heritage is almost inexhaustible. Few of us can claim to have mastered even one. And no one needs to practice more than one religion in a daily, weekly, yearly, communal way. So as a practical matter, we find ourselves having to choose a religious practice just as we find ourselves having to choose a place to live.

Choosing a Christian practice is complicated by the fact that Christianity is undergoing a major transition period in which this heritage is being rescued from many complex perversions. Nevertheless, the true gifts of the Christian breakthrough are recoverable. And the core gifts of the Christian breakthrough are different from the core gifts of Buddhism and other great heritages. Christian practice, at its best, maintains a creative balance between solitary devotion and communal nurture, between individual healing and social transformation, between transrational Spirit experience and thoughtful, timely social action. This creative balance is, in part, why I have maintained Christianity as my religious home.

23.

Christian Community as the Body of the Messiah

Christianity is a communal religion. All religions are communal, but Judaism and Christianity are more communal than many religions. In their ancient origins, these two religions were even more communal than they are commonly practiced today.

Ancient Hebrew culture was based on a montage of communal metaphors: delivery from Egypt, the wandering wilderness tribe, the tribal federation, the divinely "called" nation selected to lead other nations in Spirit realism.

Christianity, likewise, was rooted in communal metaphors: the new Israel, membership in the Kingdom of God, participation in a new humanity (a new Adam), and most striking of all – being the living organs or limbs of the Resurrected Body of Christ. The solitary person was affirmed in Christian heritage but not as an isolated entity. The solitary person was challenged to choose between: (1) being a slave in the fallen society of Satan or (2) being a freed citizen in the commonwealth of Almighty God.

In their religious practices, the disciples did not go off by themselves and be individual Christians. They formed a close-knit group. They met together; they thought together; they prayed together. The first Christians gave great emphasis to communal life.

The story of Pentecost is an interesting example. In this story the Holy Spirit did not descend upon individuals who were off alone somewhere. The Holy Spirit descended upon a large group of people speaking different languages. And when the fire of the Spirit burned that day, the result was this: a diverse group of people could hear each other through all the barriers of language and culture. The Pentecost story is almost the reverse of the Tower of Babel story. In the Babel story humanity sought a common language with which to build their own kingdom. In the Pentecost story people were moved from this divisive babble of culturally separating languages into a communication of Spirit that is universal to all humans and created by none of them.

Early Christian communities understood themselves to be the first fruits of a historical restoration of the entire family of humanity. All humans were potentially members of this communal Body of Christ. This small out-of-the-way group of Christ-way Jews experienced themselves as a beginning of restoration for all humanity. Jesus was "written up" as a portrait of a new humanity (not a new species, however, just the original humanity restored). Jesus was the Second Adam, the Adam who resisted temptation rather than fell into it.

If we do not have this strongly sociological view of being a Christian, we are practicing an impoverished sort of Christianity. Today this impoverishment is widespread in Christian groups as well as in Western culture generally. We live in an era of individualistic overemphasis. Conservative Christians want to save individual souls for their heavenly reward. And liberal Christians tend to focus on psychological well-being, personal morality, and individual vocation. The sociological intensity of Spirit community and the vision of responsibility for the Spirit healing and the structuring of justice for the whole of humankind has been largely lost in this modern swamp of individualism. The reverse side of the individualistic coin is collectivistic tyranny. When individuals insist on overemphasizing living alone, those individuals end up living under oppressive collectivities. Oppressive leaders come to power when too many individuals have lost their sense of communal responsibility. Strong democracies with responsive leadership come into being when people are talking together and acting together in an aware and responsive manner in a majority of local communities.

THE BODY OF CHRIST

The apostle Paul referred to the Christian community as "the Body of Christ." The meaning of this phrase, to Paul and his hearers, included an understanding that the events surrounding Jesus marked a change in the fundamental conditions of human life. The aliveness that was in Jesus came alive in the Christian community. Paul spoke of those motley little gatherings of Christ-way Jews as being "in Christ." The resurrection was something that happened to a community of people. The resurrection of Jesus was witnessed by a community of people. The resurrection happened to them. They became the resurrected body. The resurrection myths are not about something that happened to an individual person named Jesus. Resurrection happened to a community of people who came to view Jesus and his life and death in an expanded manner. The resurrection was not a biological wonder, but the birth of a communal body. This understanding has been clouded by our individualism, by our hope for the immortality of our individual egos, by our addiction to a miraculous escape from the necessity of an ego death. It was egoic individualism that had been crucified on the cross of Jesus. What got raised up was true humanity, a communally embodied Spirit fire upon the Earth.

This understanding of resurrection undergirds what it means to say that Jesus is the Christ. The union of the words "Jesus" and "Christ" changed the meaning of both words for those who first conceived this religious symbolism. "Christ" no longer meant the coming of a divine champion who would throw off the shackles of Rome. "Christ" now meant the coming of a divine champion who would throw off the shackles of demonic addiction of which Rome was merely one passing manifestation. The disciples were indeed rescued from Rome, but in a profoundly inward and secret way that most people could not see.

And the meaning of the word "Jesus" was also changed. The word now meant more than the appearance of an unusual prophet, a mystic teacher, a religious innovator, a social revolutionary. The word "Jesus" united with the word "Christ" meant that Jesus was not simply another individual attempt to make a difference. "Jesus" now meant a turning point in human history in which a specific ordinary person succeeded in leading the human species out of slavery to the delusions of Satan's kingdom into the fresh open air of freedom in the Kingdom of God.

Some biblical scholars have tended to dismiss the Christ interpretation of Jesus and seek instead for an uninterpreted historical Jesus as the starting point for their "theology." The value of this scholarship is that it makes probable that there actually was a historical figure called "Jesus" who actually did have qualities that make plausible all the fuss that has been made about him. But what we know about the historical Jesus is probable knowledge, scientific knowledge, knowledge that still has to be interpreted for its human meaning. Some of these biblical scholars do not seem to notice that, like the New Testament community, they also have to interpret Jesus. Some of them seem to identify more with the interpretation of Jesus that appeared in the Gospel of Thomas. That document sees Jesus not through the lens of an ego death and a Spirit birth (cross and resurrection), but through the lens of a mystic teacher of occult wisdom. This interpretation of Jesus is quite different from the interpretation that is contained in the "Gospels" selected for the New Testament. The author of the Thomas document did not call his work a "gospel." The term "gospel" or "good news" is a New Testament symbol for the Christ interpretation of Jesus. In spite of significant differences, the four Gospels of the New Testament agree that Jesus is to be viewed as the Messiah (the Christ) and that resurrection and cross are the fundamental metaphors for interpreting his Messianic significance.

It is true that Jesus did not start Christianity. A select group of his followers did. The Christ interpretation of Jesus was done by those who saw themselves as his resurrected body. They felt empowered to interpret what Jesus said and did and to expand on what Jesus said and did because they viewed themselves as Jesus – as his resurrected continuation. They saw Jesus in one another. While they failed, so they admitted, to fully realize this high calling to the full stature of Christ, they saw themselves in a covenant to grow into this full stature. Their realization of this completeness was fragmentary; nevertheless, they viewed themselves to be "in Christ." They were his body. They had died with him in his crucifixion, and they saw themselves as raised up with him into the essential humanity that he pioneered in manifesting.

The Kingdom of God

Virtually all-biblical scholars recognize that it is highly probable that the preaching of the historical Jesus frequently contained the phrase "the Kingdom of God." But a number of scholars assume meanings for this phrase that do not accurately reflect what Jesus was pointing to. "The Kingdom of God" could be translated "the Empire of God." Part of its meaning was its opposition to "the empire of Rome." In the Empire of God we experience a wholly different mode of social operation than in the empire of Rome. Below is a saying that the Jesus Seminar scholars color gray (meaning that only a small percentage of them view these words as the actual words of the historical Jesus). But I view the meaning of these words as consistent with other sayings that most scholars consider to be the actual words of Jesus.

> You know that the so-called rulers of the heathen world lord it over everyone, and their great leaders have absolute power. But it must not be so among you. No, whoever among you wants to be great must become the servant of you all, and if he wants to be first among you, he must be the slave of all persons.
>
> (Jesus, according to Mark 10:41-44)

Many things are surprising about this passage. First of all, the disciples are being understood as members, indeed leaders, in some alternative sociological operation quite different from the heathen world. Secondly, this new "empire" is not organized topdown. The leaders are on the bottom. They are the slaves of the led. This means a new style of governing and a very different style of communal life than is commonly practiced in the civilizations of this world. And let us take note that this Kingdom is something here on Earth. One of the phrases in the "Lord's prayer" says, "Thy Kingdom come on Earth as it is in heaven." Perhaps we can relate better to the power of that phrase if we reword it slightly: "May that mode of human community that is essential within the structure of the cosmos be manifest here on Earth as it already is eternally present in the essence of human authenticity."

H. Richard Niebuhr in his book *The Kingdom of God in America* suggests that the Kingdom of God metaphor went through three stages in the history of American Christian theology. In the first of these stages Christian theology emphasized that God is king. Early Calvinist and Lutheran theology emphasized the sovereignty of God. That is, they clarified that the word "God" pointed to an absolute all-powerful OTHER-THAN-HUMAN objectivity that was being encountered by humans in every natural event and in every historical event in human history. Many contemporary Christian interpreters have taken offense with this use of the word "God." They have said that an all-powerful God cannot be deemed to be benevolent, that we have to choose between a God who is all-powerful and a God who is good. But Luther and Calvin as well as Augustine, Paul, Isaiah, Amos, and also Jesus use the word "God" to point to that which is all-powerful and which they also view as good. This joining of Final Power with Final Goodness entails giving up the ordinary human views of "good." It entails seeing that all human views of good and evil are relative and basically self-serving. To say that what the all-powerful God does is good is to say that what is actually happening is trustworthy. The probability is very high that Jesus used the word "God" in the phrase "the Kingdom of God" to indicate this Kingly, All-powerful Reality which he trusted as good – as his trustworthy "Papa." Current attempts to interpret the historical Jesus as somehow rejecting this basic Old Testament use of the word "God" are simply preposterous. Jesus was not a secular, post-theistic humanist. He was thoroughly embedded in the tradition of Moses and the prophets.

H. Richard Niebuhr claims that the second stage of the interpretation of the Kingdom of God in American Christian theology emphasized the transformation of the solitary soul. That is, it emphasized making the good, sovereign God our (my, your) personal King. The kingdom comes in our own soul when we begin to trust God as the King of our own lives. Here Niebuhr is talking about the emphasis of the Great Awakenings initiated by John Wesley, Jonathan Edwards, and others.

According to Niebuhr, a third stage of American Christian theology's interpretation of the Kingdom of God emphasized building the Kingdom of God here on Earth. Here Niebuhr has in mind theological work commonly called "the Social Gospel." Niebuhr claims that there need be no contradiction between seeing God as King of the cosmos and seeing the Kingdom of God as an enactment here on Earth by human beings. When we are living in devotion to the actual "King" of the cosmos as king of our lives, then we can and do manifest the Kingdom of God here on Earth in specific material and temporal ways. We can say all this in a more secular language: "When the all-powerful Final Reality is trusted as the core loyalty of our lives, we then build interpersonal relations and social fabrics that manifest this realism."

Niebuhr claims that all three of these understandings of the Kingdom of God are valid and are implied in the sayings of Jesus. We do not have a complete understanding of Jesus' teachings until we embrace all three of these dimensions of meaning of the Kingdom of God: (1) that God is King, (2) that the Kingdom comes in our lives when we trust this King, and (3) that this Kingdom becomes visible here on Earth as manifestations of real community and justice among transformed humans and transforming humanity.

For many decades the Social Gospel made considerable headway among liberal Christians, but this sociological emphasis, this building of the Kingdom of God here on Earth became separated from the Spirit transformation implied in trusting the Final All-powerful Reality as our God, as our King. Many social-action Christians reduced the meaning of the Kingdom of God to "a society embodying my ideals." This reduction led to a neglect of communal nurture, of common ritual, of the healing magic of sharing and studying together, and of the slow preparation of the masses of people to be Spirit-effective persons. Some socially active Christians tend to go off by themselves and find some project to do that satisfies their own individualistic need to be useful. They have lost contact both with the wholeness of humanity and with the nurturing communion of Christian life together. Thus their sociology has lost its Spirit roots. Instead of being the Awed Ones living in Awe before the Awesome, they simply glorify themselves as those who do a bit of good by their own standards. Their sociology is not based on the insight that every human being is a ramp from here to Eternity with angels moving up and down. Their sociology is reduced to only dealing with the temporal elements of reality. As their temporal causes pass away, their "Christianity" passes away as well.

Though the sociological meaning of the Kingdom of God has been perverted, this aspect of understanding the Kingdom of God is an important part of the whole picture. True followers of the Christian breakthrough are the Body of Christ. They are the Kingdom of God coming to Earth. They are the perpetual manifestation of authentic community. They are a planet-wide sociological Spirit breakthrough into the historical process. This includes demanding justice for all in the tradition of the prophets.

A true and complete Christian theology will reflect this deep sociological emphasis. Jesus becomes a community of human beings, not merely one person. Jesus, like each of us, was a singular person. But "Jesus as the Christ" is a new humanity, a restored humanity, a new Adam and Eve. This new Adam and Eve remain ignorant of good and evil. When being this redeemed community, we do not eat the forbidden fruit; we allow the Primal Mysterious Reality walking in our everyday garden to be our Good, our God. As we take up our membership in this true, realistic, authentic humanity, we know first hand what it means to be "in Jesus Christ." We are his resurrection, his bodily presence in history. We identify with the New Testament stories about Jesus, however mythic or fictional they may be, however preposterous they may seem as guidelines for our living. Finally, being Jesus Christ, we create and recreate his words and his deeds for our time in history. This is Christian community. This is the Body of the Messiah.

24.

Five Spirit Stages of Christian Community

In the previous chapter, I underlined how Christianity is a communal religion. In this chapter, I will explore more deeply the "We" dimension of being Christians. A group of people who are meeting regularly as a vital Christian community take a group journey together. I see five stages in being Christian community:

> The Healing Community of Confessing Beginners
> The Wise Community of the Wordless Word
> The Invisible League of Spirit Manifestation
> The Revolutionary Vanguard of Human History
> The Communion of Saints in Absolute Rest

These five categories can be viewed as sequential stages of communal maturity, and in each stage of the maturation journey, all five of these qualities apply in some measure. These qualities may be viewed as five dimensions of authentic Christian community. They are present in each and every authentic Christian community.

The Healing Community of Confessing Beginners

Christian community begins with the public confession of our actual lives, our weaknesses, our vulnerabilities, our estrangement, our despairs, our hopes, our depth experiences, any and all aspects of our actual lives. And in this practice, we always remain beginners. In the Spirit journey we never get beyond being beginners, for the Spirit journey is and remains a journey into the unknown. We never know where we are going in comforting detail. We never have lasting certainty that we know precisely what our problems are or what help we need.

Spirit healing always comes to us as a surprise. Being sick in the Spirit sense means not realizing what we are missing in the way of Spirit health. Spirit sickness is usually, if not always, a delusion of false "goodness" that we do not realize is evil. Spirit healing entails waking up to the moldy nature of our virtues and to the shocking disaster of our vices. Spirit healing entails surprises that we could not have anticipated. In any experience of Spirit healing we feel like novices, beginners, or "dumb dumbs" who are ignorant of something crucial for the living of our lives. Healing may be exhilarating, but not in the sense of being rewarded for our fine qualities. This exhilaration is more in the nature of the exhilaration of a child who faces some fresh adventure never taken before.

Community is needed to foster such healing. Christian community has been likened to a hospital for sin-sick souls. We come together each week seeking a fresh measure of health for the week ahead. We may call it "inspiration." We may call it "moments of Awe." We may call it "refreshment." All such words point to the discovery of some estrangement for which we can accept forgiveness and hence feel welcomed back to that common ground of realism from which we have fallen. This experience is elemental, foundational for healthy Christian community. Being a society of healing confession is the process with which each genuine Christian community begins. Without healing confession, it is not Christian community; it is not even a beginning for becoming Christian community. It is something else entirely.

The Wise Community of the Wordless Word

Healing comes first, and then we begin becoming wise about Spirit matters. Experiences of healing precede our theological clarity. Someone else's theological clarity may inspire our healing, but thinking through for ourselves what we mean to indicate with our religious terms comes after, not before, our healing. For example, we cannot genuinely speak about "sin" until we experience ourselves as estranged from our own authentic life, trapped in various forms of despair, malice, and bondage. And we cannot genuinely speak about "grace" until we know what it means to: (1) confess our estrangement in personally felt detail, (2) be forgiven (that is, welcomed home to our authentic lives) and (3) choose to accept this welcome and live more realistically.

As a Christian community matures, theological clarity becomes more important. It becomes important in order to assist one another through the tangled weeds of estrangement in all aspects of our lives. It becomes important as a protection against falling into some fresh trap of delusion, estrangement, bondage, despair, or malice.

Theological clarity is a communal achievement. It is the job of all of us in a Christian community to learn to say what needs to be said to one another and to all those among whom we dwell in the times in which we live. Theological clarity is not something worked out centuries ago. Ancient words of wisdom may have been theological clarity for those Christians who lived when that wisdom was forged, but we have to work out our own theological clarity in the times and for the times in which we live.

Christian theology is a strange and paradoxical sort of wisdom, for it uses human words to speak about what we might call "an experience of the Wordless Word." Many contemporary Christians, conservative and liberal, do not understand the wordless nature of the Word of God. Whether we think of memorizing Bible verses or giving 30-minute sermons, "many words" do not equal "the Word of God." When Christian heritage speaks of "The Word of God," this does not mean sentences in the Bible. The Word of God is not human words at all. The Gospel of John states clearly that the Word preexisted humanity. Therefore, the Word preexists words. "In the beginning was the Word, and the Word was with God and the Word was God." "All things were

made through (this Word), and without (this Word) was not anything
made that was made." (John 1:1-3) This is a strange sort of Word!
It is a Wordless Word. It is a communication from the Final Reality
manifest in all things before, during, and after the advent of words.
The author of the Fourth Gospel puts in his own words this paradoxical assertion about the wordless cosmic communication – the "Word,"
"Logos," or "Logic of Final Reality."

And how do we come to hear or know this cosmic Word? The
author of the Fourth Gospel states clearly that this Wordless Word of
God walks up to us in some fleshly, breathing, living person speaking
from heart and soul to the hearts and souls of we also living breathing
persons. This Word became flesh – it is present in history as Jesus and
in those who hear this Word and live it. In New Testament thought
the term "Jesus" means something more than an individual person
who lived long ago. Jesus is the authentic human, the new Adam, the
new humanity that does not fall like Adam fell. This new Adam (and
new Eve, by the way) lives and speaks the Truth heard from that Final
Reality that this renewed humanity addresses as "God."

All human words, whether in the Bible or in the mouth of a contemporary Christian witness, are not the Word of God. Such words
may point to the Word of God, but the Word of God is beyond words.
The Word of God is a non-conceptual actuality. The God who is really
God does not speak in human words; God speaks in direct experiences
to the hearts and souls of living people. When we picture God as a Big
Person who speaks human words to us, this is metaphorical language.
Earlier eras of Christian living were comfortable with metaphorical
language. But in our time we either dismiss metaphorical language
altogether because we are aware that metaphors are not literally true, or
we make ancient metaphors ridiculous by taking them literally.

For example, the New Testament resurrection stories are ridiculous if taken literally. A dead body getting up and walking about is
at most just a curiosity, interesting perhaps to a society organized to
explore unusual phenomena. Good Christian theology does not view
the resurrection as something that superficial. According to the core
of Christian tradition, the resurrection has to do with the restoration
of humanity to its authentic life. The key to building wise Christian
community is viewing the resurrection stories as artistic descriptions

of happenings to the disciples of Jesus. This same resurrection is still happening to us. If we do not understand the resurrection as something that happens to us, we do not understand the New Testament witness.

The New Testament resurrection stories tell us how the disciples of Jesus, who had despaired over the fact that their expectations were crushed by the crucifixion of Jesus, were transformed. The disciples were raised to newness of life. We also can be raised to newness of life. After his death, Jesus lived and walked and ate fish because the disciples who lived and walked and ate fish had become the presence of the same life they had known in Jesus of Nazareth. The first disciples saw themselves as the Body of Christ. They, in their own flesh, were the resurrected body. True Christian community today is a continuation of that resurrected body. Christ is risen indeed – that is, Messianic authenticity is here on Earth in flesh and blood communal life.

The resurrection is a group experience as well as a solitary inward happening. The first disciples saw Jesus in the eyes and speech and actions of one another. We can see Jesus in the eyes and speech and actions of those who comprise our genuine Christian communities. Jesus, the Messianic human, is alive indeed. The first disciples ceased to see his crucifixion as an unmitigated tragedy or a cause for hopeless despair. As Paul put it, "We died with him that we might be raised up with him to newness of life." The resurrected community sees the death of Jesus as the death of human perversion in our own lives, thus leaving us free to be the authentic beings that we truly are.

Words, especially the words of scientific literalism, cannot tell about the resurrection or any other Spirit happening. We need to praise the first Christians for using fantastic stories and myths to transmit their wisdom to one another and to the awakening and awakenable humanity of their era. Not only "resurrection" but "God," "Holy Spirit," "faith," "sin," "grace," "freedom," "compassion" are words that point to actualities that are beyond words. Nevertheless, the Wise Community of the Wordless Word uses words to talk clearly and meaningfully to one another. Such group word-craft is called "theology." In doing good group theology, we become capable of bearing a witness that awakens humanity in our own time and place. This contemporary Christian witness can have the same effectiveness as the original New Testament witness. The words of the Bible can have power again, but only if we see them as witnessing to the Wordless Word that we also experience and witness to others in our own words.

Becoming able to do theology in this paradoxical fashion is step two in being genuine Christian community. This theologizing is an essential dynamic of Christian community; it never grows old or becomes unneeded.

The Invisible League of Spirit Manifestation

As the journey of maturity proceeds, a Christian community can become aware that Christianity is only a religion, a finite sociological practice alongside the many other religions that humanity has invented. I have taken the word "Invisible" from that part of Christian heritage that has distinguished the visible sociological Church from the Invisible Spirit Church. And I have taken the word "League" from the wonderful little book by Herman Hesse, *The Journey to the East*. This wonder-filled, imaginative and poetic book provides us with a keen sense of the wondrous quality of being on a journey into the endless deeps of Mystery and finding there our membership in an Invisible League of authentic community.

We commonly use the word "Church" to mean a group that practices a Christian religion. But Christian heritage speaks of "Church" in a deeper way — as a sociological dynamic in the entire history of humanity. People of all religions, and even people who lack a formal religious practice, can be seen to be members of this Invisible League of Spirit manifestation. And it is this Invisible League that is the true Church. The visible sociological expressions of Christian religion are, at their best, merely pointers toward this Invisible actuality. This Invisible League, the Spirit Church, is the true fleshly presence of the Body of Christ in human history. This mysterious Body existed before, as well as after, the life and death of Jesus. Jesus himself speaks of Abraham, Isaac, and Jacob as among the living. Moses and the prophets also are seen by Jesus and by his disciples as members of their community. For Christians, the life of Jesus was a revealing moment in history showing us this Spirit body, this Kingdom, this commonwealth of God, this League of Spirit manifestation. But this League that Jesus showed us is something far greater than a visible sociological body in which people explicitly speak of Jesus.

This League is "Invisible" because the extent of its boundaries cannot be known to human beings. Organizations and doctrines do not circumscribe it. Some of the people who call Jesus "Lord, Lord" may not be members of this Spirit League. And others who have never heard of Jesus may be members of this League. Being a member of this League means manifesting the Spirit of restored humanity – of the profound authenticity from which we have all fallen. Jesus is reported to have said to his disciples when they were worried about the healing work being done by people who were not of their group, "If they are not against us, they are for us."

Such awareness about the deep nature of Christian community means a complete end to every fragment of Christian bigotry. No longer can a Christian evangelist claim that there is no salvation (Spirit healing) outside membership in some Christian religious group or outside belief in some particular confession about Jesus. No longer can a Pope or some other primary leader make the claim that his or her religious organization plays the essential role in salvation (Spirit healing). Salvation, understood as the healing of our escape from Spirit living, is a universal process beyond the control of all Popes, clergy, or religious teachers of any sort. The boundary of those who have received this healing is unknown – that is, this boundary is invisible to all members of humanity.

For those of us who are a Christianity-practicing community, this vision of the Invisible League is an essential step toward realizing who we are as Christians. As we become participants in this true Church, we become clear that the essential nature of the true Church is a dynamic of the cosmos that is far more profound than anything circumscribed by our specific sociological group. This means that as true Christians we experience a detachment from our own beliefs and religious practices. Indeed, a true Christian has a detachment from Christianity as a whole. Discovering the Invisible-League quality of the true Church means realizing that being a Christian community goes much deeper than the practice of a Christian religion. Christianity, like every other religion, is only a means to the realization of membership in that Invisible League of Spirit which is the true Church.

What does all this mean for a genuine, up-to-date practice of Christian religion in our local place? It means not taking too seriously our Christian theology, Christian symbols, Christian ethics, or Christian organizations. At the same time, we take with ultimate seriousness the universal Realities to which these Christian symbols point. We also take seriously our challenge to create Christian practices that bear witness to these universal Realities. This is a paradox: we can have confidence in the Reality toward which good Christian religion points and yet have humility – understanding that we are only true Christians when we transcend our Christianity. This detachment and transcendence allows us to see ourselves as compatriots rather than competitors with all members of the Invisible League of Spirit, whatever religion these other members may practice. If they are not opposed to Sprit, they are on our side.

The Revolutionary Vanguard of Human History

The Invisible League just described is also the Revolutionary Vanguard within human history. When we ask how human society can change for the better, we discover something I am calling "the Revolutionary Vanguard." On the one hand human history is the story of the ever-recurring fall into depravity, the fall into a loss of our essential humanity. But human history is also the story of healing and restoration. Human beings, acting from their Spirit restoration, are those who shape the course of progressive history on behalf of the whole human species. The Invisible League manifesting as the Revolutionary Vanguard is the foundation for healing, restorative action toward justice, workability, and enrichment of human society.

Whenever significant change for the better is taking place, we find a Revolutionary Vanguard at the core of this happening. Human cultures and their economic and political systems have a conservative bent, an intense momentum in accord with their habitual patterns. These inherited patterns may hold positive values, but they are also a straightjacket for aliveness and a bondage to the past that is typically difficult to break. Those who start human societies in fresh directions are those who are detached from the old patterns. The Revolutionary Vanguard are those who are able to reside in a home of consciousness that is beyond the current cultural canopy. This is the locus in human living from which fresh creativity for greater justice, more workable order, and cultural enrichment can take place. Those who do this basic creativity are the Revolutionary Vanguard. And being such creativity is one of the core qualities of being the true Church. Being the fullness of Christian community includes being part of this basic dynamic within human history, a sociological dynamic that I am calling "the Revolutionary Vanguard."

This Vanguard is manifest in signal individuals who envision fresh visions and accomplish new things, but it is also manifest in the millions of ordinary people who resonate with those fresh visions and do most of the accomplishing. Martin Luther King, Jr. is an example. He was a signal individual, but the Revolutionary Vanguard that healed the United States of much of its racial sickness was much larger than Dr. King. The civil rights movement led by King and others also illustrates how the Revolutionary Vanguard starts small, but can become a mass movement with long-range historic manifestations. The Revolutionary Vanguard is people working together to affect these far-reaching social shifts.

The Revolutionary Vanguard is a group, a big "We." This "We" quality is a challenge to the individualistic overemphasis in modern society. Christianity is a communal religion witnessing to communal forms of living. The Revolutionary Vanguard is also a communal actuality. Its boundaries are unknown, but its consequences within the flow of human history are visible for all to see.

When we consider the journey of our own Christian community toward being the Revolutionary Vanguard, we find ourselves challenged to give up the image of finding some little project we happen to like. Too often this means seeking to avoid the complexities of the broad sweep of history. The Revolutionary Vanguard is concerned for the whole of history; it is that flesh and blood part of humanity who is repenting of the sins of the whole society and who knows that nothing of historical significance is accomplished alone. Within this broad "We" context, each of us chooses our own particular roles and makes our own particular contributions, but this solitary choosing does not deny the "We" context in which our solitary work takes place.

This Vanguard "We" may not be as large and powerful as the social "We" being changed, but the Vanguard is a "We" that is dedicated to becoming large enough to shift the entire course of history. And this Vanguard includes a wide variety of people, most of whom do not engage in a Christian religious practice. Nevertheless, this Vanguard is the Church from the Christian point of view.

Each of us who shares in being members of the Revolutionary Vanguard is challenged to be obedient to the tasks that this contemporary Vanguard is discerning in our particular hour of history. We choose our own specific roles and tasks, and yet we also sense that our part in the fray is being chosen for us by the times in which we live. Our action is being shaped by the evolving consciousness of the time-specific Revolutionary Vanguard of which we are members. The Vanguard as a whole is freely choosing its way amid the ambiguities of history, yet the overall agenda is being set for us by the times in which we live and by this wide range of people who are sensitive to these times. This is a deep paradox. We the Vanguard are choosing freely, and yet we are also being obedient to challenges set for us by the God of history.

The experience of being the Vanguard includes both great certainty and great vulnerability. The Vanguard has certainty about the Spirit context from which thinking and action flow, but in the actual drama of history all responses are ambiguous. Our critique of the old social fabrics is risky because those fabrics are a mixture of good gifts and deep corruption. Since we are part of this old corruption, our actions are best characterized as repentance. Our proposals for new social fabrics to replace the old are untested creations; they are risky ventures fraught with uncertainties. We have to choose and we may choose wrongly. We may see later that our choices were wrong. We may have to repent of our own choices and choose again. Being the Vanguard is a free venture into an unknown future. Such ethical risk requires a deep courage to be our essential freedom. Nevertheless, such free action is undergirded by an obedience to the Final Reality that always wins.

The choices each of us makes contribute to the ongoing consensus building of the entire Vanguard. While we contribute to that consensus through our own creativity, we also experience an emerging group wisdom to which we are called to be obedient. That group wisdom may call us to perform actions that we did not design and may not feel prepared to enact. We may experience ourselves, in large measure, as foot soldiers who carry out master strategies that are being built by the most sensitive, innovative, compassionate people of our era. These strategies are being freely created by the Vanguard, yet these strategies can seem to arrive at our door as specific callings to be obedient to the Vanguard of our times. Obedience to the Vanguard is consistent with obedience to God. Obedient to that Final Realty that confronts us in and through our historic challenges is consistent with obedience to and among the people who are meeting those challenges. The wisdom of this larger body is many times greater than the wisdom of any one of us. And yet, sometimes one of us finds himself or herself called to enrich the wisdom of us all.

The Bible can teach us much about the qualities of being this Revolutionary Vanguard. The Vanguard are those who, like Abraham, leave old cultural homes and head for some promised land where they have never been before. Similarly, we are those who leave the well-established hierarchical slave camps of our various Egypts and wander in the wilderness of freedom waiting to discern what our promised land might be. We are those who conquer a place for our vision in actual history. We are sometimes prophets of unwelcome doom and sometimes prophets of unbelievable hope. We are like those who leave fishing nets and tax offices and follow some nomadic Jesus into awakening the lost villages of our era. We are those whose righteous-ness exceeds the righteousness of the scribes of tradition and the moral teachers of past-oriented holiness. We, the Vanguard, are those who find ourselves among the subversive forces within some decaying and tyrannical Roman Empire. We are those who build within the ruins of social collapse some small monastic islands and then whole continents of alternative living. As the Christian part of the Vanguard, we are those who engage in a thoroughgoing critique of the old and stodgy forms of Christian practice and join in the perpetual Reformation of Christian living. Such qualities, appropriately crafted for each era of living, are part of the abiding nature of being Christian community. Practicing genuine Christian community means participation in this much larger constituency, the Revolutionary Vanguard in our moment of human history.

The Communion of Saints in Absolute Rest

Absolute Rest is also a quality of the fully realized Christian community. This "Rest" exists as well as the hard climbs up the various mountains of care we experience as the servant forces of revolutionary changes in our era of history. We do not "burn out" in our revolutionary action because at a deeper level we are at Rest. We are protected from the anxiety of failure or the anxiety of completing our favorite tasks because at a deeper level we are at Rest in a manner that no historical success or failure can disturb. This Rest is our sense of being at home and having a type of home that is unthreatened by any historical development. In a fully realized Christian community, we are at home with the Absolute.

And by "Absolute" we mean the Absolute Void, the Absolute No-Thing-Ness from which all things come and to which all things return. And by "Absolute" we also mean the Absolute Fullness, the Every-Thing-Ness in which all things cohere. As fully realized Christian community we are at home with everything, with all comings and all goings. We are at home with the Void out of which comings occur and into which goings return. We are at home with the Overall in which all things cohere.

Christians have called this Rest "the Communion of Saints" because it is a group experience. We look into one another's eyes and we see this Rest. We Rest in communion with a community of humans who are at Rest. These humans are saints because they are at Rest, for this Rest means being the Spirit beings we are. It is Rest in being the sons and daughters of the Absolute. This Rest is Eternal Life, here and now. It is Eternal Life because the Absolute Void/Absolute Fullness is Eternal. This Absolute God (symbolized in both impersonal and personal metaphors) does not change; the biblical God is not part of the world of change. This God is Eternal. And as we Rest in this Eternality, we are Eternal. We Rest in Eternal Life. It is Rest because we have arrived. There is no more seeking to arrive. There is nowhere else to go. This is the final destination. All historical destinations are passing things yielding to still other historical destinations. In social history we never arrive at a final destination. But as the Communion of Saints we have arrived. We are home. There is no other home to go to, and there is no possible threat to this home. This home is Eternal. This home is Rest.

Peace, Tranquility, Stillness, Silence, these are words used by Christians and by other traditions to describe this Rest. And when Christians Rest, they Rest along with the "saints" from other-than-Christian religions. It is clear that generations of Hindus and Buddhists have known this Rest. Perhaps every religious community that has lasted for hundreds of years has lasted because its members, or some of its members, knew this Rest.

Finally, this Rest is not an escape from the ongoing work of the Revolutionary Vanguard. History moves on and our participation in history does not end when we Rest in Eternal Life. Rather, we bring this Eternal Life of abiding Rest into the continuing everyday anxieties of history. We overcome those anxieties and move on to other anxieties because we do not seek our rest within those historical processes or in our victories or defeats. We have our Rest in the Eternal Now of fellowship with all the saints of every generation. We share in their blessings of security in their Eternal place where no rust can corrode nor moth destroy. We Rest as we move and act and live and serve in all the particulars of our historical era. This Rest is even our power to move more courageously and more persistently and more flexibly than those who live in history without this Rest.

In our practice of a Christian life together, we find that our coming together each week is a way to access this Rest. We return from our individual and group work to this communal place of Spirit Rest. We reinspire our participation in Eternal Rest that we may be Rested in our work during the next week. The Sabbath tradition is a rhythm well tested through many centuries. Every seven days we need Rest, Rest in the Eternal. The Sabbath tradition arose as an expression of this Spirit insight. The Sabbath is a gift to humanity not a moral rule for being more righteous. We come together to Rest and to celebrate Rest in that Eternal Now that is present in all of our living. We set aside time for Eternal Rest, so that we can have Eternal Rest in all of our time. We set aside time for communion with our fellow saints, so that this Communion of Saints can be with us, guiding us in all that we think and do in the entire round of our lives.

Rest for our deepest being is a quality of true Christian community. We have only to open ourselves to it and participate in it. This Rest is a solitary experience, and yet it is also a group experience. We are not alone in this Rest. We Rest with all the saints in every age – past, present, and future. We Rest together and we remember that we would not have come to this Rest without the ministries of our companions in Rest. Our security in being a person who Rests is also enabled by the ongoing communion of those who also Rest. We need this communion. And this communion needs us. And yet it is also true that this communion is not sustained by any of us who Rest in this communion. The community of Rest is sustained by the Almighty/Awesome, Impersonal/Personal, No-Thing-Ness/Every-Thing-Ness that is Eternal and that is the bestower of Eternal Rest.

* * * * * * * *

Perhaps this brief description of the journey into the depths of Christian community can assist us to notice more fully the Spirit journey of the Christian groups to which we belong.

Also, I want to suggest that the reflections in this chapter can assist us to further flesh out our master view of the Christian Trinity. On the next page is a master triangle that breaks down the Triune experience of God into twenty-seven inseparable, interdependent subparts. The upper-left triangle breaks down our experience of the Awesome. It contains the angels of encounter described in Chapter Two. The lower triangle breaks down our Awe-responses to the Awesome. These are the angels described in Part Two – the angels of Trust, Love, and Freedom that move up the ramp of our soul from here to Eternity. These states of being are the Holy Spirit. Thirdly, the upper-right triangle breaks down our experience of being the Awed Ones, the Body of Christ, the Communion of Saints, the socially manifesting Kingdom of God in history, the "We" dimension of being Christians. This upper-right triangle points to that third of the experience of God that the best of triune Christian theology calls "Jesus Christ."

Finally, I want to remind us once again that there are many who experience "Jesus Christ" who have never heard of Jesus or the "Jesus Christ" theology. The Awed Ones are a universal community that can appear in any culture at any time, and they have done so often.

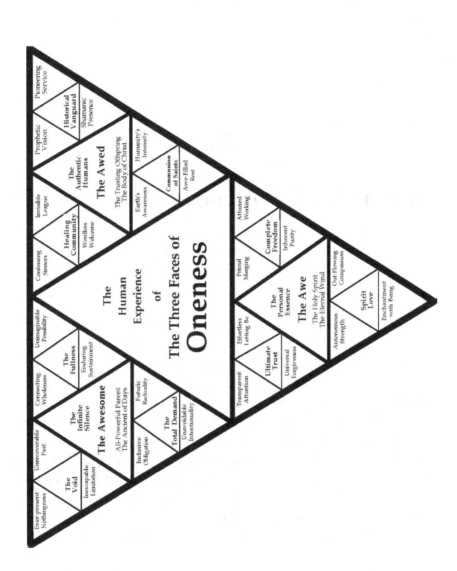

25.

Storing Spirit Wisdom in Human Vessels

"For where two or three have met together in
my name, I am there among them."
Matthew 18:20 – New English

Most likely, the above saying was put into the mouth of Jesus after his
death by disciples who were experiencing its meaning. What were they
experiencing? What did this saying mean to them?

First of all, what is meant by "met together in my name"? Surely
this means something more than pronouncing the name "Jesus" or
"Jesus Christ" or any other theological words. Meeting in this name
certainly means something more than saying words. The word "name"
in biblical lore includes the meaning "nature" or "essence." So what
is the "essence" in which these two or three are meeting? "Being the
Awed Ones," is my answer. And "being the Awed Ones" means being
true to ourselves as biological beings in our space/time coordinate as
well as being a ramp of angels coming and going between here and
Eternity.

When two or three or twelve of us meet in this way, then Jesus,
understood as the Messianic arrival of full humanness, is bodily there
in the midst of us. Christ is there because we here-and-now humans

are Christ to one another. We are the Body of Christ. We are the living embodiment of the resurrection of Jesus. Each of us is Jesus in living relationship with one another, if we are meeting in this name.

These considerations imply that we cannot be Christians by ourselves. To be Christians in the full sense of this religious practice, we need to meet regularly with one or two or five or twelve other persons. And speaking from my experience, yearly or monthly will not do. We need to meet with others daily, or at least weekly.

Primarily, this book has been written to assist circles of weekly-meeting Christians who wish to be the Body of Christ in an earnest manner. When this book is being studied by persons who are serious about growing up into the full stature of their authentic humanity, then this book is meeting the purpose for which it was written.

This book may help clarify someone's theology. It may help open up the message of the Bible and the wonder of the Christian heritage. It may challenge some demons and deliver someone to their Trust, Love, and Freedom. But if that someone is not meeting weekly with others, this book will have failed to do all that it is intended to do.

This book is a guide for growing up as Christians into our essential humanity. It might assist Buddhists and others as well, for essential humanity is not limited to Christians. But this book contains Spirit wisdom crafted for Christian groups. Its purpose is to assist Christian groups to become human vessels for the Spirit wisdom pointed to in this book and pointed to by the great writings of the Christian heritage.

But the words of the Christian heritage, including all the insights of this book, cannot be stored in a library. The core insights of this book are about authentic states of Being, and these states of Being have to be stored in human vessels. The words of this book and the charts of this book are useless if they are no more than furnishings in our minds. Theological clarity is important, but it is only important if it is part of actually living these primal states of Trust, Love, and Freedom. These three grand words point to core realizations of our inner being. They point to everyday manifestations of these primal inward states in our response to ongoing Reality.

So if we, the readers and writers of the words of this book, are not meeting weekly with others in this "name" (this essence), we have only acquired a few more mental pieces to move around in our interior chess game.

This book is written to assist us to put our bodies into a deeper game, the master game of the cosmos. By "game" I do not mean something trivial or superficial. I do, however, mean something playful. Being ourselves is play, not work. Being ourselves is Rest, not struggle. And the Christian game is not the only Spirit game on Earth. We could be playing the Buddhist game or the Muslim game. All effective religious practices are a Spirit game. Humanity must learn to take our religions playfully rather than super-seriously. Our religious play is only serious to the extent that it points beyond itself to the Eternal dynamics of Awesome, Awe, and Awed.

And the Christian religious game includes meeting once a week (or more often) with others who also play the game of being the Body of Christ. This Body of Christ game is played every moment of our living, not just when meeting with other Christians. But if we are not meeting with others regularly, we are not in the game.

And if we are not meeting with others, we are closing ourselves off from the primary journey of Spirit that constitutes this game. Christ is present in the brother or sister with whom we meet. We meet together in order to meet with Christ. Why would we ever think that we can grow up to the full stature of Christ if we don't meet with Christ, and thereby continue becoming more aware of what being "in Christ" means?

If we are not going to be "in Christ," perhaps we should be "in Buddha" or some other religious practice that points to our essential nature as a ramp from here to Eternity. And if we are going to be "in Buddha," then we need to meet regularly with others who play the Buddha game.

I have written this book as a call to Christian-identified people and to people who might opt to be Christian identified. I do not intend this to be a call to bigotry or to any sort of contempt for other religious practices. But I do intend to promote Christian practice. I intend to make this call to be the Body of Christ plausible to the most aware persons of our era.

And this call calls for wholeheartedness. Being the Body of Christ cannot be a minor sideline of religious piddling, alongside the more important things of our lives. Being the Body of Christ is the core game illuminating the whole game of our lives. If it is not, then we are not playing the Body-of-Christ game.

Being the Body of Christ is an alternative to being the body of despair. In truth, being the Body of Christ is a continual dying to the body of despair in which we also participate – dying in order to be resurrected to an aliveness beyond despair, beyond malice, beyond bondage, beyond death, beyond life, beyond all escapes from authenticity. The resurrected life is living this triune experience: life with the Awesome, life in Awe, life as a member of the Awed Ones in history.

Such a life does not take place in some far off place or future. Such a life takes place here and now, and it takes place in human vessels. These human vessels may own books and read books and write books, but the Spirit wisdom to which books point is not stored in these books, or in whole libraries of books. Spirit wisdom is stored in the human vessels themselves.

Afterword

The Ongoing Wrestle with Invisible Angels

Jacob as a young man dreamed about his true soul, about a ramp from here to Eternity with angels moving down and up. As a mature man Jacob had a second deep-night visitation. This occurred after about two decades of living with his uncle Laban, acquiring two wives (Laban's daughters Leah and Rachel for whom he had labored seven years each), many children, servants, and much wealth. One night Jacob and his large family slipped away from Laban. Laban pursued his missing family members and some missing objects. Jacob, by a stroke of luck, avoided a violent showdown with Laban. Then Jacob learned that his estranged brother Esau, who two decades ago was angry enough to kill him, was heading his way with 400 men.

He sent generous gifts ahead to his brother. He divided his company into two parts hoping at least one would escape. And he spent the night in deep prayer.

> "Save me I pray from my brother Esau, for I am afraid that he may come and destroy me, sparing neither mother nor child. But thou didst say I will prosper you and will make

278

your descendants like the sand of the sea which is beyond all counting."
(Genesis 32:11,12 – New English)

Alone, Jacob wrestled all night with a mystery figure, a nameless angel of God, one of the more severe angels. We might as well say that Jacob wrestled with God, with Final Reality; for whatever angel it was, every angel is a symbolization of a specific experience of the Awesome Final Reality. Final Reality was confronting Jacob in the coming of his brother and 400 men. Jacob had to make some kind of response to this encounter. His prayer was a wrestling match with an angel that could not be defeated.

Jacob hung onto this angel all night long. Just before dawn the angel asked to be released, but Jacob still insisted on a blessing. The angel's blessing began with a question, "What is your name?"

"Jacob," said Jacob. What was contained in the name "Jacob"? It contained all that had happened before: the tricking and cheating of his brother Esau, the tricking and cheating of Labon, the entire creative aggressiveness one might find in a typical personality type eight. Jacob was the name for this man's particular personality, a habit of living built up over the years of his life. But now, simply being Jacob, the tricking, cheating, power-dealing personality, was not adequate for tomorrow morning's encounter with Esau and with Jacob's destiny.

The blessing-giving angel continued: "Your name shall no longer be Jacob, but Israel, because you strove with God and with men and prevailed." The word "Israel" means striver or wrestler with God.

Jacob then asked the mysterious figure for his name. Here is what the figure said:

> "Why do you ask my name?" But he gave him his blessing there. Jacob called the place Peniel (Face of God) because he said, "I have seen God face to face, and my life is spared."
> (Genesis 32:29-31)

Clearly, the Genesis storyteller wants us to understand that Jacob had wrestled all night with God, the nameless God, the Eternal God that no name can contain. Jacob did not actually see a literal face of some supernatural being. He saw Esau approaching with 400 men. He saw a dream image of an angel, a messenger of profound Awe. The God of the Bible was then and is now encountered through specific events and through specific states of Awe. The encounter with God takes place through specific angels, if your mind dreams in that sort of poetry. Jacob wrestled all night with this angel, with God as God met him in this particular crisis of his life.

The all night wrestling match took its toll. The storyteller claimed that the angel had dislocated Jacob's hip.

> The sun rose as Jacob passed through Peniel (Face of God) limping because of his hip. (Genesis 32: 31)

> Jacob raised his eyes and saw Esau coming toward him with four hundred men. (Genesis 33:1)

The situation had not changed, but Jacob had changed. He limped a new walk. He had Freedom from being plain old Jacob. He was Israel now, the "wrestler with God." This new name characterized the best of his past and a hope for his future. He now had the Freedom to meet this threatening situation with astonishing creativity. If you wish to have a full picture of Jacob's creativity, read the entire 33rd chapter of Genesis. Jacob made clear his desire for peace and honor with his brother. At the same time he did not trust Esau, and he took creative steps to keep his distance.

The story of Jacob is just a story, a story told over and over, but the fictitious Jacob of this grand story is indeed the father of many descendants. These descendants include all of us who still hear and love the Jacob stories. Certainly Moses was a descendent of the Freedom told about in the Jacob stories, as was Joshua, all the judges, and all the prophets. Jeremiah certainly had his own all night wrestling matches when he had to prophesy the end of his nation and the dispersion of most of its people into various places of exile. Jeremiah recorded the pain of his nights of wrestling with severe rejection by those to whom he proclaimed his message.

Like Jacob's all night wrestling, Jeremiah's all nights also spawned descendants. Though Jeremiah had to tell the grim truth that his nation was doomed, his message was not a message of despair. It was a message of hope that this Spirit community could continue in exile without its nationhood wrapper, that a new covenant was being forged with this people, a more inward covenant located not in a land nor in a kingly organization but in the hearts of an exiled people. Perhaps we can identify with Jeremiah's deeper truth.

We also see Jacob's all night wrestling match reenacted in the Garden of Gethsemane when Jesus was confronted with betrayal, capture, rejection, scorn, torture, and death. Here is part of Mark's telling of the story:

> Horror and dismay came over him, and he said to them
> (Peter, James, and John), "My heart is ready to break
> with grief; stop here, and stay awake." (Mark 14:34)

Three times he chastened his sleeping disciples, who could not stay awake for such a grim encounter. But Jesus, with the same Freedom we saw in Jacob's all night vigil, stood up and faced his tragic morning. Though he would be tortured and killed that day, he was the victor in his own personal drama. This is what Jesus had concluded in his night of wrestling: "This is not what I want, but not my will but Thy will be done." In the conclusion of Mark's telling of this story, we hear Jesus saying these words:

> Still sleeping? Still taking your ease? Enough! The hour has
> come. . . . Up, let us go forward. (Mark 14:41,42)

The astonishing courage we can see within these words is in marked contrast with the then weak disciples who could not even stay awake to face the horror that Jesus asked them to face with him. After that terrible day was all over, the disciples spent all day Saturday in a state of sheer emptiness. Then Sunday morning (I am elaborating the story a bit) some angels spoke to some of the distraught women, and then to the men. "No longer shall his name be 'Jesus,' but 'Jesus, the Messiah,' shall be his name, for he has led you through the execution of your sinful weakness into the dark night of sheer oblivion and thus into the sunny day of life in the style of Jesus." The disciples got to their feet and gave witness to this message.

Some of us reading these words are true descendants of this happening; we see something more than a remarkable, profound, clever teacher who is now dead. We see a new humanity who is "in Christ." We see a body of ordinary human beings who are now something more than sleepy disciples who cannot face the horrors of history. We see a functioning body, a group of people who refer to themselves as the Body of Christ, and who manifest in history the life that was present in Jesus, an aliveness which could not and cannot be destroyed by all that estranged humanity can do. We see what these first disciples saw: humanity has been rescued; true humanity has appeared and can spread to all the nations.

Jacob's dreams have become enriched with meaning by all these centuries of Spirit living. And Jacob's dreams can be our own.

Appendix

A. H. Almaas and the Holy Ideas

This appendix adds little, perhaps nothing, to the main thrust of this book. I am adding this appendix as a help for those who have read or may read A. H. Almaas's book *The Facets of Unity.* Such readers may wonder how my descriptions of the nine major facets of Spirit Being correspond with Almaas's descriptions. I am much indebted to Almaas for clarifying my appropriation of the enneagram heritage, and I feel that I owe readers who are also students of Almaas some explanation about how my descriptions relate to his. If you have not read his book, these comments may be cryptic.

Almaas uses a different set of terms than I use for the same nine "facets of unity." I have used terms that make deeper contact with Christian language and with the truth contained in Christian heritage. I maintain, however, that the aspects of our "True Nature" (or "essence") that Almaas describes are the same basic aspects of our essential humanity that I am describing. Only the language is different.

It may be that these slightly different language systems illuminate these nine aspects of Spirit somewhat differently, but what is being illuminated is the same overwhelming, mysterious (beyond all conceptualization) actualities of our True Nature.

Almaas describes these nine basic facets of our True Nature with terms he calls "Holy Ideas." In his use of this term "Ideas," Almaas does not mean mental concepts. He means something like archetypal approaches to human essence. With these "Holy Ideas" he is distinguishing nine distinctive facets of our inner diamond of True Nature. By "Holy" he does not mean otherworldly or ghostly. He means our basic, essential, shining, numinous human nature. His use of the word "Holy" corresponds with what I point to with words like "wondrous," "awe-filled," or simply "Awe."

For some of the nine points of the enneagram, Almaas uses two or three Holy Ideas to describe that same aspect of our True Nature. This does not mean that Almaas is pointing to two or three different things. Each Holy Idea in his sets of Holy Ideas points to the same aspect of our True Nature. Here is a chart of the Holy Ideas that Almaas associates with each of the nine aspects of Spirit Unity as they correlate with the enneagram diagram.

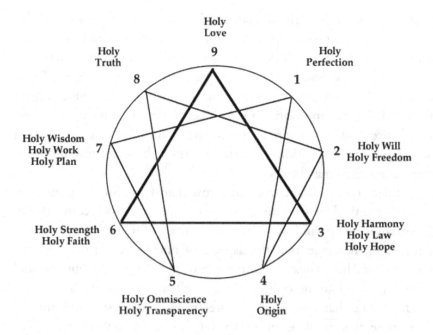

These terms hold well the insights that Almaas develops. Nevertheless, I find that Christian readers tend to associate Almaas's terms too directly with similar terms in the Christian heritage. By doing so, they create misunderstandings of the Christian terms. So, I have used Christian names for these nine Spirit facets. I have attempted to preserve the insights Almaas has expressed using the above terms, and yet provide alternate terms that I feel communicate these insights more clearly, at least to Christian readers. In some instances I use words that Almaas also uses but link them with other words that further shape their meaning.

It may also be that my renaming of these nine points adds additional insight in some instances. My basic evaluation of Almaas's writings is that he tends to overemphasize *attention* and underemphasize *intention*. Christianity is an activist tradition when compared with mystical Islam and the Eastern traditions with which Almaas is more fully conversant. This is not to say that Almaas is not familiar with Christianity. Indeed, he often expresses deeply valid and helpful interpretations of Christian heritage. Nevertheless, I find him somewhat less than fully resonant with prophetic Judaism and Christianity with regard to the sociological preoccupation found within these traditions. Judaism and Christianity are rich with Spirit-interpretations of historical developments and with the social activism that results from this historical emphasis. I mention this not to demean the work of Almaas but to partially explain the source of a somewhat different emphasis that I develop in this book.

The following chart contains the "Christian" names I am using for the nine facets of Holy Unity that Almaas also describes. Each of the nine "Holy" points of Almaas's enneagram analysis correspond to an aspect of "Holy Spirit" – three of Trust, three of Love, and three of Freedom.

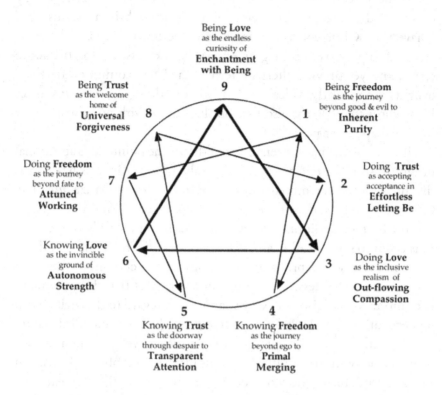

Being **Love**
as the endless
curiosity of
**Enchantment
with Being**

Being **Trust**
as the welcome
home of
**Universal
Forgiveness**

Being **Freedom**
as the journey
beyond good & evil to
**Inherent
Purity**

Doing **Freedom**
as the journey
beyond fate to
**Attuned
Working**

Doing **Trust**
as accepting
acceptance in
**Effortless
Letting Be**

Knowing **Love**
as the invincible
ground of
**Autonomous
Strength**

Doing **Love**
as the inclusive
realism of
**Out-flowing
Compassion**

Knowing **Trust**
as the doorway
through despair to
**Transparent
Attention**

Knowing **Freedom**
as the journey
beyond ego to
**Primal
Merging**

Points 6, 9, and 3 deal with those aspects of Holy Spirit that the Christian heritage points to with the term "agape" or "Spirit Love." Spirit love includes love of self, love of others, and love of the Ground of our Being. I am suggesting that point 6 is about love of self; point 9 is about love of the Ground of our Being; and point 3 is about love of others.

Almaas suggests that we might view this "inner triangle" as corresponding to Christianity's "theological virtues" of faith, hope, and love – with point 9 being love; point 6 being faith; and point 3 being hope. But I am suggesting that points 6, 9, and 3 are all three aspects of "Spirit Love," as this term is used in Christian heritage.

In Christian heritage "Faith" is another word for "Trust." And in the above diagram I am asserting that points 5, 8, and 2 reference aspects of what Christian heritage is pointing to with the term "Trust."

And, as I will explain shortly, the Christian use of the word "Hope" can be shown to be an aspect of "Freedom." In the above diagram, I am asserting that points 4, 1, and 7 reference aspects of what Christian heritage is pointing to with the word "Freedom."

LOVE

I will begin comparing my terms with those of Almaas at points 6, 9, and 3. If we look carefully at what Almaas is pointing to with the word "faith" when he uses it to describe point 6, we find that he means "self confidence." He means having faith in oneself, having faith in the goodness of one's True Nature. This is consistent with what Christian heritage points to with love of self. Also, in describing the Spirit aspect at point 6, Almaas uses a second term in addition to Holy Faith. He describes point 6 as Holy Strength, where this Strength includes an embracing of our natural autonomy – our courage to be a distinct person rather than be simply absorbed into the biological mother or into the society. Such Holy Strength is also consistent with the meaning that Christian heritage gives to "love of self."

In describing the Spirit aspect at point 3, Almaas uses the term Holy Hope together with Holy Harmony and Holy Law. As we study what he means, we can discern that point 3 can be understood to point to what Christian heritage means by "Spirit Love for others." Such Love means being essentially connected to other persons; to other aspects of biological life; to other aspects of the physical cosmos; and to the outgoing work of establishing justice, viability, and appropriateness in our modes of human society. The terms "Holy Harmony" and "Holy Law" imply that Almaas is using the term "Holy Hope" in the context of out-flowing relations with other beings.

So what happens to the term "hope" in my "Christian" renaming? In Christian heritage Spirit Hope is sometimes described as the hope that does not disappoint. Every other hope is actually the converse of some fear. When we hope that some expectation will work out, this is the same thing as saying that we fear that this expectation will not work out. Every ordinary hope is a hope that can disappoint. So what is the hope that cannot disappoint? It is the hope that full life is possible no matter what happens or does not happen. Such hope can be associated with Spirit Freedom. When we access our Spirit Freedom, we can always respond victoriously no matter what circumstances are calling for that response. In the face of failure and even death itself,

Spirit Freedom can be present as a positive response. So the capacity for Freedom is the capacity to live in a hope that does not disappoint. This is why I view the Hope that is cited in the New Testament as an aspect of Spirit Freedom rather than an aspect of Spirit Love.

In his famous poem about the primacy of love, the apostle Paul speaks of faith, hope, and love. Nevertheless, in the main body of Paul's thought much more is said about freedom than about hope. I believe that Paul's three main categories of Holy Spirit are: (1) "faith" (which means basic Trust in the Ground of our Being), (2) "Freedom" (which includes hope), and (3) "Love" (which is rooted in an enraptured affirmation of the Ground of our Being and is then manifest in merciful attitudes and actions toward self and others). Both Paul and Almaas see Spirit Love as basic to all the Holy aspects of our essential being.

TRUST

How are points 5, 8, and 2 facets of the master Christian category "Trust"? Point 5 can be depicted as a fully open curiosity about the multiplicity of Being and about our flights, fears, defenses, and resistance to that multiplicity. This openness is a state of Trust. To avoid such openness would be distrust. This description of point 5 is entirely consistent with what Almaas describes as Holy Omniscience and Holy Transparency.

Point 8 can be depicted as realizing the One Truth of the Benevolence of Being. This is also an aspect of Spirit Trust. This description of point 8 is consistent with what Almaas describes as Holy Truth.

Point 2 can be depicted as a surrender of our typical willfulness and thus letting Actuality be what it is. This is also an aspect of Spirit Trust. This description of point 2 is consistent with what Almaas describes as Holy Will and Holy Freedom.

FREEDOM

Finally, how are points 4, 1, and 7 facets of the master Christian category "Freedom"? Point 4 can be depicted as recognizing the bondage of our egoic self-image and thus experiencing the liberation of merging with the Freedom that is our True Nature. This description of point 4 is consistent with what Almaas describes as Holy Origin.

Point 1 can be depicted as recognizing the bondage of the good and evil judgments of the superego as well as the culture, and thus experiencing liberation "beyond the law." This is what the core of Christian heritage (in Paul, Luther, Bonhoeffer, and others) has meant by Spirit Freedom. This description of point 1 is consistent with what Almaas describes as Holy Perfection. In being our Freedom we are Pure.

Point 7 can be depicted as Attuned Working, as being aligned with the flow of Reality rather than fighting with Reality or knuckling under to Reality as if Reality were a fixed fate. This description of point 7 is consistent with what Almaas describes as Holy Wisdom, Holy Work, and Holy Plan.

For those who wish to study Almaas's *Facets of Unity* as well as this book, perhaps my notes in this appendix will aid those readers in recognizing the correlations between the vocabulary of this book and Almaas's witness in *Facets of Unity* to these same nine aspects of our True Nature. This dialogue with Almaas has strengthened my conviction that we can approach the same nine-faced diamond of our True Nature through many lenses of religious vision. Our mysterious Spirit essence is what it is; but the language we use to describe it can differ widely.